AUBREY

By

Aubrey Beauchamp

With love!
Aubrey ☺

2 Thes 3:3

PROMISE PUBLISHING CO.
Orange, CA 92668

M. B. Steele, Editor

AUBREY

Published by Promise Publishing Company
Orange, California 92668

Printed in the United States of America

Library of Congress
Cataloging-in-Publication Data

Beauchamp, Aubrey
     Aubrey

ISBN 0-939497-12-3

TABLE OF CONTENTS

FOREWORD by Brother Andrew
INTRODUCTION

EPILOGUE

FOREWORD

Too many books nowadays are written about people's problems - all the symptoms of a broken life, ruined relationships, marred future until some "guru" comes along (and often it's a Christian "guru") who has a solution. Sometimes it works, often not. But in either case, the circle within which the whole drama unfolds is very small.

That is my main objection to this kind of books. However, when the circle bursts open - when even MY salvation, MY happiness and MY place in Heaven do not appear to be the main, most important event and purpose in life - THEN it becomes a different story.

And such is the life story of my dear friend, Aubrey Beauchamp, whom I have known for many years. I have met her at different times but always in a different country on this planet. She is in search, like me, but no longer within the confines of that small circle. She has broken out and is searching for OTHERS - to make them partners of such great salvation.

Her main concern: Patients! Her main target: one of the most forgotten, loneliest and yet most important groups of people. Importantly, it is not because their soul is worth more or because of their greater contribution to our economy. No, it is because all of them touch our own lives and that mostly in times of crisis - sickness, accident, death:

THE CARE GIVERS!

- The health care professionals!

- The volunteers!

- The visitors!

- The church visitation teams!

Together with chaplains and clergy, nurses reach out to the sick, the dying and the hospitalized. They reach out with the Good News of the Gospel, of forgiveness, of comfort, of eternal life.

But let Aubrey tell you her own story - how she got there. All I want to contribute is to say that her life is multiplied many times over. And is that not (or should it not be) the greatest dream of a dedicated Christian?

It may help YOU to break out of your shell, your little circle, and start something in this old world that has eternal value because, yes, there IS something you alone can do. Find out what it is! My prayer is that this book help you in your search.

Yours for the suffering church,
Brother Andrew

Brother Andrew, founder of OPEN DOORS, was born on May 11, 1928 in a small village in the Northern part of Holland. He is widely known for his books, "God's Smuggler" and "The Ethics of Smuggling" and as a voice for the Suffering Church in Eastern Europe, Russia, China, Africa and the Middle East. Brother Andrew was one of the first pioneers who confronted the West with the tremendous needs of the Suffering Church. Since 1955, Brother Andrew has been a spokesman for these suffering brethren and has assisted them in many different areas.

INTRODUCTION

How many people have said to you at one time or another: "You should write a book!"? I believe all of us have. Yet how many actually sit down and write their life's experiences? Not many. I was among them. Of course, I had a multitude of reasons and excuses: too big a task, not enough time, never written a book before. If the matter was pressed a little more, the excuses would change to questions like: Who would publish it? Who would read it? Who would market it? Who would finance it?

Finally, during the summer of 1987, after the acquisition of a word processor, I decided to give it a try. Only a try, mind you, to get acquainted with that mysterious computer. Where would I start? How about the beginning? What did I remember about my youth? Memories slowly surfaced as I began to dig up the past, a different continent, a different era. With the help of my parents and my sister, Helen, the cobwebs of our memories were carefully removed one by one. History came alive again, incidents and details long forgotten resurfaced.

As chapters began to light up on the screen in front of me, my enthusiasm increased. It was exciting to relive the past, painful at times, joyful at others, yet always moving along like a fast-paced movie. I began to send some chapters to Sandy, my son in the Air Force. He was elated. One day, when home on leave, he said: "Mom, I think everyone should write about their lives. What a family heritage to pass on to our children and grandchildren. I had no idea what your life was like when you were a little girl. This is great! All the guys at work are waiting in line for the next chapter. They often read it before I do." I smiled and realized my time had not been wasted regardless of what happened to this "baby".

And a baby it was! The gestation period quickly advanced. I could feel life and movement and after three months realized that birth was near. One chapter followed another. One day, I knew it was all there! The story was complete. My life went on, of course, but that which I had endeavored to put on paper (or computer screen) was all said and done.

As you read these pages, I trust that one day you, too, will sit down and write about your life. We all have a story that is unique and of interest to others. Sadness, happiness, lessons learned, growth, tears and laughter - it's all there in everyone's life. But as for now, please sit back and relax as I take you around the world!   Life is wonderful! Life is exciting! Are you ready? Let's go!

Aubrey Beauchamp
San Clemente, California

Chapter 1

THE DUTCH TOUCH

"There's someone here to see you."

I looked up from my sandbox in our backyard where I was busy making mud pies. My mother was approaching with a blond, blue-eyed boy I had never seen before. He seemed nice although a little bewildered and tightly held on to her hand. For a moment he silently observed my sandy domain, then let go of Mom's hand and smiled.

"This is Mickey," Mom announced. "He lives down the street. Why don't you two play together?"

I moved over and handed him a sandform.

"Watch out for my castle," I cautioned, steering him away from an emerging edifice in the corner of the sandbox. Mom returned to the kitchen and I tried to show Mickey the art of baking pies and building sandcastles.

It did not take me long to discover that this kid had a problem: he did not know how to talk. Oh, he did open his mouth and produce sounds but they did not mean anything, neither did he seem to understand a thing I said. I'd ask him for a spoon and he'd just sit there and stare at me. Then he'd say something to me which made no sense at all. Patiently, I'd try to figure out what he had in mind. Finally, I gave up, deciding that communication with this kid was hopeless. I did the only sensible thing a three year old can do; I burst into tears and ran to my mother.

"I can't play with that boy," I sobbed, "he doesn't know how to talk." Oddly enough, Mom did not seem surprised. She just smiled and led me back to the sandbox where Mickey was working on his castle. She talked to him and he responded immediately with a broad smile. He talked back but what did he say? Then I realized I couldn't understand my own mother.

Speechless, I stared from one to the other.

After some mysterious dialogue, Mickey went home and Mom pulled me on her lap in the living room. We had a serious talk at the conclusion of which I had added a new concept to my vocabulary - foreign language. The foreign language Mickey spoke was English. It was foreign because we lived in Holland and spoke Dutch. Although Mickey's father was from Holland, his mother was not. She was English. His Dad had recently moved the family to Holland and settled in the village of Blaricum where we lived. Little did I know then that one day, many years later, English would become my native tongue but that, in the course of mastering this new skill, my life would take several drastic turns in unexpected directions.

Blaricum was a tiny, almost forgotten and rather sleepy village just about fifteen miles south of Amsterdam and several miles from the main highway which connected our capital with other major cities such as Apeldoorn, Arnhem, Utrecht, The Hague or Rotterdam. It was nestled in a rather wooded area around a couple of square miles of charming heather fields and surrounded by several townships of which Blaricum was the smallest. The whole region was called 't Gooi.

't Gooi was slightly elevated, quite unusual for this part of Holland (most of which is below sea level) and kept dry by man-made dykes and natural dunes. Also called "the Netherlands" or "lowlands," the most common sights of Holland are stretches of green, flat pastureland, divided into tiny plots by a maze of rivers and canals with fat black and white cows grazing contentedly in the rich grassy meadows. There are quite a variety of windmills, of course, and sparkling clean villages, scattered around tall steepled churches. All church steeples are similar yet no two are quite the same. A trained eye can, even from a far distance, tell one village from another by the shape of its church steeple. But 't Gooi was different. There were few pastures but many trees such as firs, oaks, pines, birches and huge red and white blooming chestnuts. During the summer the blooming heather covered the ground like a huge purple blanket, highlighted by scattered bushes of bright yellow Scottish Broom.

Mom and Dad were seventeen when they met in Bussum, another village in 't Gooi. Mom worked in a pastry shop, selling breads and cakes which Dad produced in the bakery in back of the shop. He was actually preparing for a career as a purser on a passenger ship so he could see the world. This career would give him easy access to explore foreign shores. One phase of his training included Food Services, hence the bakery job. Mom and Dad fell in love and Dad began to have second thoughts about a career at sea. Mom shared his sense of adventure, though, and together they spent many a day biking through Holland and neighboring countries like Belgium and Luxemburg. They also acquired a small sailboat, quite an adventure in those days, and tried out their sailing skills on the often choppy lakes in nearby Loosdrecht. Dad finally relinquished his world travel plans. They both enrolled in evening classes, taking bookkeeping and commercial math. Six years later, at age twenty-three, they were married and moved to Blaricum. They both had jobs in Bussum at Van Heel's Condensed Milk, an international firm exporting dairy products.

Most couples were unable to save enough from their meagre incomes to furnish a home in those days. Very few could afford to buy a home so most people, like Mom and Dad, rented. They moved to Blaricum for two reasons. There was a two-story, three-bedroom house available which they liked with brick walls and a thatched roof. They also liked the quietness of the little off-the-main-road town. Dad then persuaded a merchant in Amsterdam to sell them furniture on a six-month installment plan, proving his credit by two steady jobs for himself and his future bride. It was 1931, the Great Depression was in full swing and furniture sales were low. The manager finally agreed, a deal was made, and Mom and Dad began their wedded life in a fully-equipped home. The payments were made at the agreed upon times. This was a breakthrough not only in family tradition but also in Dutch customs.

Two years later, I came along, a hefty nine pounder, born at home and delivered by a midwife. Mom had a hard time and after the delivery the nurse stayed for two weeks, helping her with the baby and household chores while she recuperated. Almost three years later, she was pregnant again. This delivery was vastly different. The doctor, new and young, came from the neighboring town of Laren. (Blaricum didn't have any doctors or a hospital.) He estimated her delivery date sometime in September. Mom did not agree and felt it was much earlier, but he insisted. One day in late July, she felt some mild contractions and summoned the young doctor. He came to the house, worried, and examined her.

"Yes," he said, "you are in labor but I can feel no life. I believe the baby is dead. You will probably deliver it soon."

The nurse came, Mom was put to bed and the doctor left. Labor continued. Soon a tiny, lifeless little baby was born, still fully enveloped in a bag of unbroken membranes. The little body was surrounded by brownish-green liquid. Gently, the nurse put the whole thing aside and turned to Mom to wait for the afterbirth. With a heavy heart Dad looked at the little formless bundle on the side of the large, double bed. Suddenly however, he thought he saw a small movement.

"Nurse!" he shouted, "Something's moving inside!"

The nurse looked up, grabbed a pair of scissors and cut the bag of water open. She pulled out the limp form by its tiny ankles and gave it a gentle pat. Its little arms jerked, the tiny mouth opened, it took a breath and screamed!

It was alive! A little girl! Everyone laughed and cried at once.

"Quick," the nurse instructed Dad, "we need several hot water bottles to keep her warm." She hurried off to the neighbors who owned a phone and called the hospital in Laren. They prepared a special heated crib ready for this infant who needed to be admitted for observation.

In all the excitement, Mom was left unattended for a while, her uterus filling with blood, then clots. Finally, the doctor came and cared for her. It was very painful. The bleeding stopped but she had lost so much she remained anemic for many years. Nobody suggested iron pills until fifteen years later. Meanwhile the baby did fine, was named Helena Elizabeth after her grandmother, weighed in at four and a half pounds and was discharged from the hospital three days later.

Our family was a happy one. We were not wealthy but we were loved and secure. We had no car or garage, just four bicycles in a shed. We had no telephone, refrigerator or oven; not even hot water or a bathtub. On the other hand, crime, immorality and violence were just about unknown. Life in Blaricum was simple, wholesome and predictable. Dad, dark and tall, was a serious and responsible breadwinner. Although quiet, he had a quick sense of humor and was active in our local soccer and ping-pong games and in the drama club. Mom, who quit her job after I was born, was a tall, blue-eyed brunette, outgoing and innovative. From a couple of orange crates, for instance, she fashioned several sturdy and attractive cupboards for our home which had no built-in closets. She covered the sides with cloth, painted and papered the shelves and hung a hand-embroidered burlap curtain in front. She shared Dad's sense of humor and there was always a lot of laughter in our home. Mom was one of the main actresses in the local drama club, the Korenbloem (Corn Flower). Most plays were comedies, performed in Blaricum's one and only theater, a 200 seat auditorium called Enzlin. It was behind the store of our local baker. In fact, backstage was the bakery, always warm and cozy and permeated with the mouth-watering smell of fresh bread.

We lived on the Huizerhoogt, a cobblestone road which connected Blaricum with the next village of Huizen. Our home was about one mile from the heart of Blaricum. A blackened little steam tram, nicknamed the Murderer, huffed and puffed its way through 't Gooi, belching clouds of smelly smoke into the air while pulling two cars carrying commuters, high school kids and shopping housewives, from one village to the other. Downtown Blaricum was actually just a bend in the road. We even boasted a bandstand next to City Hall, a rather dull, red-brick building. Right behind it was our elementary school which housed seven grades in four classrooms. Mr. Kranen, the Principal, was a quiet, unassuming man who lived next to the school right behind the bandstand. Across from City Hall was a garage, actually a converted farmhouse with a thatched roof, where a man named Jan Klaver fixed cars and bicycles. There were other merchants, a barber, a grocer, an impressive Post Office and a large fabric store. Merchants lived right behind or above their shops as did the dentist and the vet. Mixed among these businesses were farmhouses complete with haystacks, chickens, outdoor water pumps and cows who were kept inside the large stables during the long, cold winters. The farmer and his family lived in these stables also. Their quarters were separated from the lowing, munching animals by a single thin wall. It was always nice and warm in there but the pungent smell of fresh cow dung was something to which you had to adjust.

Our favorite place in Blaricum was Kooy's Ice Cream Parlor across from the Post Office. I can still see the huge, red flowering chestnut tree in front of the white building and the many bicycles haphazardly parked in front. Besides ice cream, Kooy also served scrumptious yogurt concoctions. In the area of yogurt, by the way, Holland was rather ahead of her time for it would be many years before this dairy product caught the imagination of other countries. Alas, these delicacies were only permitted on special occasions. I also clearly remember the little candy shop of Pietje Riga. It was hidden at the end of a small alley behind a photography store and just before the Police Station. A little bell attached to the low door jingled when someone entered. Pietje, an old, heavy-set woman, would shuffle in from the back where her living quarters were.

"May I help you?" She would lean her stout, short frame against the counter, her face blank, polite, without any emotion. She knew exactly what we wanted but waited for the official order.

"A penny from the tray, please," we'd pipe up at her from our lowly height of three feet.

From below the counter she'd produce a large tray covered with all kinds of candies. For a penny, we could choose any one of these. Oh, how we must have tried her patience as we gloated over these delectables. It was so hard to make a choice.

Come to think of it, we were seldom given any choices in matters of food or drink. You ate what was set in front of you. All of it. There was no choice. We never ate out. Nobody else did, either. Perhaps we'd have an occasional sandwich at a cafeteria when Mom couldn't make it home in time for lunch. The only exceptions were the roadside ice cream vendors during the summer months. On Sunday afternoon bicycle trips, Mom would usually ignore those people but Dad had a sweet tooth and we could often persuade him to produce a nickel from the depths of his pocket when one of the vendors came in sight. The man then pulled a long metal cylinder out of his cart which contained the ice cream. The front of the cylinder was open. The vendor covered the ice cream top with a wafer. Then with a flat scoop he'd cut a slice off, cover the other side with another wafer and we had our ice cream! The thickness of the slice depended on the price or, as I frequently suspected, the vendor's mood.

We had two Police Constables in Blaricum. One was an impressive man named Jacobs sporting a large, drooping moustache. He wore a black uniform and his only weapon was a rubber stick. I'm not sure what filled Jacob's days although he always showed up at dances, parties or official events around closing time. Good-naturedly, he would accept a beer from the exuberant crowd. Then he'd stand up, clear his throat and announce:

"Time to go home folks! Everybody out! Remember, if you give me a hard time, I'll have to call the police."

Another Blaricum character, although far below the social status of Jacobs, was Tinus the Trumpeter. Nobody knew much about Tinus except that he carried a trumpet which he could not play because in the summer it was too hot and in the winter it was too cold. He was always dressed in rags. An old hat covered his long, dirty hair. He had some teeth missing, needed a shave and was always looking for handouts.

Occasionally, we had the opportunity to buy fresh fish from a man with a large basket in front of his bike. He'd stop at certain crossroads, clang two cymbals together and announce his presence through a bullhorn.

Besides these odd figures, we had regular vendors like the grocer, milkman and the fruit and vegetable man who made daily deliveries to the house on their bikes. One day the grocer pulled up at our front gate. He leaned his bike against the little brick wall next to the gate, picked up a basket with orders and walked around the house to the kitchen. I was standing on the balcony upstairs where Mom was cleaning and saw the man coming. As he walked right under me, I quickly pushed a can of cleanser from the edge of the balcony. It was a direct hit! The can smashed right into the basket, all over the groceries! Mom was furious but the deed was done and I secretly congratulated myself.

After my encounter with Mickey, the neighborhood produced additional playmates. There was Adri, an enterprising girl, three years my senior. When she was little she called herself Doe (as in "I do"), a name she retained as she grew up. Next to us lived Thys and Donald whose Dad was away in the service. Other neighbor kids included Woodrow, Ria and Gieneke. We often played together. There were no TVs, stereos, VCRs or movies. Our radio featured an hour-long children's program on Sunday morning. However, we had plenty of imagination and fresh air. Doe often invented games. We played hospital. Woodrow was the doctor, our scooter the ambulance, Doe the nurse. I was the patient and an old flower bed served as the hospital.

When Doe turned six it was time for her to leave our playful endeavors and start school. There was no kindergarten. Elementary school was from nine to noon and from two to four in the afternoon. Everybody walked to school and everyone came home for lunch including Dad, who pedalled six miles across the heather from Bussum four times a day. First graders, however, did not have to go to school in the afternoon. The first day our leader, Doe, was gone, we were at a loss. The morning was long and boring. When she finally came home, we swarmed around her in the backyard.

"How did it go?" "What did you learn?" "What was it like?" We all yelled together.

Dramatically, Doe rolled back her eyes, threw up her hands and fell into a lawn chair.

"Please," she begged, "don't talk to me right now. I've learned so much I'm exhausted."

Now our playtime moved to the afternoon. Doe became involved in several plays which she put together and directed. She memorized long poems which we acted out as she went along. There was one about a witch with a large wart on her nose which she wanted to get rid of. Everyone always got a part. If there were no parts left, we invented one. My part usually involved that of stage manager, prompter or MC. We needed an audience, of course, so we often waited for birthdays to come around. Birthdays in Holland were visiting days and family gatherings. Nobody was invited, everybody just showed up.

One memorable birthday, I believe it was my sixth, we had worked hard on the play with the witch and her wart. For this occasion, I was cast in the role of the witch. Early in the day, we took possession of the living room, actually the drawing room, used mostly for special occasions. It was divided by a heavy brown curtain from the sunroom, a perfect set-up for a stage. Dutch homes are always meticulously clean but for special family gatherings many extra hours are spent cleaning and polishing and dusting. Mom, although not quite as fanatical about house cleaning as most Dutch housewives, nevertheless had made a supreme effort to get the house sparkling and dust-free. Although my folks knew we kids had prepared something special for the occasion, they were given no details other than that it would be a surprise.

When the first visitors arrived, Doe's brother Guus, who was ushering, went into action.

"This way, please!" He directed everyone away from the front door and around the house to the sunroom entrance. Many neighbors began showing up as well. Some of them had never been to our house before.

"What are all these people doing here?" Mom whispered to me as we passed in the hallway. She looked worried.

"..Eh, we just invited them for the play, Mom," I said, avoiding her eyes. "We're just about ready to start. Why don't you go to the sunroom?" Grandpa, who had also been directed to the sunroom, noticed an empty basket on the table.

"What would that be for?" he inquired of Guus, the usher.

"Oh, that," Guus said, "is for donations."

Mom just walked in and overheard his remark. Her embarrassment grew as did her forebodings about what we were up to. Little did she know what lay ahead. When all was ready, my sister, Helen, in one of her first official parts, opened the drapes. I heard Mom gasp!

The first act was supposed to take place in a forest. To change a living room into a forest is no easy task. We had to haul in lots of branches, leaves, moss and pine cones along with a few rocks. To Mom, her sparkling clean room was a total disaster but to us it was a terrific forest. An angel came into view, floating across the forest. It was Gieneke. Her dress, Mom noticed, strongly resembled one of her best slips. An elf stumbled across on high heels. Her shoes looked very familiar. In a corner sat Ria, hunched in a stuffy gunnysack. A paper beak indicated she was a bird. Her part consisted of just one line which she forgot. She could not see a thing and almost suffocated inside that sack. Happily, the play got underway. The plot was simple. The witch wants to get rid of her wart but none of her magic potions work. Finally, walking through the woods one day she slips and falls, hits her nose on a sharp rock and the wart is gone! However, I had used a little too much glue and after I dutifully fell on the rock, the wad of tissue that was my wart refused to come off my nose. In the excitement of the moment, I didn't notice. But Doe, the prompter, did.

"Your wart!" she hissed.

No response.

"YOUR WART! It didn't come off!" she was yelling now.

I gave her a bewildered look and suddenly got the message. Oh no! What should I do? Undaunted, I fell again. And again. No results. Finally, I grabbed the wart and pulled it off. It hurt. The audience roared but I could have died. Luckily, it was time for intermission.

When everyone had feasted on lemonade and cookies, we continued our performance. For this act, actually another mini-play, we had changed the forest into a family room. A number of people sat around the dinner table. We were using our best china. Mom held her breath. I don't remember the plot but at the end of the meal someone gathered the dishes to take them to the kitchen. As soon as the dishes were out of sight, I was ready for our special effects. Standing behind the drapes, I grabbed two old cracked plates I had found in someone's trash and smashed them with great gusto on the floor. The effect exceeded our expectations. Mom screamed! Others jumped up to investigate. There was instant pandemonium! We gloated. Helen closed the drapes.

"Perhaps you should explain," Doe cautioned in a nervous whisper, not sure of our safety now. I agreed and picked up the real, unbroken, dishes and I stepped in front of the drapes again.

"It wasn't real," I beamed. "Look, here they are!"

I don't remember the rest of the day except that Mom never lets me forget it. Somehow, the living room survived and life continued.

The front of our house faced a street called the Dwarslaan, actually an unpaved trail. It ended in a number of fields where local farmers planted rye, corn, potatoes and beets. These fields were hemmed by low shrubbery, ideal places to play hide and seek. I also loved to watch the farmers at work. An old, muscular horse slowly trudged across the field pulling a large hoe while the farmer in his wooden shoes plodded behind, keeping even furrows. Later, the farmer would hand-seed his field pulling handfuls of seeds from a large pouch around his waist, scattering them with an even hand as he slowly walked back and forth along the furrows. Irrigation from our ever-active "sky sprinklers" was guaranteed and soon young, green shoots appeared which eventually became a waving sea of golden rye, dotted here and there with bright blue cornflowers. In the fall, farmhands would join the farmer for the harvest. Wielding large, curved scythes they would mow the ripened rye with slow, even movements. Later, long rows of sheaves stood across the fields like miniature Indian teepees. Above them white, billowing clouds floated lazily overhead playing hide and seek with the warm September sun.

In grade school, we quickly mastered a variety of subjects including the basics of the three Rs. Swimming was also part of the curriculum. Every six-year-old could swim, tread water and rescue someone else. One part of the finals for this class was swimming with a full set of clothes on (including shoes). I always felt the girls were at a disadvantage here since our skirts wrapped around our legs making swimming almost impossible. We also had to retrieve an object from the bottom of the muddy pool. Actually, our pool was a modified pond and the water was never clear nor chlorinated.

The Dutch have been fighting water for centuries. Most of the western half of Holland consists of so-called "polderland," drained lakes surrounded by dykes to keep the water out. Our nearby village of Eemnes was such a "polder." Cows grazed in pastures lower than the water level of the surrounding canals. Mr. Ploeger, our third grade teacher, told us one day of the biggest "polder" of all, the former Zuiderzee.

"The Zuiderzee," he started, "used to be an inland sea connected to the North Sea right here." He pointed to an area about fifty miles long between the provinces of Friesland and North Holland. "The Zuiderzee then had tides and white, sandy beaches. But then," he continued, "we needed more land. Why did we need more land?"

"We have too many people," someone guessed.

"Right. How many people do we have in our country?"

"Ten million?"

"Almost eleven and how big is our country?"

No answer.

"Well, about 100 by 200 miles." He covered the whole country with one sweep of his hand.

"So we needed additional land. What would you do first to dry out the Zuiderzee?"

"Build a dyke."

"Right. We did built a dyke to separate the Zuiderzee from the North Sea. When the dyke was built the Zuiderzee became a lake. Then what do you think happened?"

"No more tides," one bright kid observed.

"Right, no more tides and the water changed from salty to fresh. It gets fresh water from rivers like the Ÿsel, right here." He pointed out.

"So they renamed the Zuiderzee...?"

"The Ÿsel Lake!" We all said it together.

In fact, I could see the Ÿsel Lake from the end of our street. It was choppy and often covered with angry whitecaps but there were no tides and not much of a beach. The whole Zuiderzee project, by the way, came to an abrupt halt in 1940 when World War II erupted. Afterwards, when the country had somewhat recovered from five years of occupation, it was eventually completed. But by that time Holland's population had swelled to fifteen million.

Water, however, wasn't our only danger. Fire was another. Our thatch-roofed home was attached to two others but the house on one side had a tile roof. This type of roof was often interspaced as a fire deterrent. It didn't always work, however. One day a plumber was working on a home two doors from us and caused a fire with his welding torch. This house shared a thatched roof with its neighbor. Strong winds fanned the flames and within minutes both homes were ablaze. Wouldn't you know it! That day it didn't rain! Fire engines screeched in from both Blaricum and nearby Huizen. Our street was roped off. We stood in the front yard and watched in horror. The house next to us was the only structure separating us from the blazing inferno. Burning reeds shot into the air like fireworks. Soon one landed on the thatched roof of the house directly across from it. Additional fire engines arrived to battle this new blaze. They were unsuccessful.

After many anxiety-filled hours, the fire still raged on. Huge clouds of black smoke drifted all over Blaricum. Our sun-room had, by now, become the Fire Marshall's Command Post and Emergency Center. Firemen received orders there, Red Cross workers treated people for smoke inhalation and eye injuries. The national press sent reporters, Constable Jacobs and additional law enforcement agents tried to control the large, gawking crowd. Suddenly one of the burning reeds touched the roof of the home directly across from us. There were three homes sharing this roof. The red-hot reed smoldered then quickly ignited. Flames leaped upwards. An alert fireman tried to pull a hose over to it but the flames were too high. Precious minutes were lost until someone hauled in another ladder.

"Is there anyone at home there?" a fireman shouted at Mom.

"No, they're at work," she said, "but their dog is inside."

The firefighter broke a window and Mom helped to get the scared dog out. Fortunately, the winds began to die and this last fire was quickly contained leaving only a gaping hole in the master bedroom. The other three homes burned to the ground. Eventually they were rebuilt - again with thatched roofs.

Our family was healthy and nobody had ever been hospitalized. Babies were born at home. When kids were sick, the doctor made house calls. However, I was soon to have my first encounter within the walls of a hospital. One day, when I was about five, Mom noticed a lump in my right groin. She took me to Dr. Holtman, a general physician, who lived and practiced in Laren. I can still see that large whitewashed impressive home, rather somber, surrounded by huge trees. The actual office was in front, the waiting room in the back, while a wide stairway led to the second floor where the doctor and his family lived. The waiting room was plain with a high ceiling and a variety of chairs against each bare wall, filled with sober, unsmiling people who either read old magazines or just stared into space. When our turn came we entered the consultation room where a faint smell of carbolic acid ushered us into the presence of Dr. Holtman who was seated at his cluttered desk. He was an elderly, kind man who always seemed to exude hope and confidence. Just to be in his presence made us feel better. He examined my abdomen and discovered not one but two hernias, an inguinal and an umbilical one. They had to be surgically removed, he told Mom. Of course, for this I had to be hospitalized. Now Mom faced a problem.

I had never been away from home, never wanted to stay overnight with relatives or friends. How was she going to get me to the hospital? She finally hit on an idea - a fabricated a story:

"When I was a little girl," she began a few days later when we were quietly sitting at home, "I also had a hernia, just like you. Luckily," she continued, "I was able to go to a hospital. I got all kinds of presents and games and people came to visit me." There were more enticing details.

I listened attentively. Finally, I asked the hoped-for question: "Do you think there is a chance that I can go to a hospital, too?"

"I doubt it," she said, "but if you like I'll ask the doctor."

During the next few days, I kept asking Mom: "Did you hear from the doctor yet? Can I go?"

Finally, I got the good news.

"Guess what?" Mom announced, "I spoke with the doctor today and he said it was all right. You can go to the hospital."

Delighted, I packed a small bag and climbed contentedly in my bike seat behind Mom who pedalled to St. John's hospital in Laren. Our footsteps echoed through the bare, uncarpeted halls. The smell of disinfectant reminded me of the doctor's office. Most of the nurses were nuns, kind and efficient, their faces almost invisible behind large, starched caps which were part of their cumbersome habits. I was taken to a semi-private room and put to bed. Mom left me some coloring books and games and pedalled home. I was little apprehensive but didn't cry or object. Her strategy had worked.

The next day, I was transported to the operating room, placed on a table and covered with a sheet. A nurse was fussing with some instruments on a nearby table. I waited. The silence hung heavy in the large, well-lit room. Dim sounds from the outside world came through the windows. Someone mentioned that the doctor was delayed. He must have arrived eventually for a pleasant nun sat down at the head of the table and put something over my face. It was an induction to ether.

"Just breath deeply," she instructed.

I didn't like it and wanted to pull the mask off but discovered my hands were tied down. Then suddenly, I was back in my room, a little foggy and with an awful taste in my mouth. I noticed I had a roommate, a girl my age. Her parents were visiting. That reminded me of my parents. Where were they? A sudden wave of homesickness swept over me and I started to cry. Ouch! That hurt. Panicky now, I cried even louder resulting in more pain. Frantic, I stood up in bed, grabbed the siderails and screamed. This brought immediate action. Two nuns rushed in. They were very angry and pushed me down, flat on my back again. Then, to make sure I'd stay there, they tied two straps over the blankets and fastened them clear down under the bed. They also gave me a sedative.

During all this frantic activity, my folks arrived. They were stopped in the hall and allowed to see me only after I was securely tied down. The surgeon was also notified and he ordered several extra days of complete bed rest for me. After Mom and Dad left, I quieted down somewhat and eventually adjusted to my enforced rest. A few days later, still flat on my back, I gingerly explored my abdomen. I felt two dressings. Probing underneath with a finger, I encountered some metal objects attached to my skin. Years later, I realized they were Michelle clips, sometimes used instead of conventional catgut stitches. I also found out that the poor nuns thought I had ruined my surgery by standing up in bed so soon. I smile now as I see patients walk in and out of surgery after their hernias are repaired under local anesthesia. Alas, times have changed. Way back in 1939, I was discharged ten days after surgery. I didn't share Mom's enthusiasm for hospitals at all and was glad to be home. Hospitals were definitely not for me!

Even though our little family was close and happy, we never went to church, never talked about God, never prayed or read the Bible. Yet, we inherited a solid lifestyle from my parents with high moral standards and principles. Discipline and hard work was part of living; so was thrift. Everybody had a savings account. And even though we did not attend church, we did get some religious instruction at our school. In sixth grade a pastor came in once a week to teach us the rudiments of the Bible. It was an optional class. Those who were excused had a free period. Unfortunately, we were not. I don't remember much of the pastor or his classes. Most of us were unchurched and had little use for spiritual matters so the poor man was sowing on rather dry ground.

Later, my folks decided Helen and I should go to Sunday school. We had one Protestant and one Catholic church in Blaricum. Since we were not Catholic, we were enrolled in the Protestant church. Each Sunday morning we were herded into different classrooms adjacent to the huge, cavernous church sanctuary. Here we were exposed to fascinating Bible stories. We sang hymns, prayed, colored pictures, gave something towards the offering and learned Bible verses. At the end of the year we received our very own little Bible. Unfortunately, the print was so small and the text so ancient no one ever looked at it again.

The highlight of Sunday School was Christmas Eve. For once we were allowed to enter the mysterious, awesome sanctuary. Our parents were there, too. Most of them, like mine, never darkened the massive front doors of the church during the year. The huge pipe organ, towering high above the ornate pulpit, played familiar Christmas carols. Dozens of real white candles serenely glowed on the tall, brightly trimmed pine. A long stick with a wet sponge at the end stood nearby just in case. Huddled in our warm winter clothes, our eyes reflecting the soft candlelight, we listened to the beautiful Christmas story with the angels, the shepherds, the wise men, the manger and the Babe. We knew the whole story. Yet, that's all it was. Just a story.

A few months after Christmas, Dad announced that Mickey's father, Mr. Schintz, was leaving. He was taking his family back to Canada.

"I don't like what's going on in Germany," he told Dad.

World War I had ended twenty years before. Holland, at that time, had not been involved or occupied. Now, not many people paid much attention to Adolph Hitler. One rainy day early in 1939, Mickey and his family left. They boarded a boat and crossed the Atlantic. A few months later, they were unexpectedly followed by the Dutch Royal family who were fleeing their country.

Hitler's troops had marched boldly into Holland.

Chapter 2

THE LEAN YEARS

I was seven years old that spring day in 1940 when German troops invaded our little country. Our military defense put up a brave fight for three days but were no match for Hitler's huge, well-trained military forces. One night, a sudden air attack wiped out the entire commercial section of Rotterdam, one of our largest cities with a strategic international harbor. It was all over. Holland surrendered and our government and Royal Family fled to London. Queen Wilhelmina's daughter, Princess Juliana, her husband Prince Bernard and their three children escaped to the security of Canada. We were now an occupied country although Hitler insisted his troops were there to "protect" us.

It was a good thing I was seven - not quite old enough to realize the serious implications of living under a foreign dictatorship yet old enough to clearly remember those difficult years. It definitely influenced the rest of my life. We learned many valuable lessons which helped all of us in later years as we adjusted to other major changes. At first our "protectors" seemed rather benign. No major changes were apparent. In reality, however, we had lost our freedom in every area of life. The government, the police force, the press and radio were all under the control of our captors.

Take the Dutch military, for instance. Officially, all officers were prisoners of war. They were not arrested but were placed on parole until further notice. One day, all the officers were asked to check in at a large military base where they would be officially discharged from the military and freed to return to civilian life, or so the message said. A close friend of my parents, Jan Bottema, was included in this list. He seriously debated whether to show up. If he didn't go, he would have to go underground which would be dangerous and complicated. There were no indications of foul play so, together with hundreds of other officers all over the country, he checked in at his particular precinct.

For hours they just sat around, waiting for some action or official word. Finally, everyone was herded into a large auditorium. An official roll call was taken. Then without warning, all doors to the auditorium were suddenly locked. Guards and guns appeared.

"You're all under arrest!" an official barked. "Don't try to escape, the building is surrounded! Do as you're told and you won't be harmed."

Aghast, Jan realized they had all walked right into a well-planned trap.

"Get up!" the voice commanded. "Everyone leave through the back door."

They were marched to waiting buses and quickly transported to the nearest railroad station. There, a heavily armed guard forced them to board a waiting train headed for Nürenberg, Germany.

Just before the German border, Jan jumped off the train. He was bleeding and had a dislocated jaw. In great pain, he managed to stop a passing truck.

"I've been in an accident and need medical attention," he told the driver, "Can you get me to a doctor?"

The man probably guessed what happened. Word of the betrayal of the Dutch officers had quickly spread. He helped Jan into his truck and took him to a doctor.

"I'm an officer," Jan admitted to the doctor when they were alone, "can you help me? My life is in danger. I jumped the train."

The doctor treated Jan and kept him in his home for several weeks. When recuperated, Jan still felt it was not safe to contact his wife, Mien. Several months later, Mien received a letter from the Wehrmacht, the German army, stating her husband was missing and presumed dead. When Jan finally made it home he joined the Dutch underground and became an active resistance worker. Later, he was betrayed and was executed a few months before the war ended in 1945.

Official news about the war was biased and incomplete but we quickly discovered Radio Orange, a shortwave station from London, made available by the British. Our Royal Family belonged to the House of Orange, hence the name. This station broadcast daily news on the progress of the war along with messages of hope and encouragement to the Dutch nation. Soon, however, our captors got wind of these links and banned all short-wave radios.

Tucked into our beds upstairs, I distinctly remember hearing the deep hum of hundreds of Allied planes flying high over Holland to Germany each night. It was a familiar sound that would continue for many years. After dropping their bombs, the planes would return to England, again crossing Holland at a high altitude just before daylight. Reports of these raids were picked up by Radio Orange and received at a low volume from our radio now hidden in the basement. News bulletins were printed and distributed to those without a radio although this soon became too dangerous and we had to rely on word of mouth.

To prevent the Allies from recognizing landmarks as they made their nightly crossing, no lights of any kind were to be seen after dark. That meant a complete blackout with no street lights and heavy, black blinds on every window. There was also a curfew. Later, electricity was cut off so we used oil lamps. Illegal wiring produced some power for our radios and lamps. The latter had to be used with great care so that no one would know of our illegal source of light.

Some Dutchmen believed the smooth talk of our oppressors and fell for the favors and privileges they offered to those who would cooperate with them. They joined an organization formed by Hitler in the mid-'30s, called the NSM (National Socialist Movement). These Dutch Nazis wore black and orange uniforms. They marched and sang and held meetings promoting the virtues of the Third Reich. They also sneaked around to see if anyone broke the law by listening to clandestine radio stations. They faithfully reported their findings to the authorities. Some, at the request of their superiors, operated under cover so they could spy more effectively. We quickly learned to recognize friends from foes, not to divulge clandestine information and generally to keep a low profile.

After the first two years of occupation, our situation became progressively worse. Food, which had been rationed for a long time, became very scarce. Rations were grossly inadequate. Most of Holland's food (dairy products, fruit, vegetables and meat) was confiscated and shipped to Germany. By now, the Germans were starving too, their men fighting on foreign soil, leaving women and children in charge of farms and factories. Our rations consisted of bread, cheese, potatoes and some margarine. The cheese was a substitute, barely edible, and the little milk the milkman brought was diluted, non-fat and bluish. Soup kitchens appeared, so did long lines. We stood in these lines for hours to get just a pot of hot, flavored water with some cabbage leaves in it.

It was then that my folks approached a farmer in Blaricum, entreating him to keep some milk for our family after milking his cows. He was instructed to deliver all milk to the authorities but promised to keep a liter for us every day. Helen and I took turns at night, groping our way through the pitch dark streets to and from the farmhouse, clutching a glass milk bottle under our worn coats.

Clothing also became very scarce as was fuel, coal and wood to keep our homes warm during the bitterly cold winters. Our beautiful, old, giant trees, the pride of 't Gooi, slowly fell to the axe one by one. The winter of 1943 was extremely severe. Germany suffered, too, and so it was decreed that each Dutch citizen could only sleep under two blankets. All extra bedding had to be taken to local collection depots. When these "excess" items were received, we were issued a receipt. The Nazis also began their dreaded "razzias" or home searches for these items. Anyone unable to produce a receipt would be subjected to such a search. All excess blankets found beyond the decreed quotas were immediately confiscated.

One day, we got word through the grapevine that a blanket "razzia" was under way. Since we lived on the edge of town, we often got advanced warning. Dad disappeared through the backyard and we were told to keep playing and be quiet. Schools were closed because the buildings were not heated. Besides, the Germans used our schools as field offices and collection centers. Mom stripped our beds, hid the extra bedding and left only two thin blankets on each bed. No sooner had she finished this task than the doorbell rang. Quickly, she opened the door. "Guten Morgen!" she beamed in her best German, her acting talents in full swing. She faced a mere boy, a teenager too young to shave but decked out in full uniform. Surprised by her friendly greeting, he stammered, "Eh.., Morgen."

Then, trying to gain his composure, he suddenly barked, "I'm here to search for blankets. Where is your receipt?"

"I'm sorry, but I don't have one," Mom apologized, "we have nothing left to give."

Before he could reply, she opened the door wide and smiled, "Why don't you come in and see for yourself?"

He hesitated, his bluff gone. Peeking past her shoulder, he spotted our coat rack in the vestibule. All our threadbare coats and sweaters were clearly visible, displayed at this strategic location on purpose.

Trying to maintain his bravado he demanded, "How many children do you have?"

"Six!" Mom proudly announced.

"Oh my," the kid seemed relieved, "I'm sure you don't have anything to spare. Guten Tag."

He quickly turned on his heels and marched to the next home. And so, during the bitterly cold winter of 1944, we kept warm during the night at least.

Holland's economy had always heavily depended on import. Our largest supplier was the Netherland East Indies, now called Indonesia, which had been a crown colony of Holland for three hundred years. From these islands, we received rubber, rice, bananas, pepper, spices, coconuts and a host of other items. Indonesia was now occupied by the Japanese and imports of any kind had been cut off a long time ago. During the third and fourth year of the occupation, many of these items became extinct. Rubber was one such commodity. That meant no bike tires or shoes. Bikes were our only mode of transportation, so the inventive Dutch managed to fashion substitutes from strips of old truck tires. The advantage of this kind of tire was that it needed no air, the disadvantage was a very bumpy ride. Inventive cobblers also nailed wooden soles to old shoes, making walking a rather heavy and cumbersome experience. The famous Dutch wooden shoes, worn mostly by farmers as they trudged through their muddy, wet fields, became acceptable shoes for many non-farmers too.

Since the German work force in their own homeland was greatly depleted, all men in Holland between the ages of eighteen and forty were instructed to check into a local precinct. The word got around that they would be shipped to Germany as forced laborers so few men showed up. Angered, the Nazis continued their "razzias," now searching for people. Unexpectedly, they would appear at our doors, search homes and arrest all males between eighteen and forty. These men were then herded onto freight trains and shipped to Germany. We had several close calls, the most frightening one came on April 20, 1944.

Dad was inside. He happened to look through the window and to spot two uniformed Nazis at the gate. He froze. No time to leave the house. He was trapped.

"They're here!" his voice was tense as he called Mom.

She immediately sized up the situation. "Quick," she said, "get in your hiding place."

Dad opened the door of a closet in the living room. It had several shelves full of cups and plates and other china. Squatting down, he hastily removed a small panel from the side just below the lowest shelf. A tiny opening became visible. Quickly he slid through it, feet first. Then Mom handed him a panel which he used to close the opening again. He was now inside a built-in couch adjacent to the cupboard. The doorbell rang long and loud just as Mom closed the cupboard door.

She took a deep breath, walked towards the door and opened it. She faced two grim-looking Nazis in their mid-thirty's with the familiar steely, cold look in their eyes.

"Guten Morgen!" she said, smiling. Ignoring her greeting, the older of the two pushed her aside and entered the hallway.

"We're searching the house," he curtly announced.

"Come in," she smiled, ignoring the fact they were already in.

They marched straight to the living room. The room was decorated with paper streamers for my birthday which would be the following day. But that day, April 20, also happened to be Adolph Hitler's birthday. The Nazis realized it would be highly unlikely we were celebrating the Fuhrer's birthday. On the other hand, rumors of German defeats and an approaching D-Day where in the air everywhere.

"You're celebrating a bit early, aren't you?" he sneered.

"Oh no," Mom smiled. "This," she pointed to the decorations, "is for my little girl's birthday tomorrow."

His face seemed to soften a little. Looking around the room his gaze fell on a picture of me on the piano. Following his eyes, Mom continued, "That's her. She will be eleven tomorrow."

He walked over to the piano and stared at the photograph. Mom could only see his back now. She didn't move and held her breath. Then, breaking the silence she quietly asked, "Do you have any children?"

There was no answer. For a long minute nobody spoke or moved. The atmosphere was strangely charged. Finally, almost in a whisper, the Nazi said, "Yes, I have a little girl back home."

"How old is she?" Mom asked, pursuing his line of thought.

"She will be eleven soon."

"Oh," Mom continued, "how wonderful. I am sure you miss her."

Another silence. Mom still could not see his face.

"Yes," his voice was almost quiet now, his thoughts far away. "Yes, I miss her very much."

"But you will see her again? Soon perhaps, won't you?" Mom gently probed.

Another awkward, long silence. Nobody moved. A noisy fly hit the window. Some kids played outside. Finally the Nazi spoke, his voice barely above a whisper.

"No," he said, mostly to himself, "no, I will never see her again."

His voice broke. Mom realized that his next assignment was probably Russia where thousands of Hitler's troops were dying from either starvation, sub-zero temperatures or gunfire. In spite of the bizarre circumstances, she suddenly felt compassion for this man who, like her, had little control over his present or future.

Suddenly embarrassed, the Nazi roughly wiped his face with his sleeve.

Abruptly, he turned around and barked, "Where's your husband?" The steel glint in his eyes had returned.

"I don't know." Now Mom's voice became unsteady, her lip trembled. "They took him away six months ago. I haven't heard from him since. I have no idea where he is." She was in tears now. "If you want to search the house, go ahead," she said, opening the door.

He briefly observed her, a strange mixture of cruelty and sadness in his eyes. Then, briskly, he turned towards the front door and left, followed by his bewildered companion who hadn't said a word during the entire incident.

Dad, who had heard every word, stayed in his hiding place for another hour till he was sure the coast was clear.

By now, the Dutch underground was well organized. Their immediate concern was to destroy public records and personal data kept at

Government Record Departments. They quietly raided City Halls at night, destroying vital data. In retaliation, the furious Nazis would randomly stop a number of pedestrians on the street, execute them and issue a news bulletin stating the reason for their punishment.

To look older than forty, many men began to let their beards grow. Those with dentures stopped wearing them. Falsified IDs were issued by the underground. When "razzias" were in progress, the local grapevine got into action. Men went into hiding or fled to nearby brush country surrounding the farm fields. Often, angry and frustrated Germans searched through these areas, shooting at random at their elusive prey.

Just outside the little village of Putten, about fifty miles from us, some German officials were gunned down one night by a small group of the underground Dutch resistance forces. It was September, 1944. In retaliation, the furious Wehrmacht authorities issued a monstrous order. The next day, Sunday, the entire village was surrounded by soldiers. Women and children were herded into the church, all men arrested. Orders were then given to burn down the entire village! Eighty percent of the homes were brutally torched. That night from the end of our street, we could see an enormous red glow in the distant sky. We knew something terrible was happening but only later heard the gruesome details. For many days women and children, trying to save some of their belongings from the rubble that used to be their homes, were chased away. Six hundred and sixty of the arrested men were taken to Amersfoort where about sixty sick and elderly were released. Thirteen others managed to jump the train on their way to Germany. The rest of them, five hundred and eighty-nine, were shipped to brutal concentration camps in northern Germany. Only forty-four survived.

Cruelty and scarcity continued. Suddenly, copper became a forbidden item. It was needed for the German war machine. One day, we were instructed to bring all copper items from our home to a central collection center. We only had a few such items, mostly ornamental, among them a large, shiny umbrella holder. Helen and I were told that everything was taken to the authorities but the truth came out after the war when they were dug up from underneath the floor of our bicycle shed, all green and sandy. However, after some vigorous cleaning and polishing, they looked as good as new and graced our home once again.

As food became less and less available, we became more and more inventive and resourceful. Our small front yard which had boasted two lawns bordered by flowers and shrubbery, was converted into a tightly packed vegetable patch. Rows of beans crawled up on tall stalks. We had cabbage, kale, carrots and even tobacco, another extinct import product. The tobacco leaves were gathered and bundled, then hung upside down behind the stove to dry. Some expert would finally shred them. Smokers carried a pouch of this home-grown tobacco and rolled their own cigarettes. We also learned to eat carrot greens and dandelions. City folks, we heard, consumed tulip bulbs, birds and even rats and mice. Pets had disappeared, also. After all, who could keep a pet if we could scarcely find enough food to keep ourselves alive? Cats and dogs were slaughtered, their meat sold or given away to be consumed. Occasionally, we kids became suspicious when my folks would not eat much of a hearty meat soup Mom had cooked. Once I recalled the disappearance of a large dog from the neighborhood just before such a meal. It was not until later that I put the two events together.

One day, somewhere during the second year of the war, I saw two neighbor ladies on the street. They lived just a few doors from us and were sisters. Sewn on their coats were large, yellow stars. In the middle, in black, was the word, JEW.

"What's a Jew?" I asked Mom.

She explained but I did not quite understand. These ladies looked and talked like us and had lived near us all their lives. Why were they different?

Some Jews, I heard later, actually managed to hide their identity and successfully posed as Gentiles during the entire war. But most were not so fortunate. Dad worked with a sales rep who was Jewish. He too, wore a star, the star of David, with the word JEW in the center. One day, he disappeared, arrested by the Nazis and taken to Germany. He never returned.

Signs appeared in shops: "Jews not admitted." Most shopkeepers did not want to display these signs but were forced to do so. In busses and trains similar signs appeared: "No Jews" or "Jews in the Back." Cafes, the few that were left, also banned Jews. Later, people with stars began to disappear, most of them arrested and hauled to Germany's infamous deathcamps. All of the Jewish people we knew disappeared; none of them returned. Some had gone into hiding, hidden by Dutch families who risked their lives for their countrymen. They spent many years cramped in attics or hollow walls. Providing food for these people was a major problem but many survived and lived through the ordeal.

One interesting phenomenon of the war years stands out clearly in my mind. Even though I was very young, I could grasp certain trends and moods. Before the war, Holland was divided into many political factions, religious denominations and other splinter groups. During the war, however, these differences no longer existed. We seemed to be all of one mind. There was just one clear line of demarcation: the Germans and the Dutch Nazis were on one side and we, the occupied people of Holland, were on the other. Protestants, Jews, Catholics, atheists, Democrats, Socialists, all were of one accord. The rich, the poor, the middle class, farmers, city dwellers and suburbanites, these differences didn't matter any more. Divisions and walls had dissolved. Hunger, danger and loss of freedom had melted us together. Members of the underground would risk their lives for people they had never met. So would many others not involved in the resistance movement.

However, the moment we were liberated and had regained our independence, these divisions and social barriers reappeared. An amazing phenomenon. I often think of these years between 1940 and 1945. They were years of oppression and terrorism which resulted in the unification of the entire nation through acts of compassion and heroism never heard of before. How strange that the best in people is often brought out during times of suffering and calamity while prosperity and affluence tends to result in callousness, greed and indifference.

Early in 1944, the persistent rumors about an impending invasion became stronger. When and where it was to take place was up for speculation. Tension mounted. Would it be successful? Would we finally be liberated? In June of that year, it finally happened! Normandy was invaded and the Allied troops steadily advanced through France, Belgium and then, about three months later, they reached the southern part of Holland. But then, unexpectedly, their tanks and heavy artillery became stuck in Holland's muddy soil just below our major rivers, near the city of Arnhem. They had reached the last bridge. Heavy fighting ensued, costing hundreds of lives but no progress was made. Half our country was liberated but the other half, the northern part where we lived, was not. In fact, it became a deathtrap, filled with starving people and desperate Germans. This crisis was to last six long months, the most difficult months of the entire war.

Angry and hungry Dutchmen in the northern part of Holland became bolder and more daring. Many went on strike, cutting down utilities and public transport services. The underground resistance also grew bolder and stronger. Enraged, the Nazis embarked on bicycle "razzias," hoping to curtail our only mode of transportation and communication. Cars had long ago been outlawed, as had private telephones. A few scattered and overcrowded trains still ran between major cities for commuters. Dad's office had been moved to Amsterdam some time before the war. Whenever things looked fairly safe, he would take his old, worn bike with its rubber hose tires and pedal to Bussum's railroad station where he would try and catch a train to Amsterdam. Since all export business was stopped, there wasn't much to do at the office but even shuffling papers was better than just sitting at home avoiding home searches or feeling hunger pains. One day at the office, he got a call from a colleague in Bussum.

"Fred," the man's voice was urgent, "I just heard the Nazis raided the bike parking lot at the railroad station in Bussum."

Dad grabbed his coat, rushed to Amsterdam's Grand Central Station and took the first train he could get. In Bussum, he ran to the bike parking lot. When he had left his bike there that morning there had been hundreds of worn out bicycles, neatly stacked in rows. Now, in front of his astonished eyes, there was a completely empty lot. Nothing left. A solitary attendant sat forlornly near the entrance.

"What happened?" Dad asked.

"They just came and started loading bikes on their truck," the man said.

"Do you know where they went?" Dad asked.

"Someone mentioned the soccer field near the high school."

"Thanks," Dad turned on his heels and walked over to City Hall a couple of miles down the road, hoping to get some more information. As he entered the building, he spotted an old schoolmate now a frustrated City Hall employee. He grabbed him by the arm.

"What do you know about that bike "razzia" at the railroad station, Jaap?"

"Not much," came the answer, "I did hear that people working in the food and health sector could get their bikes back but I'm not sure if that's true. Better ask Information."

"Great! Thanks a lot." Dad found a line and waited. When his turn finally came, he could prove that he worked in dairy products and he got a permit, allowing him to retrieve his bike. Now he had to walk another couple of miles to the soccer field near his old high school. Sure enough, the field was roped off and stacked with rows and rows of old, rusty bikes, guarded by some Dutch Nazis.

"Go ahead and try and find yours," the guard reluctantly agreed after Dad showed his permit.

After a long search, he found his old, faithful vehicle. Relieved, he quickly pedalled home. Later, he heard that in Amsterdam thousands of bikes were confiscated and stored in deserted harbors. They were kept under guard and stayed there 'til we were liberated. By that time they were huge heaps of rust, having deprived Amsterdam's starving population of their only means of food procurement and transportation.

One of the worst times during this desperate period came when our water supply was cut off. A few people in our neighborhood had water pumps in their backyards which had originally been just for a novelty. Now these folks became heroes and generously allowed us to pump our own water. We'd take a huge pail on our scooter (with wooden tires) and carefully haul it back home, sloshing as little over the edge as possible. Bathing now became a luxury as was a simple drink of water. The whole family used one small pan of water to bathe once a week. What a relief when this period ended and during certain hours, an abundance of cold water once again flowed from our faucets, a deeply appreciated luxury.

The winter of 1944-45, when the northern half of our country was still occupied, was one of the coldest in history. Freezing temperatures and heavy snowfalls held our emaciated country in a firm and prolonged deathgrip. For us, it became known as the Hunger Winter. Food was our first priority, second even to safety. Thin, gaunt people began to wander all over the country, searching for something to eat. These searches became known as "honger tochten" or hunger trips. Shabby, hollow-eyed women, skinny children and toothless, bearded men pushing delapidated old handcarts or rusty, tireless bicycles wandered from one end of the country to the other.

These trips were extremely dangerous for many reasons. As these hungry and worn-out people slowly trudged over Holland's war-torn highways, they were passed by many a German convoy, trucks filled with troops or arrested Dutchmen on their way to German labor camps. These convoys were under constant attack from the air by powerful and fast Allied planes. There were no warnings and hundreds of casualties lay unattended on the frostbitten roadside. Another danger was the grim fact that Dutch Nazis could confiscate our precious food or vehicles at any time to add to their own dwindling supplies. German soldiers could arrest or shoot anyone at any time, no questions asked, no explanation given. Yet, the stream of weary, determined pilgrims continued to move at a snail's pace across our bullet-ridden, snow-covered highways, driven by relentless hunger pains and a starving family at home.

The export firm Dad worked for owned a dairy plant in Kampen, a city ninety miles east of Blaricum. If he could reach Kampen, his brother-in-law, Auke, who also worked there, could get him some milk, eggs, cheese and potatoes. Dad was thirty-seven and should have "volunteered" for forced labor in Germany a long time ago. Arrest, death or confiscation of food were stark realities if he ventured out on the highways. Yet, during that long, icy winter, he successfully completed several of these suicide missions. Later he recounted his last trip:

"For weeks, I knew the time was getting closer to risk another trip to Kampen. I relied on some sort of inner guidance and waited for a green light. When it came I just knew the time had come.

"I'll be leaving tomorrow," I told Mom.

"She helped me pack the few things I needed, strapped them on her bike and I was off. It was necessary to take a lady's bike because a hundred pound sack of potatoes would just fit in the frame between the seat and the handlebars. Money had long ago lost its value. Some farmers would exchange food for linens, jewelry or wedding rings. So, I took whatever I thought I might need, including fake ID papers and a month's growth of beard. I kept my dentures in my pocket."

"Riding the bike was difficult," he continued, "the tires were worn, roads full of potholes and slippery with a thick crust of ice and snow. City folk I met looked even thinner and more malnourished than I did. The farmers in our rural and suburban areas had helped a great deal to keep us alive. City people were deprived of these food sources. Many of them collapsed and died on the roadside. At night, I stopped at a farmhouse, asked for some food or ate the little I had brought, then slept in the stable on a pile of straw. Cows munched and stirred nearby throughout the night and also provided some warmth.

"I made it to Kampen where I was welcomed with open arms. Your Uncle Auke took me into his home and his wife generously shared with me their meagre meals, for their family included four children. Auke had collected a liberal supply of food for us. The next morning, he helped me strap cheese, eggs and powdered milk to the front and rear of the bike. The huge sack of potatoes fit in the frame. Riding was now impossible. I needed all my strength and attention to just keep the load balanced. My energy was limited. I had lost forty pounds. Avoiding other traffic, I pushed slowly and carefully, keeping a weary eye out for roadblocks or air raids.

"In Harderwÿk, almost halfway home, I was overtaken by our neighbor, Kees Mellegers and his daughter, Sjaantje, also returning to Blaricum. They still had air tires and were not as heavy laden as I was. We briefly stopped to chat. I asked Kees to tell Mom I was on my way. Suddenly Kees said: 'This is not a very good place to stop, let's move over there.'

"He was referring to the fact that V-1 and V-11 rockets, the forerunners of guided missiles, were launched by the Germans from Harderwÿk to bases in England. We often heard them whiz overhead. Harderwÿk was a constant target for Allied air raids. No sooner were Kees' words out of his mouth than fast, low-flying planes roared overhead. We pushed our bikes into a ditch and took cover. Bullets riddled the street where we had just stood. The noise of the whining engines, guns firing and explosions were deafening but we knew they were instigated by our Allies, wiping out some of our oppressors' arsenal. Sirens shrieked. Citizens rushed into nearby shelters. But the raid was short and soon Kees and Sjaantje continued home on their bikes while I resumed my walk.

"Progress was painfully slow. I had set goals for every day and tried to stick to my schedule. One day I was particularly exhausted and discouraged. I hadn't slept well for several nights, afraid someone would take off with my precious cargo. My goal for the day was to reach the village of Nÿkerk. All the signs along the road had long been removed from our highways so I wasn't sure where I was. My eyes kept searching the snow covered horizons for Nÿkerk's church steeple. Somehow, I knew if I could only see it, I would be able to make it. Nÿkerk was almost two thirds of the way home.

"Suddenly, across the bright, snowy fields, I saw the church spire clearly and distinctly against the evening sky. It appeared suspended in the air, sharply outlined yet somehow transparent. My heart leaped. Renewed strength surged through my aching, weary limbs. I was going to make it. But when I finally reached the town, I was not in Nÿkerk at all. I was in Putten, the village that was so brutally burned down and all its men shipped off, still ten miles from Nÿkerk. Where did that tower I saw come from? Was it a mirage? A hallucination? I don't know but I do know that the vision of that tower gave me the strength to continue. I was convinced I was closer to home than I actually was but when I realized I was only in Putten, somehow I had enough strength to continue pushing that loaded bike to Nÿkerk."

After the war, on one of our camping trips with Dad, Helen and Doe, I remembered this story as we pedalled between these two villages. The road seemed endless even on a lightly packed bike with air-filled tires.

Mom continued the story: "When Dad was gone, I never knew where he was or when he would be back, whether he was able to get food or had been shot or arrested and taken to Germany. This last trip had been an extra long wait even though I did hear from Kees and Sjaantje he made it to Harderwyk. There were increased Allied bombings and raids as the stalemate at the rivers continued. It was obvious Hitler was in deep trouble. As a result, the military as well as the Dutch Nazis became more irrational and ruthless.

"Finally," Mom continued, "one day as I looked through the window, I saw Dad coming. He walked slowly and deliberately, a little unsteady. I held my breath. Just a few hours before, the Germans had put up a roadblock right in front of our home. Would he lose everything at the last moment? My heart almost stopped beating. I dared not look. He was now behind the hedge of our neighbor's yard and I couldn't see him.

"Suddenly, there he was, almost in front of our gate. I ran outside.

"'Quick, get into the house,'" I urged, "'I'll take care of the bike'.

"He got to the back door and hid in the house. The bike was parked against the little brick wall next to the low, wooden gate. I tried to steady the heavy load and almost lost my balance. Gathering all my strength, I slowly managed to push that loaded bike to the shed in the backyard. I barely made it. How Dad ever managed to push that load over ninety miles, I will never know.

"To my great relief," she concluded, "the roadblock soon closed and no one searched the house."

Shortly after this memorable hunger trip, some Dutch Nazis conducted a food "razzia." After searching our home and finding nothing, they knocked on the door of our neighbor, Mr. van de Laar, who lived kitty-cornered from us. Van de Laar was a retired military man, very outspoken and patriotic. He shared his home with his sister, a spinster lady. Showing obvious disgust at his fellow countrymen, van de Laar reluctantly let the two men into his home. In the living room, they spotted a large picture of the Dutch Royal Family. Sarcastic remarks followed,

"The great Queen who fled in panic! What's so great about her?" they sneered.

To hear his beloved Queen being ridiculed by his own countrymen was too much for van de Laar. Furious, he exploded, shouting insults at his intruders,

"Traitors, all of you!" he yelled. "Don't you dare insult our Queen. Get out of my house!"

But instead, both he and his sister were arrested and led to a waiting car. The two men remained in the house. By now, the whole neighborhood was on the alert, silently watching the commotion from inside their homes. What would happen next? They didn't have to wait very long.

"They're going to torch the house," Mom said, her voice tense.

She and Dad gathered our belongings and some valuable papers and pictures, ready to evacuate our home. I happened to be in the dining room. My hands were clutching the back of a chair, my eyes fixed on van de Laar's home.

This can't be happening, my mind insisted. The war should be over by now. In fact, it is over for most of our people. We got through all these years without losing our home. They can't... I couldn't finish. The two men were now circling the house, smashing windows with their rifle butts. Kerosine was poured throughout the house then it was lit, the picture of the Royal Family first. Giant flames leaped through the broken windows. The thatched roof was instant fuel for the hungry flames. Huge black clouds and massive flames soon leaped high into the air. The two men remained outside, standing guard to see that no one attempted to fight the fire or alert the Fire Department.

Every neighbor was now outside, watching in horror, clutching their meagre belongings. Only one burning reed, flying across the street, could set off a massive chain reaction. A strong wind was blowing in our direction, six homes in its path. I still stood frozen inside our living room, my hands clutching the back of the chair, transfixed, unable to move.

Suddenly, at the height of the inferno, the winds miraculously changed direction. The guards had left. Folks started to breathe again. The worst was over. Small groups of neighbors kept watch over the last smoldering embers. A few broken walls, a broken chimney, surrounded by charred grass and rubble was all that remained of the large, brick, two-story home with its immaculately-kept garden. What happened to van de Laar and his sister? Were they still alive? Did they know their home was gone? Later, we learned they had been detained for a few days, then released. The burning of their home had been unauthorized. It was merely a last-minute impulse of some angry, defeated Dutch Nazis, their last act of vengeance. Van de Laar eventually rebuilt his home and lived there for many years.

Fighting along our large rivers continued. The Germans now desperately needed an additional workforce. They began patrolling our streets, picking up every available male they saw: mail carriers, mechanics, delivery boys, anyone at all. They were marched to Amersfoort, fifty miles to the south, then forced to walk to the battle areas along the rivers, an additional forty miles or so. They had nothing with them but the clothes on their backs and were unable to get messages to their families. One of these men was Jan Klaver, the auto mechanic from Blaricum. When he finally arrived at the battle zone, totally exhausted, he was ordered to fix broken-down cars. After three months of this forced labor, a German officer who seemed to like him and appreciated his work, released him. Somehow, he made his way back to Blaricum. Many others were not that fortunate.

Finally, the Allies made it across the rivers and pushed through to the main cities using our major highways. The highway through 't Gooi leading to Amsterdam was one of the first ones to be conquered. Since Blaricum was not on any major highway, we remained in a sort of a twilight zone for a few days. In Bussum, celebrations were in full swing with parades, street dancing and much flag waving. One day during this period, we walked to Bussum to watch some fireworks. But on our way home, as we crossed the heather fields now totally bare and devoid of any trees, reports of sniper fire and danger forced us to hide our flags, lower our voices and sneak quietly into a silent and very dark Blaricum. It took yet another few days for the entire country to be freed.

Then we finally met our heroes, wonderful, smiling, gum-chewing Canadians. What a difference from our previous "liberators." These Canadians didn't come from the battlegrounds near our rivers but had come from Morocco in North Africa where they had landed about a year earlier. Then, via Sicily they fought their way through Rome and the rest of Italy. Pushing through France and Belgium they finally reached Holland just after the breakthrough of the battle at the rivers.

There were parties, victory marches, dancing and singing in the streets throughout the country. We were free! Free to sing our beloved patriotic songs, free to go out whenever and wherever we wanted, free to keep our drapes open at night, to listen to any radio program we wanted. The government returned, so did the Royal Family.

Celebrations continued. Skinny, pale Jews appeared, squinting in the bright light they had not seen for years. We invited the Canadians into our homes. Every family adopted a few. Elated, we brushed up on our English and tried to entertain them, showing our gratitude and excitement. We even put a show together for our benefactors. I got involved in a choir. Clad in a sheet, exposing one shoulder, hoisting a Canadian flag, we vigorously sang the Canadian national anthem: "O Canada, our home and native land..." Few of us knew what we were singing but everyone in the audience stood at attention, whistling and applauding when it was over.

I was twelve then, still in pigtails and rather undeveloped. Just as well. When several months later, our Canadian friends returned to their homeland, they were soon followed by boatloads of Dutch brides leaving their small, ravaged country for the majestic prairies of Canada. Somewhere in Canada, in the state of Alberta, my former playmate, Mickey, and his folks still lived. Dad had kept in touch with them for many years and never quite forgave himself for not listening to Mickey's Dad in 1939.

A few months later, word got around that Winston Churchill would be visiting Europe, including Holland. He was scheduled to pass through Bussum.

"I want to go," Dad announced.

When the day arrived, he and Mom walked to Bussum to wait along the main highway between Amsterdam and Amersfoort where the great man would make several stops. They found a place towards the front of a large crowd just behind two restless horses and their riders.

"Too bad these horses are right here," Mom remarked, "the riders can see anywhere from their elevated position. Why stand so close to the road?"

Waiting patiently, the crowd burst into song again, singing our national anthem and other patriotic songs, laughing and waving flags. Standing in line was something they were used to, anyway. Besides, this was going to be an historic moment, the cherry on the cake. Nothing could dampen anyone's enthusiasm.

Finally, the crowd stirred. Several motorcycles and cars were spotted in the distance. Slowly, they came closer. Seated in a large convertible was a smiling Churchill, complete with his legendary cigar and victory sign. What a sight! Soon the party approached the designated stop along the way. Hundreds of skinny, shabby, elated Dutchmen crowded and pushed together, anxious to get a better look. They waved and screamed and jumped up and down. The two horses in front of my folks suddenly got nervous and jumpy. One rider was thrown off, the other one had to dismount to hang on to both of the frightened horses. When the motorcade stopped, they were far removed from the action.

Churchill, in the meantime, was shaking a sea of outstretched hands. Two of them belonged to Mom and Dad.

"Thank you, thank you for all you did!" "We love you!" "We appreciate you." "You're the greatest!"

It was a very emotional moment, a tremendous finale to five years of oppression, fear, terrorism and starvation.

Our liberators, in spite of their endless supplies of gum and chocolate, were not equipped to feed us and we were still pretty hungry. But then a wonderful American by the name of Marshall got into action and provided tons of food for Europe. At first, when distribution centers were not set up, large war planes would fly low over our heather fields. The bay doors opened and, instead of bombs, large sacks of food would plummet down. What a rush to get there first! Sweden also became involved and provided large, fluffy bread, a delicious treat we mistook for cake at first.

In the midst of the celebrations, there was also anger especially towards our fellow countrymen who had cooperated with the enemy and become traitors. Now, THEY were the ones who had gone into hiding. Quickly, posses were organized to raid the homes of these people. As an act of revenge, their heads were shaved. They were then put in open carts and paraded through the villages. Later, when things quieted down somewhat, most were taken prisoner and placed in specially constructed camps. Many were eventually released and accepted back into society.

It would take many years for Holland to recover and rebuild its neatly organized and tightly packed country. But during those exhilarating post-war weeks, nobody cared much about the future. The future HAD to be good. After all, we were free. That was all that mattered.

Chapter 3

FOREIGN SHORES

As we began digging up our radios, flags, copperware and other former contraband, something else surfaced as well - Dad's travel shoes! They weren't hard to find, actually, as they had not been buried very deep. He had never forgotten Mickey's father's departure to Canada in 1939. All through the war years, he patiently bided his time, waiting for an opportunity to leave tiny, crowded Holland and explore other shores. Well, the war was over now but normal travel and foreign relations still were a long way off. Over the next two years, Europe's war wounds were slowly beginning to heal and as our economy showed signs of recovery so did Dad's dreams of adventure.

In the Fall of 1947, Dad and I crossed the choppy Ÿsel Lake on a commercial passenger boat to Lemmer, a city in the northern province of Friesland. We just wanted to get away and visit some friends we hadn't seen for many years. It was a cold and rainy day. Gusty winds whipped angry white caps against the hull of our boat. The engines were groaning. Low, grey clouds hurried overhead. I shivered and walked briskly up and down the windy deck, trying to keep warm. Dad was inside the smoky lounge in deep conversation with an old schoolmate he had just met. They hadn't seen each other for years and seemed to have a lot to talk about. We finally arrived in Lemmer, visited our friends and returned home the next day.

A few weeks later when we were sitting quietly at home one evening, Dad cleared his throat and made a startling announcement.

"Remember Japie Scharf, that old friend I ran into on the boat to Lemmer?" he asked me.

"Yes, I do," I said, "what about him?"

Helen looked up from her homework, Mom stopped her knitting. She had a look on her face I hadn't seen before.

Dad looked at us, cleared his throat again and continued: "He's been in touch with our Government in The Hague. They need people in their Transport Department in Batavia."

We sensed something important was coming. Dad had our full attention. I knew that Batavia (now Djakarta) was the capital of Java, a large island in the Indian Ocean, south of Thailand and the Philippines. Java, along with the islands of Sumatra, Borneo, Celebes and hundreds of smaller ones, were known as the Netherland East Indies. (Now Indonesia) It had been a Dutch colony for over three hundred years.

"I went to The Hague this week for more information and an interview," Dad continued, his voice betraying excitement.

"You did? What happened?" I heard myself ask.

He dropped the bomb.

"My application was accepted. They offered me a contract for three years."

Dumbfounded, Helen and I stared at him. Leaving Blaricum? Our home? Move from the Dwarslaan? But we were born here! We never lived anywhere else! Leave our friends? Move to Indonesia? That was clear around the world! We finally found our voices and overloaded Dad with questions. What about school? I had two years of high school to complete. Helen was still in grade school. Do people speak Dutch there? I remembered fragments from history class. Indonesia was hot, right on the Equator, covered with palm trees, rice paddies and rubber, coffee and tea plantations. They provided all those products we so sorely missed during the war. There were also snakes, tigers, lizards, monkeys and...

"What is it realy like there, Dad?" "When are we going to leave?" "How are we going to get there?"

"I will have to go first," Dad explained, "to get settled and find a place to live. You know, the Japanese occupied these islands during the war so they are going through a post war recovery period, too.

"I will fly over," he continued, "later you will follow by boat."

A boat trip around the world? I had never been further away from home than a hundred miles. Was this really going to happen or was it just a dream?

As the news spread in Blaricum that the Hoffmanns were leaving, reactions varied. Many people envied us yet expressed doubt that they would ever take a giant step like that. Most Dutchmen in Indonesia had been interred in Japanese camps during the war or were sent to Burma to build the infamous railroad in thick, malaria-invested jungle. Not many survived. A few of those who did had come back to Holland, broken and old.

"Indonesia has changed," they said, "it will never be the same."

My folks chose to ignore those reports, however, and continued to plan for their departure from Holland. There was much to be done. We had to go to The Hague to get papers signed, birth certificates, health certificates, pictures, physicals and shots for lots of tropical diseases. Soon, Dad was packing two suitcases. No warm clothes needed. How odd. Our faithful friend, Jan Klaver, the mechanic, had access to a car and offered to drive us to Schiphol, Holland's international airport in Amsterdam.

"What about my hat?" Dad said. "They don't wear these in the tropics." He gave it to Jan as a farewell gift.

This is it, I thought. Dad is really leaving. When we see him again, it will be on the other side of the world. Mom bravely tried to hide her tears as we huddled together in the busy, windy terminal. Dad hugged and kissed us goodbye one more time, grabbed his flightbag and quickly walked away to the gate. He looks strange without a hat, I thought.

Clutching his bag and ticket, coattails flapping in the wind, he climbed the stairway of the waiting plane. At the door he turned, waved and disappeared. It was Spring, 1948.

Dad's plane was a Skymaster, a prop, and only flew during daylight hours. The first leg of his journey was to Rome where everyone spent the night in a hotel. Later Dad wrote:

The next day we flew over the Mediterranean. It was a beautiful day, the sun sparkled on the clear, blue waters. Below us were hundreds of ships - all going east. The captain explained these ships were filled with Jews from all over the world. After centuries of exile, they were returning to Palestine, their homeland. It's now known as Israel. Right below me I saw history in the making.

His journey continued with stops in Port Said, Basrah, Karachi, Calcutta, Bangkok and Singapore, with time for sightseeing at every stop.

Mom, in the meantime, faced an extremely difficult time. She had never been separated from Dad for any length of time. Now alone, she had the sole responsibility to dispose of all our furniture and other household items and pack our suitcases and trunks for a permanent move to a strange country on the other side of the world. Helen and I were in our early teens and more concerned with goodbye visits and parties than Mom's packing problems.

Letters and pictures began to arrive from Djakarta. Dad, clad in white shirt, shorts, socks and shoes with tropical hat standing under tall coconut palms, holding a bunch of bananas. He described an abundance of flowers, strange food, sunny weather, smiling brown-faced people and he threw in some words he called "pasar maleis," the simple, native language of the land. The official language in Indonesia is Dutch, he wrote, but in order to communicate with the servants, shopkeeeprs and other people, we had to learn their language. Servants? Would we be having servants? In pre-war days we had a woman come in once a week to help Mom with the heavy cleaning but you could hardly call her a servant. What kind of servants would we have in our new country?

It didn't take Dad long to find a home for us, or rather, part of a home. We had to share it with two other families. He wrote:

It's in Depok, a small village about an hour by train from Djakarta. The government has rented several homes in Depok for their employees. It's a beautiful little town, full of banana, palm and bamboo trees. You'll love it!

Passage was booked for the three of us on the "SS Indrapoera," a large oceanliner scheduled to sail from Rotterdam in a few weeks. Mom was in the last throws of a giant garage sale and faced daily decisions about what to pack and what to leave behind. Rumors had it there were no brooms in Indonesia. That would never do for a Dutch housewife. She stocked up on them only to discover later that Dutch brooms were useless in the tropics.

The big day finally arrived. A relative drove us to the bustling harbor in Rotterdam where we boarded a huge ship. The outside of the ship looked like an enormous wall the size of a city block with rows and rows of tiny portholes. We lugged our baggage across the narrow gangplank and were quickly absorbed in a vast network of narrow passageways. Hundreds of fellow passengers were milling around on the various decks and lounges, wandering through the endless corridors, trying to find their way. It was fortunate that we had never been on an ocean liner before. We had nothing to compare this one with. The "Indrapoera" had been converted into a troop ship during the war and had not been changed back into a passenger vessel. We were led to an enormous cargo space somewhere in the "innards" of this gigantic ship. Here we faced rows and rows of canvas bunkbeds with tiny walkways in between. Hundreds of women and children would coexist here for the next four weeks. Right now, everyone was trying to settle in. The din was enormous, muffled only by the deep growls of the ships' engines which seemed to vibrate right under my feet.

Excited yet bewildered, we dropped our luggage on our assigned bunkbeds and found a deck to await departure. Three piercing, slow whistles signalled it was time for visitors to leave. Soon, paper streamers were thrown from the decks to the waving crowd, the last tie between passengers and their homeland. A brass band played the National Anthem. The ship's whistle screamed again. Slowly, the mammoth vessel was pulled away by two little tug boats. One by one, the paper streamers snapped. The sea of waving arms and handkerchiefs faded in the distance. We left the busy harbor, passed huge freighters from all over the world, busy dry docks and other passenger ships. Whistles echoed in greeting. Finally, Holland's flat coastline faded from view. We were on our way.

Our first meal was quite an experience. In the first place, it was a miracle we found our dining room. There were several and, in order to accommodate the capacity crowd, we were served in shifts. Dozens of small Javanese young men, dressed in white with colorful brown head coverings, moved gracefully around the crowded tables. We had *"Rysttafel,"* the famous Indonesian fare, featured now in restaurants all over the world. One large bowl of steaming rice in the center of the table was surrounded by dozens of smaller dishes with all kinds of unknown, yet delicious, spicy foods. We discovered most waiters only spoke Maleis. A friendly couple at our table gave us a quick crash course.

"*Trima kasi banjak* means thank you," they explained. "A waiter is called a *djongos*. You raise your arm and flap your hand to get their attention." "Hot food is *pedis*, fried rice *nasi goreng*, yes is *saja*, no is *tida*."

"This is fun," Helen said flapping her hand to get the waiter's attention. "Look! It works."

Exhausted after the days adventures, we found our sleeping quarters again. The engines now vibrated full blast below us, muffling the wails of crying babies and children. The next morning the ship was heaving and rolling through the infamous Gulf of Biscay just off the coast of France. Immediately, we were exposed to the horrors of seasickness. Instantly, our entire perspective on life changed. Nothing mattered any more. Life was not worth living. Only death would bring relief. The next day was worse. We could not keep a thing down. Finally, tired of hugging the railing and throwing up, Helen and I crawled into our canvas bunks and waited for the end. Mom tried to get us up. She didn't feel too good herself but put up a good front.

"Just leave me alone," I groaned.

"You need some fresh air and something in your stomachs." she insisted.

"Please, don't mention food," Helen begged. She kept her eyes closed and was careful not to move. The dining rooms were deserted. All bathrooms constantly occupied. A few brave passengers got up and dressed, then limply sank into a deck chair. There was no conversation, only soft moans. Fortunately, Gibraltar was not far off. On the third day, we passed this impressive rock and entered the calm, clear blue waters of the Mediterranean. What a relief! Perhaps life was worth living after all. People began to pop out of their various hideaways to stretch their legs again. The dining rooms filled up once more. Green faces turned pink, then tan as white bodies were exposed to the balmy, ever-present sunshine. The ships Dad had seen from the air just a few months earlier were gone, the blue waters quiet and sparkling.

Our first stop was Port Said in Egypt at the beginning of the Suez Canal. As we moored right in the middle of the murky waters of the busy harbor, we spotted dozens of tiny boats loaded with all kinds of merchandise, swarming around our ship. They looked like an army of ants surrounding an elephant. In between the boats small, agile boys dived after coins tossed into the water by amused passengers. The smiling merchants, heads wrapped in turbans, quickly made contact with the wide-eyed passengers leaning over the railings of the various decks, high above the little bobbing vessels. After some pointing and shouting, a rope was thrown up to one of these decks, then a basket with the desired item hoisted up. No one spoke a common language, we did not have Egyptian currency yet deals seemed to be made fast. I noticed a tall passenger on my deck gesturing to one of the merchants. He leaned over the railing, pointing to his wrist. He wanted to see a watch. The merchant held one up. He must have done some quick calculating for he also held up four fingers - forty guilders. The tall man laughed and held up two fingers. Somehow, I knew they'd settle for thirty. I was right. A line was thrown and the basket pulled up. It was empty.

"Money first!" the merchant yelled.

Reluctantly, the man wrapped thirty guilders in the little bag in the basket and lowered it down again to the vendor. The watch came up immediately. Eagerly, he grabbed it.

"Hey folks, look at that!" he shouted, "A gold watch for thirty guilders. What a bargain!"

A crowd gathered around him. It certainly looked like an excellent watch, they admitted.

"It's not very heavy," someone noticed.

The tall man produced a pen-knife and opened the back of his new possession. He gasped! The watch was empty! Just a shell. Furious, he ran back to the railing, scanning the sea of bobbing vessels below. Finally, he thought he recognized the villan.

"Come back!" he yelled, "you cheated me!"

There was no response. In fact, his voice got lost in the din of hundreds of other bartering passengers leaning over and shouting from every deck.

"Come back, I said!" he yelled again. "I want my money back. You're a thief!"

Suddenly he coughed. His hand flew to his mouth but it was too late. His upper dentures plummeted down and disappeared in the murky waters below. None of the little urchins dived after them. Stunned, the man realized he just lost his money, his dentures and still did not have a watch. I felt sorry for him but learned a valuable lesson. Before going ashore the next day, we were warned to be careful. It did not fall on deaf ears.

After Port Said, we faced the unique Suez Canal. A very narrow, straight waterway cutting through miles and miles of hot, dry dessert. From our elevated decks it seemed we were moving through a vast sea of sand with here and there a forlorn, waving palm tree, a few camels and in the distance, the majestic pyramids. The Canal ended in the Red Sea so-called, I believe, because it was red hot! We had no air conditioning on board and the showers only produced salt water. The pool was also filled with tepid, salt water. Besides, Helen and I had developed three huge, open sores on our thighs from our small pox vaccinations and were not allowed to swim. Every morning, we waited in line at the doctor's office for a dressing change. The sores looked ugly and the doctor warned that if they did not heal by the time we arrived in Djakarta, we could not leave the ship. I don't know if he was serious or just tried to make a point but we strictly followed his orders. It was only one day before we reached our final destination that they had completely dried up, leaving quarter-sized, permanent scars.

We stopped again in the port of Aden in what is now Southern Yemen, a dirty, dusty and sinister town, hemmed in by bare, harsh-looking mountains. Suspicious-looking characters offered all kinds of services, merchandise and tours. Old, noisy cars, bicycles and haughty camels meandered through the pot-holed streets lined with shabby, crumbling buildings. Our stay there was short and soon we entered the wide, open waters of the Indian Ocean. For ten long days, we saw nothing but water and sky, an occasional school of flying fish and the same bored faces of our fellow passengers. Finally, we reached the friendly little town of Sabang on the northern tip of Sumatra. Fascinated, we wandered through the lush, tropical village nestled between waving palms, huge banana trees and an abundance of bright, beautiful but unknown flowers. Especially eye-catching were large clusters of delicate pink blossoms, called Bride's Tears. Friendly natives in roadside stalls tempted us with delicious but also unknown fruit and pastries. Small, dark women, dressed in sarongs, gracefully walked along the edge of the unpaved roads carrying what seemed to be bundles of laundry on their heads. Merchants, called tukans, shouldered yoke-like poles with huge baskets on each end filled with merchandise. They trotted barefoot through the streets which were crowded with playing children, cackling chickens and lazy dogs. Relieved, we noticed the town lacked the aggressive tourist thrust we had faced in other ports. No one seemed in a rush, everyone smiled. What a paradise! Was Depok going to be like this?

A few days later, we maneuvered through some small, palm-filled islands and entered the busy port of Jakarta. Dad was waiting. He looked different in white shorts and shirt, no tie and no coat. We jumped up and down to get to him first.

"Did you have a good trip?" he smiled, hugging us.

We all talked at once, glad to be reunited.

"Get your *barang*," Dad laughed.

"*Barang*?"

"Luggage! That's what it's called here."

We lugged our suitcases to the waiting car provided by the Government. A native chauffeur deftly maneuvered through noisy, smelly traffic. Nobody seemed to observe any rules. Djakarta was a huge, sprawling metropolis, a giant ant's nest. Thousands of hooting old cars; open, crowded buses; drab military vehicles and pedestrians milled around the busy streets. Added to this were the merchants and thousands of three-wheeled taxi bicycles, called *betjas*, which squirmed around the tree-lined boulevards and market places. Under large, shady, flowering trees barbers cut hair, vendors displayed their smelly, fly-covered meats and fruit, women stood and gossiped with babies strapped to their backs, black hair pulled back in enormous buns.

Wide eyed, we tried to take it all in. A totally different world, different people, food, trees, flowers, homes, languages, climate, money, smells. Nothing was familiar. But we loved it! We arrived at Dad's temporary home, a large white brick building he and other employees occupied while they were waiting for their families to arrive from Holland. Here we noticed that even the bugs were different! Cockroaches on the floors, green and yellow lizards all over the walls and ceilings, even snakes among the trees, we were told. Scary? Yes, but also fascinating.

A few days after our arrival, Mom and I ventured into a rickety *betja* together. They were brightly-painted, had little roofs for shade and an upholstered seat.

"We'll never fit in there together." Mom observed.

"Let's try it anyway." I ventured.

We squeezed in till we were firmly wedged inside the small, wobbly vehicle. Off we went to the *Pasar Baroe* (Big Market). Once there, Mom dislodged herself and got out. I tried to get up but realized that both my legs were asleep. They would not hold me up and just folded under me. Helplessly, I crumpled to the pavement. Quickly, a circle of wide-eyed native pedestrians gathered around me.

"Come on!" Mom called out, "what's the matter with you. Get up!"

When I didn't she got concerned. "What happened?"

"My legs are asleep. I guess the blood supply got cut off when we squeezed into that *betja*."

I rubbed my legs and soon the familiar "pins and needles" feeling signalled the return of normal circulation. I staggered to my feet, the crowd dispersed and we were soon absorbed by the milling crowd of the *Pasar Baroe*, a large open market in the heart of Djakarta. It was the first and the last time we used a *betja* together.

Three days later, a military truck came to take us, our trunks and other luggage from the hotel in Djakarta to Depok. As soon as we left the city limits, we passed through vast stretches of neatly terraced rice paddies, edged by clusters of the now familiar banana trees and large, gently waving bamboo stalks.

"They harvest the rice here three times a year," Dad explained, "can you believe that?"

A few large mountain peaks loomed on the horizon.

"Those are vulcanoes," he explained, "most of them have been extinct for years. This, by the way, is the main road to Buitenzorg (now Bogor), another large town. But long before we get there we're going to turn right to get to Depok."

Sure enough, pretty soon the driver left the wide, paved road to turn sharply into a winding, reddish clay dirt road. More tall, coconut laden palm trees along the road and a dense forest of banana and bamboo stalks.

"Look! There's a *kampong*," Dad pointed out.

We glimpsed a number of small, well-kept homes, built on short stilts with walls made out of some sort of woven leaves. Dried palm leaves covered the roofs.

"*Kampongs* are the villages where the natives live," Dad explained, "they're well hidden and hard to reach except by foot."

We crossed a long, stone bridge.

"That's the *kali* down there," Dad pointed. "Look! Way down there."

Far below us rushed a muddy, winding river.

"The natives use this as their swimming pool, bathroom and laundry place," he laughed.

As we crossed the bridge, I could see a long, narrow, wooden boat coming down the river, navigated by an almost naked man holding on to a long pole.

We crossed the bridge and made another sharp turn.

"Now we're entering Depok." Dad explained.

White, brick, red roofed homes with broad verandas, surrounded by an abundance of flowers, well-kept gardens and tall shady trees, passed us by on either side of the dusty dirt road. Soon, we stopped in front of one of them. This one had a smaller building attached to it on one side.

"This is it, folks!" Dad proudly announced.

We stiffly tumbled out of the truck and explored the still empty home. It was cool inside. All rooms had high ceilings and clean, whitewashed walls. We opened the windows. None of them had screens. A center hallway divided the house into two parts with three rooms on each side and a large common room in the back.

"We have a choice," Dad said, "half of the large house or the pavilion, the little house next door. Two other families will live here as well. They will arrive in a few weeks."

The pavilion was small with two bedrooms, a tiny dining room behind a half wall, dividing it from the sitting room in front with a little veranda at the entrance.

"That's more private," Mom observed. "I would prefer that part."

We all agreed. In the back of the building, Dad pointed out a kitchen with charcoal stove, no refrigerator, a *mandi*-room, toilet, storage room and well.

"What's a *mandi*-room?" we wanted to know.

"Here, let me show you." Dad took us inside the small room. There was nothing in it except a high built-in square tub full of water.

"This is not a tub to sit in," Dad explained. "Here, see this little handbucket? When you bathe you dip this in the water and pour it over yourself. Then you soap and lather and you dip it in again to rinse off. There's a drain in the corner there on the floor. It's a great way to cool off and does not take much time. Most people *mandi* (bathe) three times a day here."

"What's that big hole in the wall above the tub?" I wanted to know, thinking of my privacy during this procedure.

"That's where the *kebon* stands when he fills the tub with the water he draws from the well. See, the well is right here." We walked outside to the well.

"What's a *kebon*?" Helen wanted to know.

"A young boy who runs errands, takes care of the yard and draws water. Here, let me show you."

Dad lowered a little bucket into the well. As the rope rolled off the squeaky spindle, it seemed to take a long time before the bucket hit water. Finally, there was a distant splash and Dad reeled the full bucket up again.

"It's yellow!" Helen said "Yak!"

"Just looks different," Dad smiled, "Actually, it's excellent water. Here, taste it."

He was right. It was quite cold and very refreshing. We walked through the pavilion again. Some furniture had been provided. There were beds, pillows and sheet-covered mattresses.

"You don't need blankets," Dad explained, "not even a sheet."

"What are those poles for?" Mom asked, pointing to the vertical poles at each corner of the bed joined at the top by four horizontal slats.

"That's for your *klamboe* or musquito net. See? Here they are. You leave them folded over the top during the day."

"Hey, they also have lizards in this room! Look! They are all over the wall." Helen and I noticed the creatures at the same time.

"They're called *tjitjaks* and are quite harmless," Dad said patiently. "Besides, they can't get to you at night when the *klamboe* is down."

"Why are the legs of my bed sitting in little cups of water?" Helen asked suspiciously.

"That's so the roaches and ants don't get to you. Come," Dad quickly changed the subject, "here's our *kebon*. Let me show you something."

A young boy was standing by the well. Dad pointed upward to something that looked like a bunch of green footballs in a tall palm tree.

"See those coconuts?"

"I thought coconuts were brown?" I said.

"The brown part is the pit. The outside is green."

Dad somehow communicated to the *kebon* that he wanted some coconuts. The lad understood. He was barefoot and clad in only a pair of faded shorts. A knife was stuck in his belt.

"How is he going to get up there?" Mom wondered.

Clasping the trunk with both hands, that kid walked up that steep, tall trunk as though it was a ladder. We watched in amazement. When he reached the top he grabbed his knife and cut off some of those green footballs. They came whizzing down like rockets and hit the ground with a thud.

"They're huge!" we yelled.

The *kebon* climbed down with the same ease he had made his ascent. He picked up a coconut and started slashing off chunks of it with his knife. Finally, the familiar brown hairy center appeared. He hit the three "eyes," the weak spots, and gave us each a cool drink of cocowater. Then he knocked off the entire top and we scooped out the soft, white lining. It was delicious.

"The coconuts you buy at the store back home," Dad explained, "are old and the white meat is hard. These are young, not yet fully matured. They have less meat but it's softer and easier to eat. Most people here prefer them this way. They shred the white meat and squeeze it to get cocomilk which is used for cooking."

We quickly settled in and explored the neighborhood. Next door to us was a small military settlement with an interesting assortment of young, friendly Dutch soldiers. There were also quite a few new families from Holland, we discovered, many of them *baroes* or new arrivals, like us. We were easily identified. We walked too fast, sweat too much and did not take siestas in the afternoon.

However, within a few weeks the sweltering heat and humidity caught up with us and we started to do things *plan plan* - slowly. The best way to live here, we discovered, was to get up early, take a nap in the afternoon and stay up late. There were other interesting discoveries, too. None of the roads in Depok were paved. After short but heavy tropical downpours, the roads were quickly transformed into rivers of slippery, wet mud. With the reappearance of the hot sun, however, the whole area quickly turned into a powerful steamroom and an hour later all dampness was gone and the roads dry and firm again.

Helen enrolled in the local elementary school just down the road. Dad, together with his Dutch colleagues, commuted to Djakarta by train. A few weeks later, he was joined by Mom who got a job at an architectural firm on the Koningsplein, a large, park-filled square in the heart of Djakarta. The little railroad station in Depok was a kaleidoscope of colors, sounds and smells. Very early each morning, at the crack of dawn, amidst the constant highpitched whirs of crickets and bird calls, a conglomeration of people from all over Depok gathered at the small platform. Vendors with baskets of fruit and vegetables, including tightly-packed live chickens, patiently squatted beside their merchandise, puffing on homemade cigarettes while discussing the latest local news. *Baboes* (native women) with tiny babies wrapped close to them in their *sarongs*, chewing their favorite *pedis,* red hot peppers, shared the latest *kampong* gossip. Scattered among this company were Dutch and Indonesian businessmen carrying their briefcases and newspapers, clad in white starched shorts and shirts, discussing the latest political developments, business transactions or sporting events. The platform was framed by brilliant Bouganvillia and the ever present clusters of pink Bride's Tears. Finally, the smelly, noisy, smoke belching engine would roll into the station and slow to a grinding halt. It pulled several passenger cars as well as cargo cars. The waiting crowd quickly disappeared into the train. When it pulled out only the crickets and birds were left behind to continue their concerts.

I signed up at a public high school in Buitenzorg (now Bogor) sixty miles from Depok in the opposite direction from Djakarta. Every morning before dawn, a large military truck picked up commuters from all over Depok. It was pitch dark when I climbed into the back of that canvas covered truck with its hard, wooden benches. By the time we crossed the kali bridge, the truck was full. All I could see was the tiny glow of lighted cigarettes from some of my fellow commuters. But by the time we reached the main road, full daylight had dispelled the darkness of the night. Buitenzorg was a lovely, cool city with a magnificent botanical garden. It was nestled between two large, extinct volcanoes.

Every afternoon huge clouds gathered around the peaks of these two towering mountains. They'd grow heavier and darker and finally, between four and five each afternoon, they dumped a refreshing downpour on the city, right during siesta time.

School in this country was a new experience, too. Located just across the impressive entrance to the Botanical Gardens, the school itself was a low, one-story complex of buildings, the familiar whitewashed kind. There were Chinese, Javanese and Dutch-Indonesian students. I was the only tall, blue-eyed, white pupil. I felt rather out of place but soon got to know some Dutch-Indonesian girls who invited me over for weekends. Social life in Buitenzorg was lively with lots of fun things to do. Just the opposite of Depok which, although pretty and quiet, could also be rather dull for teenagers. Teachers at school all taught in the Dutch language but during breaks every student spoke "Pasar Maleis" the secrets of which I still had to unravel. Subjects were pretty much the same as in Holland although perhaps a little easier and more relaxed. In Holland, our high school curriculum included four languages; French, German, English and Dutch; Biology; Math; Commercial Math; Science; Chemistry; Geography; lots of History; Geometry and Algebra as well as PE and Art. Curriculums were fixed. Everyone took the same classes. Evenings were filled with homework, only weekends offered some free time. I had to struggle to keep up in Holland.

Here, in my new country, there were no lab facilities for Science or Chemistry so they were dropped. We were also far removed from Germany and France so those languages were not taught, either. Instead, we learned shorthand and typing, a very practical substitute.

My problem was Bahasa Indonesia, the official and very complicated native language, taught by a teacher who did not speak Dutch at all. It didn't take me long to figure out I could never catch up on this subject before graduation. What to do? The principal was a Dutchman, a rather crusty, retired, marine officer. One day, I gathered my courage, knocked on his door and explained my dilemma. He leaned back in his chair, stony faced, took a puff on his ever present cigar and said,

"What is it worth to you to be dropped from this class, Aubrey?"

What an odd question, I thought and gave him a blank look. What was he driving at? We looked at each other. His poker face didn't change, the lighted cigar now balanced on an ashtray. Suddenly, an idea hit me.

"How about some Dutch cigars?" I suggested. "Dad brought some from Holland." His smile exploded.

"It's a deal!" he roared, slapped his desk, got up and ushered me out. Back home Dad agreed to the arrangement and thus the matter was settled. Mom, in the meantime, had acquired the services of two native women, a *baboe* and a cook. The *baboe* took care of home chores, the cook made daily trips to the local market (where she proved to be a shrewd barterer) and concocted delicious meals. They both lived in their own *kampong* somewhere in the thick jungle in back of our house. We got used to the *mandi*-room and came to tolerate the roaches and lizards. We even encountered an occasional snake. Though poisonous, they were slow to attack and quick to slither away to a safe place. Depok, although dull at times, was never far away from surprises. Action could be right around the corner at any time. One evening the four of us were sitting outside on the veranda. It was a quiet, dark night - just the crickets and us. Suddenly, without warning, we were surrounded by a cloud of black, flying insects.

"What in the world is this?!" Mom threw her magazine down and jumped up.

"They look like ants," Dad noticed, hitting the swarming creatures with his newspaper.

"Look! They're dropping their wings." Helen yelled.

We watched and sure enough, hundreds of tiny wings were forming a carpet on the stony veranda floor. Now the little critters were crawling.

"They sure do look like ants," Dad admitted. "I remember hearing about them."

"What do we do with them?" asked Mom, trying to brush the crawling creatures from her dress. We were all up and around by now, waving and swatting madly.

"Let's close the doors and go inside," Dad finally suggested.

We did, then sprayed the veranda. The next morning baboe swept up a mountain of dead ants. She also gave some interesting advice. In fact, we couldn't wait to try out her advice and almost eagerly awaited the next flying ant invasion. After a couple of weeks we got our action. They returned - a huge swarm.

Quickly, Mom got a large bowl of water, lit a candle in the middle and turned off all the lights. Immediately, the ants flew to the candlelight, scorched in the flame and drowned. Within a few minutes the bowl was filled and the ants gone.

"It worked!" we screamed, "they're gone!"

And so another exciting evening in Depok came to an end.

Another highlight of Depok social life took place on the soccer field which was not up to size, slightly slanted and in front of an elaborate cemetery. The Dutch military, native police, Indonesian and Dutch citizens all formed their own soccer teams. With four teams, exciting matches and competitions were put together. We sat on a lone shaky bamboo bleacher while the players often took unscheduled breaks during sudden downpours or when some of the older team members needed a respite from the fierce heat. Playing time was shortened to two half hours. Come to think of it, it was rather crazy to play soccer in such heat except that it seemed unthinkable to live with a bunch of Dutchmen and not have a soccer team.

A few months after our arrival, Dad arranged for me to spent a weekend in Djakarta with a colleague of his, Tom de Rond. Tom and his wife, Joke, and their little toddler lived in Kebajoran, a nearby suburb. The day after my arrival, I decided to go shopping at the *Pasar Baroe*. Joke gave me specific instructions how to get there by bus.

"Don't talk to people you don't know," she cautioned, "you're new here and you don't know the customs or the people. Things are different here, you know, not like in Holland."

I promised, caught the right bus, found the Pasar Basar (remembered my sleeping legs after the *betja* ride) and had a great time nosing around the various stalls and merchandise, ranging from carpets, clothes and jewelry to smelly fish, coconut cookies and fried frog legs. Nothing was priced, everything had to be bartered for. I was beginning to get the hang of it but had brought little money so my purchases were few. All too soon, it was time to catch the bus home. I found the bus stop easy enough but the directional signs were confusing. Which stop was mine? Uncertain, I looked around and spotted some uniformed, native policemen on the corner across the street. Surely I could trust a policeman, I thought. Determined, I crossed the street and confronted one of them. His head barely reached my shoulder.

"Excuse me. Can you tell me which bus goes to Kebajoran?" I began.

Stunned, the man was obviously surprised that I spoke to him. Then, a quick smile showed a mouthful of pearly white teeth. He answered with a torrent of words but, like my encounter with Mickey in the sandbox so many years ago, I had no idea what he said. Undaunted, he turned to his colleague who stood nearby next to his motorcycle. The two entered into a lively conversation. Finally, still smiling broadly, the colleague turned to me and said in broken Dutch:

"You want to go to Kebajoran?"

"Yes," I confirmed, "I want to go to Kebajoran - on the bus. Which one do I take?"

Triumphantly, he pointed to the back of his motorcycle and announced: "Me take you there."

Incredulous, I stared at him. Me? On a motorcycle? No way!

"The bus!" I repeated, "I want to go on the bus. Which one?"

"Last bus gone miss," he announced, still smiling.

Gone? The last bus was gone? That couldn't be true, I thought. But... what if it is? It's after five o'clock and will be dark in an hour. Good grief, I'm stuck here on this corner. There isn't much you can do, my dear, I said to myself, but to trust this little man and get on his motorcycle. After all, he IS a policeman.

Reluctantly, I gathered my skirt and mounted the back of his bike. The little fellow quickly seated himself, revved his engine and we roared off in a cloud of dust. I had to hang on to him for dear life. He careened through heavy traffic and passed many busy intersections where he waved wildly to fellow traffic cops showing off his "catch." My heart sank. How did I get into this mess? Maybe I'd never see my family again. I was sure we were going in the wrong direction. Clutching my purse and skirt with one hand, hanging on to my "kidnapper" with the other, I considered my options. There weren't many. We entered a residential section. Slowing down he turned and yelled:

"You engaged miss?"

I pretended I didn't hear him but he persisted and asked again.

"Yes, I'm engaged!" I yelled back, feeling a white lie was justified by the circumstances. It didn't work. Unintimidated, he yelled back: "I take you to my family!"

"NO!" I screamed in his ear, "I want to go home!"

"Not take long" he assured me, "you like my family."

Spooky stories about abductions and white slave markets crowded my imagination. I had no idea where we were. Even if I ran away I didn't know where to go. We stopped in front of a nice home on a pleasant, quiet, palm-lined street. My escort led the way into a bright living room where several ladies were having tea. I was introduced even though no one knew my name. Nobody spoke Dutch. Someone offered me a cup of tea.

"No, I'm sorry, I can't stay," I repeated, "my friends in Kebajoran are waiting for me. I have to go."

I looked for my host but he was gone. Through sign language with the ladies, I gathered he had left on an errand but would be back soon. Still smiling, they poured me a cup of tea. I watched carefully and noticed they all were served from the same pot. Only after they drank their tea, did I touch mine. It tasted good. About fifteen minutes later my police escort returned. His name, I learned, was Sen.

"Could you please take me home," I begged, "right now?"

"*Saja non,*" (yes, Miss) he smiled, bowing and showing those pearly teeth again. I parted company with the ladies and mounted the motorcycle again. We took off. Presently, Sen continued the conversation.

"When I see you again, Miss?" he yelled.

I can't tell him where I live, I panicked, or he'll be back. Relieved, I recognized the street - we were almost home.

"Stop!" I yelled, "I live right here!"

Surprised, he stopped and let me off.

"Here?" he queried, "you live here?"

"Yep! That's right. Right here. Thank you so much for the ride. Goodbye."

I watched him turn and drive off in a cloud of dust. Relieved, I looked up and for the first time noticed the house I had him stop at. No wonder he was surprised. The house was under construction. Only the framework was up. I ran home to a very worried Joke and Tom.

"What were you doing on that bike?" they wanted to know.

How did they know about the bike? They couldn't possibly have seen me getting off the bike. It was dark by now and I was at least ten homes away when Sen and I parted company. Sheepishly, I told them the whole story, including the tea party.

"How did you know about it?" I finally asked.

"Your Mom called from Depok," she explained. "The military guys went to get supplies in Djakarta and saw you on that motorcycle. When they got back to Depok they told your Mom that would be the last they'd ever see of you."

Well, they were wrong. My gallant lawman had meant no harm after all but I was glad the adventure was over.

December came with continued heat and sunshine. Strange, not to have any seasons. The one and only protestant church in Depok put on a Christmas cantata. We all went, mainly because there was little else to do. The church was crowded and hot, its plain wooden benches hard. Like most other buildings there was no glass in the windows so that every little breeze from the outside could be caught. There was no Christmas tree, either. The pastor, an elderly man named Rev. Boon, had noticed our presence and visited us a few weeks later. Would we like to join the church? Dad assured him we all believed in God and that he, himself, felt closest to Him when out in nature. The Reverend nodded and left us alone.

A few weeks later someone tapped Dad on the shoulder in Djarkarta. "Hi Fred! How are you?"

Dad turned around and saw the smiling face of Henk Koevoet, a man from Blaricum. He had lived only a few doors from us.

"Henk!" he exclaimed, "what in the world are you doing here?"

"I'm with the Military Police," Henk grinned, pointing to the badge on his uniform. "What about you?"

They sat down on a park bench and Dad told his story.

"You live in Depok?" Henk said, "that's quite a distance. Nothing much going on there, eh?"

"Well, we have our home there," Dad said, "but yes, it's rather quiet."

They exchanged addresses. The following weekend Henk and his buddy Hans Vossenberg from Utrecht, drove to Depok to see us. Soon, they became regulars and picked us up for movies or dances in Djakarta. Dad didn't care for these things, Helen was too young, so it was usually Mom and I who climbed into the open jeep and hit the potholes as we careened out of Depok. Often our visitors dropped in for just the evening, lonesome for their own families back in Holland. Usually those evenings were filled with tall tales, jokes and laughter. Oh, those happy pre-television days. We actually talked and got to know people.

After our departure from Holland my uncle Auke, the one from Kampen who supplied Dad with food during the war, also got itchy feet and landed himself a contract with a coconut product company in Indonesia. He was to go to the Isle of Celebes but had to be in Djakarta for a briefing first. The day after his arrival from Holland he came to Depok for a visit. The house next to us was still empty so Dad put up a canvas field cot in the large, empty room next door complete with mosquito net on poles. Auke was a large man with a booming voice. When he laughed, which happened often, windows vibrated, cats disappeared and *tjitjaks* scurried behind pictures on the wall. He was tired after his long trip and retired early. Dad carefully explained about the mosquito net, the bathroom and the lightswitch. He also explained about the roaches and lizards.

"But you have nothing to worry about," he finally concluded, "this room is safe. Just don't forget about your mosquito net."

Uncle splashed himself in the mandi room and retired. However, in the middle of the night he woke up from a deep sleep, thirsty for a drink of water. He got up to turn on the light switch near the door but forgot about the mosquito net. He lost his balance and fell, the cot folded over him and the mosquito net wrapped around him like a giant spider web. He let out a roar that shook the house.

"HELP! Somebody is killing me!"

Mom and Dad shot up out of bed.

"It's Auke!" They said it together and rushed next door.

Dad turned on the light. There on the floor was a huge white tangled ball of mosquito netting with Auke hysterically roaring from somewhere inside. They quickly freed him from his "attackers." Sheepishly, he crawled back into his resurrected cot. The rest of the night he slept like a baby.

A year after our arrival in Depok, Dad was offered accommodations in Djakarta. Actually, it was a garage with two bedrooms in the adjacent house. We were ready for a change. Our faithful cook, Anna, decided to come with us and live in the small quarters in back of our new abode. One day, bright and early, a military truck came by to move us and our worldly possessions. Helen and I ended up in the back of the truck together with Anna who clutched a live chicken she brought along for supper. Since there were no refrigerators this was a common custom. After a long and bumpy ride, we arrived at our new home on the Panaroekanweg near the Menteng Movie Theatre and close to a cozy restaurant.

"Look!" Helen picked up something from a basket in front of her in the truck. "An egg. That chicken laid an egg."

Everyone gathered around her. The hen, unconcerned, pecked away at the basket.

"We can't eat a chicken who has just laid an egg." I said.

Anna and Mom agreed and spared her life. In gratitude, our scrawny hen laid an egg every day for many months to come...

We still didn't own a car but Mom and Dad were picked up for work by a company bus, Helen bicycled to a nearby school and I took the tram to my new high school which was close to the *Pasar Baroe*. One day during recess, I heard a soft voice behind me.

"Miss!?"

I turned and saw a little uniformed policeman. He beamed! Yes, it was Sen all right, my gallant motorist of more than a year ago. Surprised, I smiled albeit a little awkward. Luckily, the recess bell came to my rescue.

"Do you know that guy?" asked my classmates.

Reluctantly, I told them the story. They roared!

"I would have given anything to see you peeling out on that motorcycle."

"I'm glad you didn't," I retorted, "it really wasn't that funny. Besides, he was a decent fellow."

Some months after our move to Djakarta Dad made an announcement.

"A group from work is going to Monkey Island this weekend. It's a deserted island just off the coast with great beaches and swimming. You are all invited."

The next Saturday, a small boat took us and about thirty others to a small island in the warm Java Sea. It was indeed surrounded by white sandy beaches, a perfect setting for a super picnic and swim.

"Let's eat first, I'm hungry." Mom suggested.

We sat down on the beach, together with the others and looked for monkeys.

"There's one up in that tree!" someone pointed.

"There's another one! And another!"

Sure enough, there they were, perched on several branches, watching us intently from a safe distance with curious little round eyes.

"Aren't they cute? Look at those little hands and fingers."

"Here Monkey, have a cookie," a little boy yelled.

The monkeys kept their distance, however.

"Let's go for a swim," someone suggested.

We quickly changed and raced into the balmy waters. There was no surf which made it easier to swim. After lots of fun, splashing and frolicking, I lazily turned over and floated on my back, counting little puffy clouds in the sky.

"Hey look!" my reverie was rudely disturbed, "the monkeys!" "They're stealing our clothes!" "They got my camera!"

Suddenly everyone waded ashore. Sure enough, deftly perched on their high branches were our cute, little monkeys. Dozens of them now, each caressing an item of clothing, bag of food, sock or camera. We yelled! We screamed! We threatened. Nothing persuaded the creatures to give up their loot. There was no one to go to for help. The island was deserted except for us and the boat. After many fruitless attempts to get our possessions back we decided the monkeys were not so cute after all. Defeated, we finally left their enchanted island, carrying less equipment and wearing incomplete apparel. So much for monkey business.

High school finals were coming up fast. We had a month off to study. I had always been an average student and had to work hard to pass exams. Now I crammed ten hours every day for three weeks. Some subjects, like biology were especially difficult as tropical animals and insects were so different from the ones we had learned about in Holland. Since I could not study every creature, I decided to concentrate on one only. For no particular reason, I picked the cockroach. Imagine my joy when I was given three choices, one of which was the familiar roach. I passed all other exams as well and we got ready for graduation. Usually, there were no official graduation ceremonies at high schools but somehow, here in Djakarta, I got involved in an effort by our graduating class to present a variety show for the faculty and parents.

"Do you sing? Can you dance? Are you able to play an instrument?" I quizzed my classmates.

We started rehearsals and I was amazed at the hidden talent our class displayed. I MC'd the event and did impersonations of all the teachers, a rather daring stunt but since school was over, I took the risk. The evening was a hit and the entire graduating class beamed as they took several curtain calls. Smiling, I recalled our plays in Blaricum. I knew Doe would have been proud of us.

Vacation time followed. Dad had rented a bungalow in the high, cool mountain city of Bandung. It was owned and operated by the Government and available for employees. We travelled by train. For many long hours, we passed through desolate, rugged and mountainous jungle country, crossing high, fragile-looking bridges over incredibly deep ravines. Finally, we arrived in Tjoembuluwiet, a friendly suburb of Bandung where our comfortable bungalow was waiting. We loved it and enjoyed the cool weather and the friendly mountain people. One day, a small party got together to climb a nearby volcano, the Tanguban Prau. The Prau was about 10,000 feet high, its peak permanently hidden in the clouds. It had been inactive for over eighty years. A truck got us to the foot of the mammoth mountain. There, the giant towered above us, still partially hidden in the ever present clouds. A guide joined us and we slowly started our ascent. It was a paved path winding through a thickly wooded area. Wild flowers bloomed in abundance, bird songs were heard from the tall trees around us. We trudged slowly up the steep path, pausing now and then for something to drink, to catch our breath and to take pictures. Finally, the shrubbery thinned out, then disappeared altogether. Trees became scarce and soon the path curved through bare rock. We were now in the clouds. It was misty and chilly. Shivering, we realized we should have brought something to keep us warm. The guide announced we were about to arrive at the edge of the crater and cautioned us to be careful. The path under our feet was now brittle and crunchy. We were walking on lava rock. A little dizzy in the high altitude, we finally stood on the rim and looked down into an incredibly deep, enormous crater. At the bottom stretched a large floor with a small lake. White puffs of smoke drifted from its surface. Silently we took in this unusual, mysterious sight.

"That water must be boiling hot," someone observed.

"Smell that sulphur?"

"More like rotten eggs."

"I wonder if you can get down there?" One of the men, of course.

"Yes, let's try," another piped in.

The guide warned against it and wouldn't go.

"Too dangerous," he kept saying.

But the men wouldn't listen and decided to go down anyway, leaving us watching from the rim. They slid down the crater's slippery slope and were soon walking on the hot bottom. They looked like tiny specks. Half an hour later, their curiosity satisfied, they started their ascent to the rim again. Progress was slow. The lava rock kept crumbling away under their feet. The rarified air made breathing difficult, the sulphur fumes didn't help, either. Clawing at the brittle rock for added grip, they cut their hands on the razor sharp edges. Now, the men realized why the guide had warned them. Fear turned into panic which produced additional adrenaline.

Hours later, totally exhausted, they all arrived at the rim again. After some explicit dialogues, we silently walked down the darkened path. Little did we know that just a few weeks later the silent Prau would suddenly and violently erupt! Tons of red hot lava would shoot high into the air, then come crashing down around the crater rim before blazing a fiery path down the mountain, following the same route we had walked. Just as well we didn't know. After a most enjoyable and relaxing time in Bandung, we boarded a small, windowless, single engine cargo plane and flew back to Djakarta. We sat on boxes and bags and couldn't see a thing. It was our first flight together but by no means our last.

A few weeks after graduation, I enrolled in secretarial school to sharpen my typing and shorthand skills and get a diploma. A job opened up at the "Nederland," the large shipping company where Dad's brother, Willem, was employed as one of the directors in Holland. They had a large branch office in downtown Djakarta. I liked it and felt quite settled. However, Dad's three year contract would soon be coming to an end. There were rumors of political unrest and a possible government takeover. Dad's job and its future became uncertain. Mom and Dad decided to take a dream vacation to the lovely and famous Isle of Bali. Perhaps this would be their last chance. It was. One week after their departure, our Dutch government under postwar pressure of an emerging native leadership granted complete independence to Indonesia, withdrawing all troops and severing all government ties.

President Sukarno took control as Indonesia's first president. Who was this man? What were his intentions? Nobody knew for sure but he took some immediate and drastic measures. Needing lots of instant cash, he allocated half of the national capital for government bonds. Bank accounts were cut in half. Our paper rupias, the equivalent of the Dutch guilder, had to be literally cut in half. The right side was to be deposited in government bonds (without dividends), the left side was ours but was now worth only half its original value. Also, overnight, the rupia devaluated. It now took three rupias to buy one guilder. A Bank account of 1,200 rupias which one week before had been the equivalent of 1,200 guilders was now first cut in half to 600 rupias by mandatory government bonds, then only worth 200 Dutch guilders. It devastated our savings. Wealthy plantation owners went bankrupt overnight.

Suddenly everyone wanted to leave. No one knew what to expect next. Mom and Dad hastily returned from their dream vacation, devastated by this sudden turn of events. Dad's job was being phased out. His contract would not be renewed. We suddenly needed a passport to get out of this foreign country. A hastily constructed consulate office began issuing passports for Dutch and Dutch-Indonesian citizens wanting to return to Holland. I was asked to help out there and soon spent hours filling out passports for an ever lengthening line of people. We didn't want to leave our new homeland yet staying would be too dangerous. Besides, we would be jobless. Dad considered Australia but he had to go there by himself first to find a job and accommodations and it would be too risky to leave us behind. Besides, his contract included a free trip back to Holland so this, after much discussion, seemed to be the only option. And so in August of 1951, we once again gathered our *barang* and boarded the "SS Ormonde," an old P&O liner, on its very last journey back to Europe. Another chapter of our lives was coming to a close.

To stifle boredom, I offered my secretarial services to the Ship's Purser. This also got me in touch with the crew but they were all English and with my two years of high school English, I was not able to follow much of their conversations, let alone participate. I did learn how to throw darts, however. Slowly, we retraced our steps back to Holland through the Indian Ocean. This time we had a two-day visit to the lovely island of Ceylon, now Sri Lanka, and its beautiful capital of Colombo. Then came the hot Red Sea, followed by the Suez Canal and the balmy Mediterranean. The Gulf of Biscay was rough again, so was the choppy North Sea. Finally, the flat coast of Holland came into view. We passed the coastal city of Hoek van Holland where the "Ormonde" slowly turned and was tugged into Rotterdam's harbor. I stood alone on one of the deserted decks. It was bitterly cold. Angry winds blew through my thin, borrowed sweater. We had no winter clothes left. I realized that I had almost forgotten what it was like to be cold. The skies were low and grey, rain came down in huge waving sheets.

I felt overwhelmed by the enormous contrast of these two countries I had grown to love. Where do we go from here, I wondered. What would the future hold? Chilled to the bone, I returned to our tiny cabin and helped carry our *barang,* which had now become luggage again, to the exit. Another era had come to an end.

Chapter 4

DOWN UNDER

Housing in Holland was extremely difficult to find. Our small, over-populated country, still recovering from the war, had strict rules as to where people could live and how much space they needed. We had to return to Blaricum where we had been registered before our departure. Our former home was rented to another family. Kees Mellegers who still lived across the street, made part of his three-bedroom home available to us. We had our own living/dining room and two bedrooms but had to share the kitchen and bathroom. His own five children slept in the attic. It was a temporary arrangement till we were allotted other accommodations by the Housing Department, if and when something became available. This, we were told, could take years.

After several months, we got in contact with an elderly widow in Bussum. She lived with her daughter and was willing to rent half of her home to us. By then, we all had found jobs in or near Bussum and welcomed her offer which would mean more space and privacy for all of us. We moved in but since we had no official permit to live in Bussum, it was an undercover arrangement.

We continued to talk about Australia. Thousands of Dutchmen, as well as other Europeans, were emigrating in droves to that vast continent down under. However, the Australian government preferred farmers, blue collar workers and people under forty. Families in these categories were provided with free boat passage, free accommodations in resettlement camps where jobs would be provided and some initial cash to get settled. Dad was forty-three and neither a blue collar worker nor a farmer.

"There is no shortage of accountants in Australia," an official told him at the Immigration Department. "You may apply for emigration but you'll need proof of accommodation before you leave Holland. You won't be eligible for any government assistance, either. And you will need to pay for your own passage over there."

That meant four expensive tickets for the five-and-a-half week boat trip and no job or settlement assistance. Our savings from Indonesia were virtually gone after Sukarno's drastic measures. We were in a tough situation.

"Didn't Henk Zwart move to Australia?" Mom asked one day.

Henk, his wife Bets and two children were also from Blaricum. Henk had been a private chauffeur.

"Yes, he did," Dad said. "Maybe he can help us with accommodations."

We quickly got in touch with them. Their response was very encouraging. They loved their new country, they wrote, and were delighted about our plans to join them. Within a few months they had rented an apartment, a so-called holiday flat for us (for whenever we would arrive), and mailed proof of this arrangement back to us in Holland. Our Dutch courage was flying high by that time and Dad formally applied for emigration for the four of us.

Our papers were accepted but there was a long waiting list for available boat passage. Notice for departure, we were told, could be very short. Indeed, it was. Early in 1952, two years after our return to Holland, we were booked on the SS Johan van Oldebarnevelt leaving Amsterdam in three months. Physicals, passports, shots, termination of jobs, packing trunks and suitcases and saying goodbyes to friends and relatives followed in quick succession.

This ship belonged to the *Nederland*, the same company I had worked for in Djakarta. Dad's brother, Willem, was one of the directors. He officially came on board to see us off. We even dined with the captain and were given a private cabin for just the four of us. What a luxury! Most other passengers were still accommodated in large, crowded holds. The trip, by now, had become familiar. Everyone got seasick in the Gulf of Biscay, everyone recovered in the Mediterranean. Shopkeepers in Port Said remembered us, the Suez Canal was still the same as was the hot Red Sea. Aden hadn't changed either, and was as sinister as ever.

From Aden, we crossed the vast, balmy Indian Ocean once again, this time heading for Freemantle near Perth, the southeastern tip of Australia. For two whole weeks, we again gazed at water, skies, occasional schools of flying fish and hundreds of bored faces. Perth, when we finally reached it, was a lovely city, very British and unlike Holland. Everyone drove on the left side of the road and spoke English with an accent. While living in Bussum, I had taken some lessons in conversational English from my Uncle Henk, a professional English teacher. He had converted Sir Conan Doyle's *The Hound of the Baskervilles* into a text book. Following Sherlock Holmes' and Dr. Watson's exploits in English was a rather fascinating experience and it did increase my English vocabulary but I still lacked a great deal of confidence. One Dutch passenger seemed surprised after a sightseeing tour through Freemantle.

"I can't believe it," she exclaimed, "even little children speak English here!"

A week later, we arrived in Melbourne, a modern, large metropolis where a number of passengers disembarked. Two days later, we finally turned into the magnificent Sydney harbor, actually a large arm of the sea. I will never forget the sight. It was a bright, sunny day with just a little breeze. Miles and miles of mountainous shoreline weaved in and out of the huge harbor. Hundreds of homes were clearly visible among brilliant patches of flowers, shrubbery and trees. All this was drenched by the warm, brilliant sunshine with millions of reflections winking at us from the deep blue waters of the harbor. Sandy beaches snuggled in rocky coves, ferry boats made straight, white paths as they took their cargo and passengers from one shore to the other.

In the distance, the famous Sydney Harbor Bridge came into view. Small at first, it slowly became an semi-circle connecting the city of Sydney with the sprawling North Shore communities. As our ship quietly moved closer, the bridge's enormous height and width and the intricate design became clearly visible against the blue skies. Stately white clouds provided a majestic backdrop to the magnificent structure. Finally, the "Johan" moored almost under the Bridge and we realized with great excitement that we had arrived in yet another homeland.

Henk Zwart, his wife Bets and two small children Roef and Mieke, were waiting for us on the crowded quay. We laughed and hugged and everyone talked at once as we hauled our luggage to the waiting car which Henk had borrowed. Soon we crossed the Harbor Bridge and had an even more spectacular view of the sparkling Sydney harbor. The bridge supported a wide, multi-lane highway which included bus lanes, railroad tracks and pedestrian walkways. Traffic was heavy and we marvelled that cars did not collide driving on the left side of the road. We also had our first glimpse of Sydney's famous double-decker busses. They were everywhere, transporting thousands of commuters from Sydney to its vast conglomerate of suburbs. We were heading north and soon crossed the narrow Spit Bridge which led us to Pittwater Road. This highway gracefully followed the weaving shoreline, connecting towns like Dee Why, Collaroy and Narrabeen to Palm Beach on the Hawksbury River.

We passed a large, white building with a sign: TOP DOG.

"That's a garment factory," Henk said. "We're almost in Collaroy."

The ocean sparkled again to our right. A reef covered with lush green grass jutted far out into the water. There were glorious white beaches all along the edge of that bright blue water.

"That's Long Reef," Henk pointed out, "a beautiful place to walk." He turned left at a movie theater, Odeon, next to a few small stores.

"We live in back of that first store," Bets explained.

We were on a narrow, rather poorly paved road, flanked by homes on either side. In the distance, it sharply ascended to a high, flat-topped hill.

"That's the Collaroy Plateau," Bets pointed.

Henk brought the car to a halt in front of a two story, red brick building called "Sea View."

"Welcome home!" he beamed, opening the car doors. "This is it."

We met the landlady, an old, wrinkled but remarkably perky woman who lived downstairs in the back.

"I'm Mrs. Twight," she chirped. "Let me take you upstairs."

She shuffled up the steep stairs and showed us our flat which included a roomy kitchen/dining room, a sitting room, one bedroom and a sunroom in front with daybeds for Helen and me. Also, there was a bathroom with sink, shower and toilet. The latter was filled with sand.

"The toilet does not work," she said matter-of-factly, "but there are three in the back, one for each family. I'll show you."

Down the stairs we went to three outhouses in the backyard. Well, we can always use a commode at night, Mom thought. No problem.

We met the Morgans, a friendly couple who lived below us.

"Let me know if we can help you with anything, *mate*," Mr. Morgan told Dad.

"*Mate*" smiled and looked at our luggage. Mr. Morgan got the message and willingly helped to haul the many suitcases and trunks upstairs. Helen and I quickly explored the beach which we could see from our sunroom. The sand was white and soft, the water blue with a gentle white-capped surf.

"Look!" Helen pointed, "there's a swimming pool."

We walked over to the right side where the beach made a slight curve. A low rectangular cement wall had been built in the water, making a perfect saltwater pool. The wall kept the water inside the pool during low tide. Benches for spectators were hewn out of the rocks on the edge of the pool. From here, we had a splendid view of the rest of the coast which weaved in and out of the ocean.

There seemed to be a private beach for each village since the rocky, hilly shoreline dipped in and out of the clear, blue Pacific. Lifeguards in colorful shorts and caps paraded up and down the beach. In the future, we would see them marching and competing with other groups in dory races, relays and other events, popular Australian pastimes. There were also frequent shark warnings and there were schools of playing dolphins which often frolicked around in the surf.

"Let's go to the movies," I said to Helen a few days after our arrival. After all, with a movie theater almost next door, no transportation was needed. I will never forget our first show. We saw "The Day The Earth Stood Still," a movie about a flying saucer starring Michael Renny. The reason I will never forget it? No Dutch subheadings! Ouch! This was getting serious.

Life became interesting and full of surprises now. We noticed the Aussies often put an "n" or "r" behind their word. Idea became idear, etc. To meet people, Helen, who had whiled away many an hour on board ship playing deck tennis, joined a tennis club. Coming home from a practice session one day, Mom asked:

"How did it go, Helen?"

"Oh, fine," she said, "but there is one thing I don't like."

"What's that?"

"They keep calling me an onion."

"An onion? You're kidding!" Mom said, "Why would they call you that?"

"I don't know but every time I hit a good ball they yell 'Good on'yun, Helen!"

The Australians actually simplified their language. The word *now* for instance could mean now, no or know. *Die* could be die, dye or day.

Mr. Morgan came up one evening and announced:

"Tomorrow is rubbish *die*."

Uncomprehending, we stared at him, so he repeated, a little louder:

"Rubbish *die*, you NOW?!"

No, we didn't know. Finally he grabbed Dad by the hand, took him downstairs and pointed at something.

"Aha," Dad suddenly smiled, "trash day!"

"That right, *mate*. Rubbish *die*."

We found the Australians to be both friendly, casual and eager to help. They always praised our efforts to speak English and kept telling us how marvelous we were doing. One man offered to give me driving lessons. I gladly accepted. Driving along one day he suddenly said,

"Pull up."

I looked around for something to pull up. Would it be the hand brake? No, I didn't think so. But there just wasn't anything else to pull up. Was he getting fresh and talking about my skirt? He didn't seem the type.

"Pull up!" he repeated impatiently.

Frantically, I searched again for something to pull up. Finally he screamed:

"STOP!"

I immediately slowed down and stopped.

"Why didn't you stop?" he yelled.

"Why didn't you TELL me to stop?" I retorted, "and what in the world did you want me to pull up?"

Shortly after our arrival, I got a two-week relief job in the nearby town of Manly with the gas company.

"You will be answering the phone," the lady who interviewed me said, "and be making morning and afternoon tea. You will be earning ten guineas a fortnight less tax, of course."

I searched my memory for words. A guinea, I had learned, was one pound and one shilling, a fortnight was two weeks but what in the world was tax? She saw my lack of comprehension. As so many other people had, she repeated the word but louder this time,

"Tax, you know. TAX!"

The closest word I knew was taxi. Would that be it?

"Oh no," I said casually, "I'll take the bus to work, Ma'am."

It's a wonder I got the job.

Making tea, I was soon to find out, was quite a traditional art and my Dutch tea brewing techniques had to be totally abandoned.

"Never pour hot water in a cold pot, put one teaspoon full of tea in the pot for each cup plus one for the pot," I was told.

"That makes very strong tea," I ventured.

"Correct, but we use lots of milk."

I slowly learned. Not so simple were the phone messages. I simply could not understand people. When a caller realized I was a "New Australian," poor in English, they would spell out their name and address for me. That only made matters worse. I could understand when someone said: Mrs. Brown but B-R-O-W-N didn't mean a thing to me since I had never learned how to spell in English. In Holland, when something needs to be spelled we use words. Brown would be something like "boy, river, old, william, never." After a few days someone else was put in charge of taking telephone calls.

During morning tea breaks, I carefully listened to the chatter of my fellow workers around me. Here and there, I picked up some words but couldn't really follow a whole conversation. Some of the girls talked about the latest hit movie playing in Manly. It was called, "Singin' in the Rain" with Gene Kelly. Had I seen it? No, I hadn't seen it and didn't want to, either. Forlornly, I served out my fortnight behind the tea-trolley, cut off from the lives of those around me by the ever-present language barrier.

We heard about a Dutch employment agency. The lady in charge got me a live-in job at a surgeon's home in the exclusive area of St. Ives on the North Shore. They had five children and were going away on vacation. I was to be the housekeeper and baby-sitter. A kind man picked me up from the train station. I took him to be the surgeon but he laughed and said he was only the gardener. We came to a large, ranch-style home with an orchard in front and lawn and paddock (meadow) in the back. Housecleaning had never been my forte and I knew very little about cooking. I did a lousy job with both responsibilities. The kids were nice but rather independent and I still could not converse very well. I packed lots of lunches and watched them trot off to school every morning, neatly dressed in their school uniforms, a common sight in my new homeland. Housecleaning came next but my heart wasn't in it. I was lonely and miserable. When the couple returned, the vacuum was broken, the bathtub full of rings (we never had a tub - how could I know about rings?) and the house was dirty. I was promptly fired. Rather relieved, I packed my bags and had the gardener take me back to the train station. In Sydney, I switched to a double-decker bus and happily resettled in our sunroom in Collaroy.

Dad, in the meantime, had made several trips to the Employment Office in Sydney with little results. The immigration man in The Hague had been right; Australia did not need accountants or bookkeepers. Dejected, he sat down one day at Sydney's beautiful Botanical Gardens on Maquarie Street overlooking the harbor. These gardens used to be part of a huge estate now maintained by the state as a public park. Nearby was the old, ornate Conservatory of Music building, formerly the stables for the estate. Many years (and lotteries) later the famous and impressive Opera House would be built here, right on the water's edge. Munching on his sacklunch, Dad absentmindedly threw some breadcrumbs to a pigeon near him. Soon he was surrounded by flapping wings as a multitude of eager and friendly pigeons settled on his head, his arms, his shoulders, his lap and even his hand. Amused and intrigued, he almost forgot about his employment problems. Suddenly, a voice broke his reverie.

"Mind if I take your picture?"

He looked up and saw a young man with a camera in front of him.

"Are you a photographer?" he asked, a little suspicious.

"Oh no," said the young man. "I just happened to see you with those pigeons around you. You're quite a sight, you know. If you let me take your picture, I'll give you a copy."

He seemed sincere so Dad let him take his picture.

"My name is Bob Murning, mind if I sit down."

"I'm Fred Hoffmann," Dad replied. "I don't mind. Please sit down."

"Where are you from?" he asked, noting Dad's accent.

Dad took another look at the stranger next to him. He seemed to be in his thirties with an average build, dark hair and eyes. A little shabby, but soft-spoken and sincere, perhaps a little sad. Dad needed someone to unload on so he told Bob about Holland and our recent arrival in Sydney, how we loved the country but couldn't find work. He told him about Helen and me as well as his own frustrations. Bob was quiet and listened intently. Once in a while he asked a question. Finally he said:

"Well Fred, seems to me your daughter has to get another live-in job. That's the only way she's going to learn to speak our language. Staying home is the worst thing she can do. If she does not like to be a housekeeper perhaps she can work in a hospital as a live-in aide for awhile. And you," he continued, "you said you like gardening. Why don't you try some gardening till an office job opens up?"

His advice made a lot of sense. Encouraged, Dad went home, bought a newspaper and answered several gardening ads. Eventually, he worked every day at several large homes. This continued for two years. He earned a living and felt and looked extremely healthy. Intellectually, he was rather unchallenged but it got him through a few tough years. Eventually, he got an excellent job as office manager in Sydney's business district. Mom, meanwhile, worked behind the counter of the grocery store next to our movie theater. Later, she joined Dad's office and became his assistant. Helen, who had finished school by now, initially got a job at a small children's rehabilitation hospital right in Collaroy. Later, she became an efficient long-distance telephone operator with the phone company in Sydney.

When it was first suggested that I work in a hospital, I cringed. That was absolutely the last thing in the world I ever wanted to do. One day, many years before, while walking home from school in Holland, I had passed the leftovers of a small dog that had been run over on the Huizerhoogt. There were pieces of dog all over the street. My stomach turned and the gory sight haunted me for weeks. Besides, the few nurses I had known from a distance were not exactly role models. They seemed to be brisk, plain, flat-chested, no-nonsense women, overworked and underpaid, with no fun or laughter in their lives. No, nursing was definitely not my bag.

However, I did have a problem. If I wanted to pursue my secretarial career, I had to get a better command of the English language. Living among the Aussies, away from home, seemed to be a good "idear." Bob, who by now had become sort of a family friend, arranged an interview for me with the Matron (Directress of Nursing) of the prestigious Royal North Shore Hospital near Sydney. I spoke at length with the very kind lady. She gave me some textbooks explaining simple nursing procedures, then I looked through the ad section of the Sydney Morning Herald and called several hospitals. A small hospital in Randwick was looking for a nurse's aide with on-the-job training. It was, like most nursing jobs, a live-in position.

The Matron explained which tram to take to get to Randwick, a suburb south of Sydney near the popular Bondi beach. This was unfamiliar territory for me but her directions were clear and soon I walked through the quiet suburban streets looking for Helena hospital. (The"d" in Randwick was not pronounced, while the "i" in Bondi was like the "i" in white.) I opened the iron gate in front of a fairly large, two-story home. Was this a hospital? There was a colorful, well-kept garden with lots of flowers and blooming shrubbery surrounding the building. I rang the doorbell and was ushered into the private office of the Matron, an elderly, friendly lady. She had me fill out an application and hired me on the spot, offering me a small salary and one and a half days off each week. Then we walked through the hospital and the nurses' quarters. The latter was a small separate building on the grounds.

"You will have this room." She pointed to a light and airy room with two single beds, a large chest of drawers, small table and two chairs. "You will have a roommate, of course."

She also gave me instructions about uniforms which I had to have made by a seamstress. Tired but excited, I finally took the tram back to Sydney where I boarded a double-decker home to Collaroy. I didn't realize then that my life would never be the same.

"Please stand up when Matron walks in," Sister Sabian said. She was tall and skinny, clad in a blue uniform, her hair covered with a huge, starched white veil. We were having lunch with about eight other employees in the small three-table dining room at Helena Hospital when the Matron arrived. Everyone stood and remained standing till the Matron was seated. Sister Sabian was an RN assigned to teach me the rudiments of nurse's aide care. I learned a lot that first day. All RNs were called Sisters, students and nurse's aides addressed as Nurse. All Sisters wore starched veils, blue uniforms, white hose and shoes. We sported a long-sleeved mauve uniform, partially covered with a large, high-bibbed apron. A white, starched cap covered most of our hair. Other starched items were white cuffs, belt and a Peter Pan collar. Black hose and shoes completed our new appearance.

There were a few other new employees, among them my roommate, a shy, blond, blue-eyed girl from England, Daphne Challoner. Our lessons were interesting and rather easy to follow. With Daphne's help, I was able to either translate or understand most of the procedures.

"What is pneumonia?" I asked her one day.

She tried to explain. It must have something to do with your chest, I figured. On my next day off, I brought an English-Dutch dictionary to the hospital. "Pneumonia: Longonsteking," I read. Aha, that's what pneumonia meant. It was sometimes hard to explain that I did indeed know a lot of medical words but only in Dutch. *The Hound of the Baskervilles* never had pneumonia nor did he have his temperature taken. I never knew if he had a bladder or was ever constipated. Words like enema, respirations, incision, distension, obstruction and the like, are not often found in conversational English classes.

"Nurse Hoffmann." Sister Sabian stood in the doorway of the pan room. I was scrubbing the stainless steel bedpans before submerging them in their daily bath in the sterilizer.

"Sister Davies in Room Three needs some help with her patient. Can you go right now?"

I hesitated. Sister Davies was a private duty nurse taking care of an elderly man who had died that morning. I had never seen a dead person, let alone touch or handle one. Yet I knew that's what she needed help with now.

"Sure," I said lamely. "I'll be right there."

Slowly, I dried my hands, walked to Room Three and softly knocked on the door.

"Come in!" Sister Davies called.

The shades were drawn. In the dimly lit room, I saw the contour of a still form on the bed. It was covered with a sheet. Sister was busy with a dish of warm water, soap and towels.

"Please, close the door," she asked me. Then she turned around and removed the sheet. I just stood there, kind of frozen to the spot, awkward and embarrassed, not knowing what to do or expect. Ignoring my hesitancy, Sister started to gently bathe the body, asking me to help with turning and drying. She plugged the various orifices with gauze and cotton and replaced his dentures, then tied the jaw so it wouldn't sag. An ID card was tied to the big toe, the body wrapped in a large, white shroud, another ID attached to the outside and we were done. Sister thanked and dismissed me. Relieved, yet in a daze, I returned to my familiar bedpan room. I lost my appetite that day and skipped lunch.

The next day, I felt better and did not have to work till the evening shift. The morning was bright and sunny and I decided to check out Bondi Beach. Little did I know another lesson was waiting to be learned. At first, the beach seemed similar to our Collaroy beach on the north of Sydney. It had soft, white sand, clear blue water and white, foamy surf. The beach was shorter though, I noticed. It was only about a mile long as opposed to Collaroy's which stretched out about ten to fifteen miles to the next city of Narrabeen before being cut off by a rock formation stretching into the ocean. At each end of the sandy stretch at Bondi Beach a long, high tongue of land jutted out into the ocean, ending in a sheer cliff which caught huge sprays of water from distant waves. The beach was not too crowded on this midweek day. Several swimmers frolicked around in the distant waves. I put my bathing suit on in one of the change rooms, found a good spot for my towel and beach chair and walked towards the water.

It was nice and warm and shallow. I quickly walked into the small, churning waves which playfully licked my feet. Collaroy beach sloped gently into the ocean. You had to walk quite a way before the water came up to your waist line. Imagine my surprise when I suddenly saw an enormous wall of water approaching. It came so fast, I was completely taken off guard. The water I was standing in was barely touching my knees. Yet here was this huge mass of water at least ten feet high, rushing towards me at an alarming speed! Before I knew what to do, the wall thundered over me, lifting me, together with tons of sand, inside its wildly churning center. Automatically, I curled up into a ball, clasping both hands around my knees which were drawn up under my chin. I had managed to quickly gulp some air before the deluge crashed over me. Then I was helplessly tossed around and around by tons of angry water.

I know this can't go on very much longer, I remember thinking. This wave will finish churning then I will float to the surface, wherever that is, and run for the beach, whichever way that is.

Sure enough, pretty soon I felt air on my back. That must be the surface. I raised my head and gingerly opened my eyes.

Oh no! I gasped. It can't be! I stared at another wall ready to crash over me. Quickly gulping another lungful of air, I curled up into my fetal position again, spinning around crazily inside the crashing wave.

There are other people in the water, I remembered. How are they coping with this wild scene?

As I floated up once again, I peeked around. Another colossal wave was gathering height and speed. Several swimmers ahead of me watched it coming, waited and then, just before it crashed, dove under it. I had no time to get out of the water and didn't want to spin around again so I tried the diving trick. It worked! Amazing! Diving deep under the mass of water, almost at the bottom, I avoided the swirling mass altogether. It was quiet there and I quickly surfaced after the wave crashed. Frantically, I tried to run towards the beach which seemed close but I had to strain hard against the tide of the retreating waters. With every laborious step my feet were sucked into the soft sand. Finally, I reached the safety of the beach. Exhausted, I collapsed on my towel. My heart was beating fast and furiously. After a while the adrenaline diminished and I took a closer look at the beach. I noticed something interesting.

Because the beach was so short, pushed back so far from the protruding rocks and shaped like a giant V, the distant waves were forced into a smaller and smaller area as they reached the beach. Thus, they became larger and larger until they were stopped by the sloping beach and crashed. Most swimmers ventured out farther into the water before the waves got too big but in my confusion and panic I never got that far. My hair and bathing suit were covered with sand. After showering and soaking up some sun, I returned to Randwick still quite shook up and happy to be alive. I wondered how many other things I had to learn in this country.

Helena Hospital was really a converted two-story home. Most patients were downstairs in two four-bed wards and several private rooms. The Theatre, or Operating Room, was upstairs. There was no elevator and patients after surgery, were carried on a canvas sheet, IV and all, downstairs to their bed by the entire surgical team. There was no Recovery Room, either. Part of my training included helping in the Theatre. Sister Allen, a brisk, efficient nurse, was in charge. She taught me how to wash out gauze 4x4s, ace bandages and IV tubings, make ABD dressings and sterilize them in a special metal drum with holes on the sides in the autoclave. Nothing was disposable. I also washed and sterilized instruments.

I still shuddered when I thought about bloody surgeries and didn't think I was ready to watch such procedures. ("Bloody" was a bad word here - people off duty used it occasionally when they were angry.) But Sister Allen did not agree and one day made the dreaded announcement that I was to observe a leg surgery the next day. I don't believe I slept much that night. Early next morning, we got the surgery room ready. The patient, a man in his forties, had a complicated leg fracture. He was wheeled in on a stretcher and moved to the operating table. I had a flashback of my own surgery when I saw the anethesiologist put the mask on the patient's face. He dripped some Trylene or similar induction agent to get him to sleep, then switched to a steady drip of ether. The floor nurse had shaved the man's leg, scrubbed it with soap and water, then washed it with iodine and alcohol and finally wrapped it in a sterile towel. The surgeon now removed the towel and washed the leg all over again. Then he and his assistant scrubbed their hands in a nearby sink and put gowns and gloves on (assisted by me). He then took a sterile rubber tourniquet and wrapped the leg carefully and tightly from the toes to the upper portion of the thigh. He anchored it at the thigh and then unwrapped the beginning, from the toes upward. I watched, curious yet still apprehensive. The leg was then draped with sterile towels. The anethesiologist confirmed the patient was asleep.

"Knife," he said to Sister Allen.

She was also gowned and gloved and was in charge of the instruments. She handed him a scalpel. I cringed. Now it is going to happen, I thought. Blood everywhere! I'm going to be sick.

The incision was made. The pale skin parted slightly. There was no blood. The incision was deepened. Still no blood. Suddenly it dawned on me that the tourniquet had squeezed all the blood out. Until it was released, there wouldn't be any. I breathed again. Perhaps this was going to be bearable after all. My attention focussed on the instruments displayed on a tray between the surgeon and Sister Allen. They looked familiar. I recognized a hammer, a saw, a screwdriver and screws. Intrigued, I now closely watched the doctor at work. He began to explain.

"This is the tibia. I am bypassing this to get to the fibula, the second bone in the calf. It was badly fractured."

With the saw, he removed part of the fibula, then dug around for a while, repairing damaged tissue and muscles. Finally, he picked up the bony fragment of the fibula he had removed and fitted it back where it had come from. He placed a small metal plate with holes over the severed bony ends. A screwdriver was used to place some screws into these holes and attach them to the rest of the fibula. I could actually follow the procedure and, fascinated now, noticed all the intricate steps. Finally, the wound was cleansed, closed and stitched up. A bandage was wrapped around the leg, the tourniquet removed and a cast applied. The surgery was over. I was elated. Nothing to it. I could watch anything and nothing would bother me anymore. It was as though the psychological fear of seeing "blood and guts" was lifted.

The following day, I watched my second surgery. This was a radical mastectomy on a very large woman, one of the most bloody surgeries imaginable. I watched the entire procedure from beginning to end and even held the large specimen basin for the breast when it came off. It didn't bother me in the least. Amazing! If it had not been for that bloodless leg surgery the day before, I probably would have quit my hospital job right then and there. A few weeks later, I completed my surgery stint and was transferred back to the floor downstairs.

The next test was the ultimate one! A painter had fallen off his ladder, smashing his partial dentures and swallowing some pieces. It was imperative that the doctor know all pieces were accounted for so the next week he was assigned to me. I shuddered every time I saw him coming out of the bathroom and calling for me. Swallowing hard, I got a fork, a strainer and gloves and went to work. Eventually, I found all the pieces. After that, nothing ever bothered me anymore.

There was only one RN on duty each shift. Sometimes a number of patients needed medications at once, particularly shots. One day, Sister Sabian decided she would teach me how to give pain medications. Actually, I was surprised she suggested that. Just the day before I had sorely tried her patience.

"Nurse Hoffmann," she had said, "please go and clean the sink."

Sink? What is a sink, I thought. Aha! I remembered, "sink" is a metal. I trotted down the hall to look for some. What did "sink" look like? My dictionary did not say.

"Did you clean the sink?" I heard her steps down the hall.

"Ah...yes, I mean...no, I mean I can't find it," I finally admitted.

"What do you mean you can't find it! It's right here." She pointed to a large sink in the bedpan room.

Aha, I thought, so that's called a sink, also!

"Sorry Sister," I murmured, "I thought that was a basin."

"That's right," she said firmly, "it's also a *bison*." (I thought a bison was a buffalo...)

Anyway, Sister Sabian decided I needed to learn how to give shots. She took me to the medication room where several small glass syringes and needles were boiling in a tiny sterilizer. I knew the needles were sharpened every week in the operating room upstairs. She explained the difference between subcutaneous, hypodermic and intramuscular needles and how and why they were used. With a pair of forceps she fished up a syringe and needle from the boiling water in the sterilizer and placed them in a small, sterile kidney *bison*. . . basin, to cool off. Then she lit a match and put a flame to a small kerosine burner. Next she put some water in a spoon, dropped a white Morphine tablet in it and slowly boiled the solution over the flame. Then, deftly with her other hand, she picked up the syringe, pulled back the plunger and stuck the needle in the freshly boiled Morphine solution. When it was drawn up she said: "Now wait till it cools off and we'll give it to the patient."

I had been practicing on an orange and felt pretty confident. We walked over to the patient. She bared his upper arm, swabbed it with alcohol, quickly stabbed the needle in, pulled back on the plunger and, when no blood appeared, slowly pushed the Morphine solution into his arm. Then we went back to the medication room, washed and resterilized the syringe, charted the medication in the narcotic book and on the patient's chart. Nothing to it. The next one was mine. It was an insulin shot for a diabetic patient but for this we had to get a urine sample first.

Another small room, next to the medication room, was a makeshift lab where urine samples were tested for sugar. This could be a trying experience, I found out. Again a small burner was lit and one c.c. of blue Benedicts solution poured into a test tube. Then eight drops of urine were added, the tube was held by a clothespin and the solution brought to a sustained boil for two minutes. By that time, the color had changed from blue to green, yellow or orange. This indicated the amount of abnormal sugar present which determined the insulin dose to be given. If no sugar was present, the solution would remain blue. Simple enough except for one thing. When the solution started to boil it had the nasty habit of suddenly ejecting from the tube, splattering the walls and ceiling, leaving a hot, empty tube. After cleaning the mess, the whole procedure had to be done all over again. A major headache.

After many trials and blue streaks on the walls, I finally discovered that by constantly moving the tube in and out of the flame, the concoction would eventually boil, actually remain in the tube for the prescribed time and not shoot all over the room.

After working at Helena Hospital for about a year, several things became clear. First, my English was improving, although still far from fluent. Secondly, much to my own surprise, I realized that I'd much rather work in a hospital than sit behind a typewriter all day. The nursing bug had bitten and I was hooked. A new future loomed in the distance. I did not want to be a nurse's aide all my life and considered formal training. Surprisingly, Helena Hospital was licensed to train RNs but the place was so small, without even an Emergency Room, that I decided against it. Instead, I applied at the massive and tough Sydney Hospital. It was located in the heart of Sydney on Macquarie Street overlooking Martin Place, the hub of downtown Sydney.

The training took four years, an assistant Matron told me. This did not include obstetrics or psychiatry. These were separate and optional courses, one year each, and not offered at Sydney Hospital. There was also a waiting list. Upon closer scrutiny, it was discovered that my high school diploma from Indonesia was not acceptable and I had to take a Nurse's Entrance Exam. A few weeks later, I took it and promptly flunked. If it had been in Dutch, I would have breezed through it for it was actually a simple test. But since English grammar and I were still not on familiar terms and English math was vastly different from my simple Dutch metric system, it was too much of a challenge.

I studied some old tests and noticed that each exam had one question in common. For composition choices there was always one where a New Australian (a recent immigrant) was asked to write a letter to a friend back home, describing details about his/her new life in Australia. I got to work and composed such a letter, extolling the Australians' wonderful patience as I stumbled through a new language and their marvelous understanding as I tried to adjust to their beautiful country. Then I went to Mr. Morgan, our neighbor, and had him edit this epistle. When he finished, I committed it to memory. I also polished up on the complicated system of inches, feet, yards and miles, marveling that people could make simple math so complicated. When I took the test again, I passed. My application was accepted and Sydney Hospital was to become my home for the next four years.

Chapter 5

REAL NURSES

One sunny day in May of 1954, two years after our arrival in Australia and 21 years old now, I walked through the front gate of Sydney hospital, suitcase in hand to start a strenuous four years' training program. I had been warned by many well-meaning "experts" that the training at Sydney Hospital was extremely tough and chances of finishing the course very slim. I ignored these friendly warnings but didn't really intend to finish the training anyway simply because four years was a very long time. My commitments didn't stretch that far in those days. I'll start and then we'll see, was my philosophy.

I passed the guard at the front gate and entered a small courtyard surrounded on all sides by massive, brownstone buildings. The four story building on the left housed the Nursing Office, dining rooms, classrooms and student dorms. I climbed the few steps to the front door, rang the bell and was ushered into a waiting room. About twenty-five girls, all about my age, were already there.

"Hello. Are you starting here today also?" I found an empty seat next to a blond, blue eyed girl.

"Yes," she said. "You too? Do you live around here?"

"Yes, I live in Colloray. Where do you live?"

"Dee Why."

"That's next to Collaroy." I said, surprised.

Her name was Betsy. She was soft spoken and I noticed a familiar sounding accent.

"Where are you from?" I probed, "I mean, where were you born?"

"I'm from Holland," she replied.

"You're kidding? So am I. Where did you live in Holland?" I was delighted.

"Nymegen," she said. "How about you?"

I told her about Blaricum and realized she must have had a tough time in Holland during the war. Nymegen was a city on the beleaguered rivers close to Arnhem where those fierce battles were waged by our allies. Our conversation was interrupted by the appearance of a lady, probably in her forties and clad in blue uniform, white hose and shoes and starched veil.

"I'm Sister Rodmell," she smiled "and will be your tutor sister for the next three weeks."

She looked disciplined, efficient but kind.

"You will be assigned to your dorm rooms so you can settle and unpack," she continued. "Then you'll be issued uniforms from the laundry. Some of the older students will help you with them. I will see you in the class room next door in the morning."

We were ushered to the second and third floors. The rooms were fairly large, with three single beds and three dressers in each, a high ceiling and a non-functioning fireplace and mantle. To my delight, Betsy and I were assigned to the same room. So was another girl but she wanted to room with a friend so that left just the two of us. The bathrooms, we were told, were down the hall. We unpacked and found the laundry where our new uniforms were issued. Putting these on proved to be quite a job. First, there was a blue and white striped long sleeved dress. Before putting this on, a stiffly starched white collar had to be attached to it with a safety pin. Over the dress came a large white (also starched) high-bibbed apron with a wraparound skirt. This was fastened in the back with another safety pin. The bib straps were crossed in back and held in place with two more safety pins also pinned to the back of the apron. This was quite a tricky thing to accomplish. Covering all these safety pins was a stiff, white belt. Finally, there were two stiffly-starched cuffs held in place by two white plastic cufflinks. Our heads were covered by a cap, also starched and white, covering all our hair except a few bangs (called fringes). The caps were typical of first year probationers, as we were called. Students in their second, third and fourth year had different caps so they could be recognized and treated according to their status. Completing our metamorphosis was a pair of black hose and black shoes which we had been instructed to supply ourselves.

At the appointed time, we filed into the classroom ready for inspection. Sister Rodmell was thorough and made lots of adjustments. Finally, she said we were ready to be presented to the Matron. Matron's office was small so we had to file slowly past her. Seated in a straight chair behind an impressive desk strewn with papers and files, the old, white-haired Matron sternly looked us over, one by one, then asked to see our fingernails. Polish was taboo, of course, but so were long nails. Mine were short enough but several students were sent back to their rooms to cut their already fairly short nails even shorter. Eventually, Matron had approved the entire new class of probationers, or "pro's," and we were led downstairs to the dining room for lunch.

By now, I was getting used to Australian food and eating habits. They ate breakfast, lunch, dinner (called Tea) and supper (a snack before bedtime). Tables were set with plates, knives and forks but also an extra small bread and butter plate on the side with another small knife. Roast lamb and pumpkin were popular fares for Tea which was not surprising in a country that raises millions of sheep. A special treat was kangeroo tail soup, only served in fancy restaurants. Years later, I found out why only kangeroo tails are eaten. For morning and afternoon tea, fresh scones (biscuits) with butter and jam were served. Coffee was hard to come by at first but as the influx of New Australians continued, Italian expresso and instant Nestle's coffee were soon to be introduced. Table manners were British and I was slowly getting used to eating food with a fork held upside down. Eating peas was only possible if combined with mashed potatoes. Hospital food was pretty good and we could always eat as much as we liked.

The next three weeks, we spent in the small classroom where the capable Sister Rodmell explained the arts of bedmaking, baths, enemas, bandaging, backrubs, taking vital signs, catheterizing bladders, cleaning dentures, preparing a patient for surgery and a host of other procedures. My first problem arose with bedmaking. There was a bed in the classroom to practice on. Electric beds had not been invented; neither were siderails. The matresses were hard which necessitated frequent backrubs to prevent pressure sores.

Being tall, I sat in the back of the class next to another tall girl, Mary Sharp. When my turn came to make a bed in front of the class, I thought I had done a pretty good job. So did my classmates. But when Sister Rodmell came in to inspect my endeavor she took one look and faced the class.

"Can anyone tell me what's wrong with this bed?" she demanded. The class remained silent. "Goodness me!" she exclaimed, incredulous. "You mean nobody sees anything wrong with this bed? There are two errors here. We won't continue till you tell me what they are."

We all stared at the bed. The opening of the pillow case was away from the door, both ends of the quilt hanging on the sides were of equal length. The sheet was folded over ten inches. Or was it ten centimeters? Suddenly, I realized I wasn't sure how long ten inches were. At the same moment, at the end of her patience, Sister Rodmell faced me and said: "Nurse Hoffmann, how long is ten inches?"

Oh no, I cringed. That's it.

"I don't know," I admitted. "I only know how long ten centimeters are." I had shortchanged my sheet overlap. OK, now what else was wrong? The class continued to remain silent. I racked my brain. Exasperated, Sister finally pointed to the seam at the edge of the top sheet. It was inside out, she said. I looked, stepped forward and felt the seam. Indeed, it was inside out. An unpardonable sin. We all sighed with relief, determined that would never happen again.

Changing dressings came next. "A basic dressing tray consists of a tray with two kidney basins and three small bowls in the center," Sister

Rodmell explained. "This basic tray can be used for changing dressings, giving enemas, inserting nasogastric tubes, etc. For a dressing change you put your instruments (forceps, scissors, etc.) and clean dressings in one kidney basin. Afterwards they go in the other kidney basin. Cotton balls go in one of the small center bowls, Normal Saline or some other solution in the other. The last bowl is for dirty or used cotton balls."

We each had a chance to practice. Each dressing change was preceded by a series of steps. Put a screen around the patient, flatten the bed. Remove bedcovers, expose only the site to be treated so patients wouldn't get cold. Then drape the surrounding area with sterile towels. A large dressing trolley was wheeled from bed to bed. Our basic trays were put together at each bedside from the supplies on these trolleys. Of course, preceding the dressings rounds, these trolleys or dressing carts had to be loaded in the corner of the ward where the sterilizers and dressing drums were kept. For some reason, taking blood pressures or starting IVs was strictly a doctor or intern job but removing sutures (stitches) was somehow beneath their dignity and fell on our shoulders.

In class, it all seemed so easy but later I struggled with dozens of tiny scalp sutures between the stubble of a ten-day hair growth after craniotomies or even smaller, almost invisible, stitches after adult circumcisions, a rather embarassing job, even for the most seasoned ones among us.

In our last week, we practiced with and memorized a great variety of enemas including the famous Harris Flush, the latter a procedure to relieve a patient of post operative distension due to flatus (gas). It's almost like an enema and the patient feels immediate relief.

I remember one brief moment when Sister Rodmell's efficient and business like expression suddenly softened into a merry smile. We were discussing the treatment of worms. There were tape worms, pin worms and hook worms. She explained where they came from, how we get them and how they develop and multiply. Next came the various treatments.

"Are there any questions?" she concluded.

Totally serious, Mary Sharp asked: "When do they turn into butterflies?" The class roared.

One morning, about a week after Tutor School started, we were paired off and assigned a ward to help with backrubs for a few hours. Mary and I went to Ward 9 for male orthopedic patients. I will never forget my first entrance into that ward. It was huge, lined with twenty-two beds from which I felt twenty two pairs of eyes staring at me. Most patients were in traction and hardly able to move.

The center of the ward had a desk, a sink and several portable screens. A door at the other end of the ward led to the bathrooms and bedpan room. Both sides of the ward were lined with long, narrow windows, one in between each bed. Each window had a blind which was pulled up to exactly the same height.

Most of the work and patient care at Sydney hospital was done by students, supervised by RNs (sisters). There was one sister in charge of each ward. When she was off duty, the senior student would take over. Our selfconsciousness of entering these large wards was quickly taken care off as we were put to work.

After reporting to the charge nurse, we took off our cuffs and put them under our bib, then rolled up our sleeves and began on the backrub rounds. A screen was placed around each patient, the lower back washed and vigorously rubbed with soap. Then the soap washed off and area dried. Next came rubbing alcohol and another vigorous rub. This done, the area was dried again and powder applied. After each backrub the sheet was inspected for creases and straightened out. All patients in this ward were on four-hourly rubs. A Back Book was kept and taken every morning to Matron's office to be signed. If any patient's skin broke because of a pressure sore, it was mentioned in the Back Book. This was considered a disgrace to the entire ward and drastic measures were immediately taken to correct this condition.

One of my first backrub patients was an elderly man. Because of his traction he was unable to turn over. However, he could raise his back off the mattress by pulling on a monkey bar, a triangular metal bar suspended over his bed. I couldn't see the area I was rubbing but could feel that the skin was firm and intact. As I rubbed his back, my face was close to the man's chest while he kept his arms flexed on the monkey bar. His chest was covered with grey hair. As I stood there rubbing away, I had the eery feeling that these hairs were alive and moving. Since my face was so close to it, I felt I was unable to focus and dismissed the thought. However, after the rub was completed and I had straightened out his bed, I glanced at his chest again. From my more distant perspective things still looked alive around there. I excused myself, left the screen around the bed and reported my sightings to the charge nurse. She came, looked and took me aside.

"Nurse," she said, slightly shaken, "that man's chest is full of lice. I am going to call the orderly and have him shave that area, then wash it with antiseptics. Don't say anything to him or the other patients but keep his things separate and boil everything he uses."

Lice?! Is that what I saw? Suddenly I felt crawling things all over me. I changed but still felt itchy. Luckily, a few days later the patient was pronounced cured of vermin to the relief of the entire staff.

"Nurse, I need a urinal, please."

The request came as I passed Mr. Stetson's bed. He was a big, bearded forty-year-old sheep shearer with a broken leg. He was not in traction but his legs were covered with a large metal cradle to keep pressure from the blankets off. "Sure," I said, "I'll be right back."

I was on my way to the pan room anyway. There were two racks there, one for bedpans and one for urinals. The urinal rack was empty. They must be all in the sterilizer, I figured. I put my foot on the pedal and heaved the large tray to the surface of the boiling water. There were no urinals in there, either. That's strange, I thought. We had at least fifteen of them. They couldn't be all in use. I walked back into the ward and glanced over chairs and nightstands. Not one urinal anywhere!

"Nurse, hurry!" Mr. Stetson looked uncomfortable.

Sister was busy doing rounds so I couldn't interrupt her. Perhaps the veranda. Searching through the extra nightstands, I finally found one. I rushed back to the pan room, scrubbed and cleaned it and delivered it to Mr. Stetson. He seemed surprised, almost disappointed. Strange man, I thought.

The surgeon making rounds was in deep discussion with the senior resident. Sister was right behind them, making notes as they went along. A trail of six young interns closed the ranks. Pretty soon they arrived at Mr. Stetson's bed.

"Let me see your leg, sir." the doctor asked.

Stetson didn't move. Finally, the doctor motioned to an intern who stepped to the bed and turned the covers down.

"Good grief!" the doctor exclaimed. "What is THAT?!"

Everyone stared at Stetson's bed. There, under the cradle, piled neatly and snugly together, were the sixteen missing urinals. Stetson roared!

A few days later several patients were discharged.

"Could you strip the beds, nurse.?" Sister asked. "We're getting some new admits right away."

I wheeled a large hamper in and stripped the linens off the beds. The pillows were taken to a rack outside on the veranda. The remaining mattresses were the next items to be carried out. I flipped both ends to the center and with a large heave balanced the whole thing on my shoulder and deposited it on the same rack outside on the veranda. Later, this rack would be picked up by an orderly who fumigated everything.

Another rack with clean mattresses and pillows stood nearby. Now these had to be carried in, one by one, to the empty beds to be made. Since I was tall and fairly strong, carrying these mattresses was relatively easy. But for Winnie Young, one of my smaller classmates, it was an almost impossible task. One day as she staggered (and almost disappeared) under a heavy load, the ward Sister called me.

"Look at that poor girl, Nurse Hoffmann," she remonstrated, "don't just stand there, go and help her."

After that, whenever we worked together, I was assigned to haul her mattresses as well as my own.

Our three weeks of Tutor Class passed quickly and Mary and I were both assigned full time to Ward Nine where by now, we felt quite at home. We worked various shifts. Everyone worked forty-four hours with one and a half days off each week. Our board, lodging and uniforms were free and we all got a small salary, about $100 per "fortnight," paid in cash. All the students were single and lived in the rooms provided, some at the hospital and some in the city.

After orientation, our medical classes began, led by physicians, pharmacists, dietitians, etc. These were scheduled around our workweek. We also punched a time clock, not for pay but for personal file records. Every six weeks, we were transferred to another ward. There were seventeen wards on the main premises, an Eye Hospital across the park and a Rehabilitation Hospital in Randwick, close to my old Helena Hospital.

Protocol among staff was strict, almost military. Every student who had started training ahead of us was considered our "senior." When addressed by a senior, especially a senior in charge, you stood up, put both hands behind your back and remained thus till the conversation was concluded. Rules for wearing cuffs were worse. When entering the ward cuffs were put under your bib and sleeves rolled up. When leaving the ward for any reason or when serving meals or during visiting hours, sleeves were to be rolled down and cuffs put on. A major pain in the neck. Cuffs didn't always stay behind bibs and often slid to the floor.

The day shift came on at 6 am. The night nurse had given some baths by then but we had to finish the rest. When all baths were given and beds made, someone would ask, "Where are the tea leaves?" Tea was served throughout the day and all used tea leaves carefully saved in the kitchen. Tea bags had not been invented. When baths were done, we threw these moist tea leaves under every bed, then swept the entire floor. The leaves kept the dust down.

Now the blinds had to be pulled up. It was very tricky to get them all even. Many seemed to have a mind of their own. At this time Matron or one of her assistants could make surprise inspection calls. The quilts and blinds were scrutinized first, then came any article or item not in its proper place. Standing ramrod straight, both hands behind our back we heaved a sigh of relief when the ordeal was over.

By then, the kitchen staff had brought up the food trolley. We had to dish up all meals, checking for special diets. It was a long walk from the dayroom to the last bed in the ward. By the time the patients were fed, it was 7:30 and we could relieve each other for breakfast.

A new patient came in one day. His name was Terry. He was about twenty-four and good-looking. Terry had back surgery and was on a Striker frame, a small canvas frame he was strapped on. To turn him, another frame was bolted on top of him and thus sandwiched in, the whole thing turned around. Now, he faced the floor and the top frame was removed. He was turned every two hours. I liked him and we had some interesting conversations during backrub and turning time. After he recovered, he asked me for a date. It was against hospital rules but I suffered a memory lapse and did go out with him a couple of times. It was then I discovered that a nurse-patient relationship inside a hospital is a different kettle of fish than an out-of-the-hospital encounter. We had a nice time but nothing clicked.

After Ward 9, I was assigned to Ward 3, female medical. This ward was in front of the hospital overlooking Martin Place. It was here I met twelve-year-old Julie. She was an only child of elderly parents born with severe cerebral palsy and admitted with a bladder infection. Her legs were locked in a permanent fetal position. Her arms and head were constantly shaking. She talked but it was almost impossible to understand what she said. Yet, she had a wonderful personality, a great sense of humor and a sharp mind. Her crooked smile was contageous and her beautiful, large brown eyes most expressive. Feeding her was a chore. The harder she tried to stop shaking, the worse it became. Finally, I discovered that by diverting her attention to something else she would quiet down enough for me to get food into her mouth. I greatly admired Julie's parents who were totally devoted to her and gave her excellent care at home. After her discharge, I even visited her a couple of times, much to Julie's delight.

A few beds from Julie was Mrs. Marsh, a young mother admitted with terminal leukemia. Her thin frame was almost transparent. We turned her often and spoonfed her small amounts of liquid. One morning, after a bedbath and linen change her sunken eyes searched my face. There was great fear, almost panic in her voice when she spoke.

"Nurse," she whispered, "am I dying?"

Taken off guard, I avoided her eyes and fussed with the bed. Of course, she was dying, I thought, everone knew that but patients were never told about these things. Besides, we were taught to give our patients hope and if I told her she was dying I would remove all possible hope for her. Finally, I looked at her and said softy, "We don't know, pet. We really don't know."

After all, I justified myself, nobody did know for sure when anyone else would die. But the next day, she was gone. I began to seriously consider the whole matter of life and death. Was there an afterlife? Was there a heaven? Could I truthfully tell my dying patients there was hope for them after death? Would they be reunited with their loved ones? I certainly believed in God the Creator but did He know me? Did

He know anyone else by name? To see old people die was one thing, but the death of young patients brought on all kinds of questions. We had several young men with Hodgkins Disease, cancer of the lymph glands. They were given two years to live. When first admitted they looked so healthy, yet at every subsequent admission for blood transfusions and other treatment, they had aged, lost enormous amounts of weight and within two years they were gone. Was there a God Who cared? Was He really in control?

None of our lectures dealt with spiritual matters although many classes were given in the hospital chapel. I never saw a chaplain either, or any other member of the clergy. The chapel was pretty with stained glass windows and comfortable pews. There were Scriptures on the windows. One said: *Come unto me all ye that labor and are heavy laden and I will give you rest.* It never occured to me those words could have meaning for me personally. I did not labor and certainly was not heavy laden and I didn't need any rest. Pretty words for a pretty window, that's all. I had an interest in spiritual and religious matters but somehow was not attracted to churches. I found some books on various world religions and philosophies in the city library and heard about meetings in a building close to the hospital. I devoured books by their founder but found the meetings disappointing. They were attended by only a few, very elderly people. It was stuffy and boring and I lost interest.

Meanwhile, I was developing another interest. For several weeks, I had worked with a girl named Berys. She was short and pleasant, yet serious and a hard worker. One day after we signed off she said: "I'm going to a concert tonight. Want to come along?"

We took a city tram to the huge, impressive Town Hall, a large, ornate auditorium. The Sydney Symphony Orchestra was giving a youth concert. All tickets were sold out in advance but the choir seats were on sale at the door for a few shillings. Berys and I climbed the steps on stage where the orchestra members were already busy warming up. There were several hundred young people already seated on the choir benches behind the orchestra but we found two seats not too close to the drums. Ahead of us was a vast sea of people filling both the main floor and the balconies of the richly decorated auditorium. Then the house lights went off and the entire stage was suddenly flooded with light, including our choir seats.

The conductor entered. There was applause, then he introduced and explained the program, giving some background of the composer and the composition. When done, he turned, faced the orchestra and raised his baton. The house lights dimmed, a hush fell over the audience. The conductor faced us, the crowd on the choir seats. I felt as though we were a private audience up there and that all these upturned, concentrated faces of the members of the huge orchestra watching that baton and the conductor, were performing just for us. The crowd in the rest of the auditorium didn't seem to exist anymore. A soft drumroll introduced a lively composition with a kaleidoscope of harmonious sounds from strings, brass and wind instruments. I sat spellbound, fascinated.

After a few short compositions, the conductor introduced the main soloist, a young French violinist, Christian Ferras. He was to play Mendelssohn's violin concerto. Although I had always liked all kinds of music and had diligently practiced my piano as a child in Holland, I had never heard a live orchestra nor was I familiar with the works of the classical masters.

I learned that night that a symphony is music written for orchestra while a concerto is music written for orchestra and a solo instrument. Most symphonies and concertos consist of three movements. Mendelssohn, I read in my program, had written volumes of music but only one violin concerto.

The young soloist made his entrance and for the first time in my life I was exposed to the exquisite beauty of the Mendelssohn violin concerto. For an encore, the soloist repeated the first movement. Thrilled, I thanked Berys for taking me.

"They're repeating the program," she said. "Want to go again?"

Would I? Well, of course! The following night, we climbed the stairs again and soaked up another majestic performance. As an encore, we heard a repeat of the second movement. The last night, we returned again. This time the encore was a repeat of the third movement. Within three nights, I had heard one concerto four times. Now I was beginning to recognize the various themes and melodies. I was suddenly hooked on classical music and for the next four years, Town Hall became a very familiar place.

By this time, Betsy and I had been transferred to a nurse's dorm on Young Street about one mile from the hospital. We usually walked to work although there was a hospital bus to shuttle us during night hours. On our way to the hospital, we almost passed the Conservatory of Music at the Botanical Gardens. One day, I stopped by there and inquired about piano lessons. Not only were the fees reasonable but there were also practice pianos available. I enrolled and for the next few years studied music and piano under the guidance of a kind, balding man. A side benefit was frequent free concerts performed by graduating students in the auditorium. Although I never became an accomplished pianist, I learned to appreciate good music, an excellent antidote for the stress and human misery we encountered in daily hospital life.

I was on night duty in Ward 10, Male Surgical. It was very dark and most patients were asleep. We had a small, heavy, battery operated, metal lantern to see by. Nothing else. Its weak light illuminated our report book just enough to make the necessary entries. Taking care of patients while holding on to this heavy supply of light was a real challenge. Put it down on the nightstand and you would illuminate the blinds or water pitcher but not the patient. After receiving the report from the evening nurse and walking rounds through the entire ward, we had to memorize all new admits and new surgeries including names, doctor, condition, surgery performed and medications. Around midnight, the physician in charge would make rounds with the night supervisor. Questions could be asked on any detail. The first new admit that day was diagnosed with pyloric stenosis. I had to look up what that was and managed to remember these strange words. The next patient had a hemorrhoidectomy that day. Another huge word. I was seated in the center of the ward at the desk surrounded by a screen so that my small "torch" would not waste any light on sleeping people. The trouble was you never knew who came and went through the entrance doors. I was a second year student now, the only one on duty for the night and responsible for twenty-four patients, relieved once during the entire night for supper which we had to cook ourselves.

Straining my ears, I thought I heard a rustle near the door. Yes, they had arrived. I walked towards them (an important protocol) stood straight, hands behind my back and waited.

"Good evening, nurse," the senior resident greeted me. "How are your patients tonight?"

"Fine, Sir," I replied.

"How many new patients to do you have?"

"Three came in today, Sir."

"Any new ops (surgeries) today?"

"Yes, five Sir."

"Are they all right?"

"Yes, Sir."

"What kind of medication are they on."

"Mr. Gorden is on Pethedine 100 mgm IM every four hours for pain. He's also on one million units of Aquaous Penicillin IM every six hours."

I continued my dissertation. He seemed satisfied.

"Anyone with an elevated temperature?"

"Only Mr. Cooke. It's down to 100 now from 103.6 this morning. He is on ASA gr.X every two hours and still on Aureomycin and Sulpha."

"Any problems with anyone else?" "Mr. Thomas' Nembutal hasn't worked. He is still awake. I have a call in for the house Resident."

"Fine, thanks a lot, Nurse. Good night."

New admissions could come in any time. Usually, we received a call from Casualty (Emergency Room) but not always. The supervisors had just left when an orderly quietly pushed in a stretcher.

"Better take care of him right away, nurse," he whispered, "he doesn't look too good."

"Why didn't you call me? I could have gotten a bed ready," I said a little annoyed.

"Why don't you take a look first?" he suggested.

It was then I noticed the entire patient was covered with a sheet. That's funny, I thought. I looked at the stony face of the orderly then lifted the sheet from the patient's face. My "torch" lit up the bony features of our classroom skeleton. Relieved, I smiled. Very funny.

My reaction was not what the orderly had hoped for. Rather disappointed he wheeled his stretcher out the door to the next ward.

Later, I went to supper. When I returned to the dark ward, I noticed that Lois, my relief nurse, was on the phone just outside the main entrance. She had placed her "torch" on top of it. It was shining on the wall which I was about to pass. Remembering the skeleton joke, I playfully spread all my fingers wide, stretched out my hand and moved it into the tiny sphere of light focussed on the wall. I was totally unprepared for what followed. The poor nurse let out an earthshaking, piercing scream, the phone dropped from her hand, she stumbled and then fell backward on the floor. Stunned, I quickly appeared from around the corner and helped her up. All patients were awake, not only in my ward but probably in the entire building. The supervisor and other staff would rush up any time. What was I to say? A practical joke? Not very funny. Why had Lois reacted that way? It wasn't that scary. If it had been me, I would not have batted an eye. Badly shook up, I profusely apologized to the poor girl who was trying to get herself together again.

"What are we going to say?" I whispered.

"Don't say anything," she urged, very embarrassed now, "I don't know why that scared me so much. I'm sorry."

"No, I'M sorry," I insisted, still shaking.

I picked up the dangling phone and put it back. It rang immediately.

"Let me answer it," Lois requested.

"Ward Ten, Nurse Holmes speaking." I heard her say.

"Yes Sister, I heard it also. No, I don't know where it came from. Yes, I'll let you know if I hear anything."

She hung up the receiver and left. Relieved, I gathered my wits and spent the next hour trying to put my patients back to sleep.

The weeks and months went by quickly. Only two people in our class dropped out, the rest stuck together and hung in there. Over the months and years, we were transferred from ward to ward, Urology, Pediatrics, Gynecology, Dermatology, Out-Patients, Eye hospital, Rehab, Casualty and Surgery. We worked night shifts, day shifts, evening shifts and split shifts. My days off were mostly spent at home in Collaroy. Dad worked in Sydney in an office not far from the hospital. In fact, we passed it walking from our Young Street dorm to work. One day, Betsy and I walked home from work. It was around three in the afternoon on a week day. For years, we had had a special family whistle, a few notes only members of our family recognized. Whenever we were in a public place looking for each other, our little whistle would bring immediate results.

"If I whistle," I told Betsy as we walked along the quiet street, "a door will open and a man will appear."

She looked at me as though I was crazy. I smiled, then whistled and kept walking. We continued another ten feet or so then suddenly, a door opened and Dad appeared, looking right and left to find me.

Betsy was astounded! What would those Hoffmanns come up with next?

In our third year, we did a stint in one of the Operating Theaters. The entire first week was spent washing walls and bottle tops. Each Operating Room had a shelf full of bottles, mostly antiseptics and other cleansing agents. The tops of these bottles were soaked in an alcohol solution every day. It was a serious and most important daily routine.

The instrument room held several enormous stainless steel sterilizers where large metal trays full of instruments were boiled. When a surgery was about to begin these heavy trays had to be lifted from the boiling water with large forceps and carried to the next room. I had nightmares about dropping these trays, keeping an entire surgical team waiting while everything had to be re-sterilized. Luckily, this never happened.

Sponges, drapes and dressings were autoclaved in metal drums. Each ward also had a drum for daily dressing changes. After I graduated from washing walls and bottle tops, I began to observe during surgeries and eventually scrub as an instrument nurse. My first patient had varicose veins on both legs. She was put to sleep with Pentothal. Two senior residents positioned themselves along each leg. I gathered from their conversation that they each had strong opinions about taking care of varicose veins. One insisted they should be stripped, the other maintained they should be ligated, a different procedure. They both went to work, one on each leg. Tying off bloodvessels as they went along became a hurried, sloppy procedure. The area between the patients legs was the instrument field for which I was responsible. I had to keep track what was where and which instruments to hand to the surgeons. The field, however, was filling up with a pool of congealing blood, covering most of the instruments. Undaunted, the residents continued. "Patient's blood pressure is dropping," the anesthesiolgist announced.

"Did you type and cross match any blood, Doctor."

"No, I didn't."

"You'd better make it snappy," his voice was urgent, "her pulse is 120, bloodpressure 90/60!"

My supervisor came around and noticed the mess on the surgical field. She helped me retrieve the submerged instruments and instructed me how to cover the area with clean drapes. I was nervous and very insecure. Finally, the ordeal was over and both legs bandaged and wrapped. The patient was getting IV Plasmanate by now and eventually her BP returned to normal.

My other cases were fairly routine and, all in all, I learned a lot. One of the senior vascular surgeons, Dr. Allen Sharp, had done extensive research on aortic aneurysm repairs. He had developed a special nylon patch or graft which he sewed over the weakened aneurysm. Pre-operative tests to determine the exact site and size of these aneurysms had not yet been developed so Dr. Sharp appeared in the Theatre accompanied by his wife. She, in turn, brought her sewing machine. When the patient was put to sleep and opened up, Dr. Sharp measured the aneurysm and relayed the needed measurements for the graft to his wife who then went to work on her sewing machine. When finished, the piece of material was autoclaved and sewn into the aorta. Most of his patients died shortly after surgery. Nevertheless, his pioneering efforts were of great benefit to future research in this field.

Thoroughly seasoned now with the sights and smells of blood, ether and anticeptics, I was transferred to the emergency room. Whining ambulances screeched in constantly with all kinds of paticnts, mostly accident victims or medical emergencies. Being in the center of Sydney, we always attracted lots of business. One day, I became a patient myself. Getting dressed one morning, I tried to fasten one of the safety pins in back of my apron. Trying to push it through the heavy, starched material, it slipped and disappeared instead under the cuticle of my right thumb.

It hurt but not bad. The following day, however, it was extremely painful, red, swollen and throbbing. A few days later the doctor announced I had an infection under the nail that caused a lot of pressure. It had to be lanced. I was put on antibiotics and scheduled for outpatient surgery. Skipping breakfast, I checked in a few days later.

The anesthesiologist said he would use Nitrous Oxide or laughing gas to put me to sleep. I didn't think it was a laughing matter and tried to remember my ether experience many years ago in Holland when my hernias were repaired. The anethesiologist appeared. He sat down near the head of the stretcher I was on and started fussing with the anesthesia machine.

"Does anyone know how this thing works?" he quipped.

Very funny, I thought. Sick joke. The doctor washed my finger and cracked a smile. A nurse was setting up her instruments. Then I felt a mask over my face.

"Count to twenty," the cheerful voice near my head said.

I did. At ten I felt a little drowsy.

"Is she under?" the surgeon asked.

"Yes," said the cheerful voice.

"Wait, I'm still awake! Don't start." I yelled.

Nobody heard me. Next thing I saw was the surgeon bandaging my thumb.

"Don't start," I repeated, "I'm still awake."

"All done!" he smiled. And so he was.

"You can work but don't get your finger wet," he instructed me.

"How do you do that?" I asked.

"Try gloves," he smiled.

Ten days later the infection was gone and the nail healed. However, it was permanently scarred - a special memento of the safety pin days at Sydney Hospital.

"Guess what I found in the trash?" an ER orderly asked me a few weeks later. I was restocking the medicine room during a relatively quiet moment between ambulances.

"I don't know," I replied, not very interested. "What did you find?"

He glanced around, then produced a small metal cigarette box from his pocket. Slowly, he opened the lid. On a patch of cotton was the top half of someone's middle finger.

"Why would you want to keep that?" I asked.

"Because," he whispered, "I think it's still alive,"

All right, I thought, what's the joke? Folding a stack of arm slings, I took another look at his finger. Indeed, it moved. Then I realized it was his own middle finger, cleverly stuck through a hole in the bottom of the box.

"How did you do that?" I queried, intrigued now.

He looked disappointed and I realized he had wanted to scare me, not arouse curiosity. Rather lamely, he showed me his trick. I immediately got myself an empty box of Benson and Hedges, cut a hole in it, lined it with cotton and a little red Merthiolate and, on my next visit home, I showed everyone my "souvenir" from the ER. Here, I reaped the desired effect the orderly had missed.

In spite of our hectic schedule, we managed to maintain a pretty active social life. Living in the heart of the city had distinct benefits as well as disadvantages. One disadvantange was the fact that on weekends, especially Sunday, the town was dead. Downtown Sydney was strictly a business center, filled with thousands of commuters Monday through Friday but deserted during weekends. Theatres and restaurants were open on Saturday but on Sunday you could have fired a hundred shots on Martin Place, the hub of Sydney, and not hit a soul. Advantages were the proximity of all sorts of entertainment facilities and eateries during the week. We discovered a terrific Chinese restaurant on King's Cross near the notorious red light district of Wooloomooloo, also a pineapple bar on Martin Place where thick, fresh pineapple juice, squashed before your very eyes, was served in huge glasses. Then there were the numerous milkbars, Australians famous walk-in, stand-up hangouts, found on almost every street corner.

Huge shopping centers were within walking distance, David Jones, Walton Sears, Woolworths and many others. There were theatres with double features and live intermission shows and excellent plays in a variety of theatres.

One day Berys, the cultural expert, took me to a Shakespeare play featuring Kathryn Hepburn. Our seats were in the far balcony of the crowded, narrow theater. We were almost touching the rafters and the stage seemed no bigger than a postage stamp. The wooden seats were rough and I ruined a pair of hose. My English, which by that time had greatly improved, was still not geared towards a Shakespearean vocabulary and much of the dialogue eluded me. But it was a great experience.

One movie I saw in Sydney with Betsy was "A Man Called Peter." It greatly moved me. I also attended a special evening at the Conservatory of Music where the famous Indian mystic, Krisnamurti, spoke. I was impressed with the man's apparent inner tranquility and his words of wisdom. I resolved to read some of his writings.

During my fourth year, I was in charge of Ward 15, a busy male and female surgical floor, divided into two wards with about fifteen beds each. I worked with a second year student, Sally. She was a bright young lady, a good worker who often felt she could take over some of my responsibilities. When the residents made their rounds, rather than call me, she would walk along with them herself, taking verbal orders which she would later relay to me.

"Oh, Nurse Hoffmann, I couldn't find you" or "I knew you were busy" would be her excuse. I knew I had to face this issue but wasn't looking forward to it. Finally one day, I found a few minutes after dressing changes and medication rounds.

"I need to talk to you, Sally," I said. "Let's go to the veranda."

"Sally," I began, "you are a good nurse and I like to work with you but you know, one of these days you are going to be in my shoes. You will be a fourth year student and in charge of a ward."

"When that time comes," I continued, "you wouldn't want a second year student to take over your responsibilities, would you?"

"No, I wouldn't," she admitted.

"Well, then Sally," I concluded, "you'd better learn now to stick to your own job. If I am busy or you can't find me, look for me anyway and, if I am not in the ward, get the next nurse in charge."

Much to my surprise Sally was grateful, not angry with me at all, and our teamwork greatly improved. Confrontation was difficult but the results well worth it.

From Ward Fifteen, I was moved to Ward Two, Male Medical. It was a genial bunch of men, most of them ambulatory and eager to help with meal trays and other small tasks. Many were diabetics and I spent the usual time in the blue walled lab room testing urine samples. Benedict's solution, when boiling, still shot from the test tube now and then. However, my speed with these tests had greatly improved.

One night, we got a new admit, Mr. Stafford. He had advanced carcinoma of the trachea and was admitted for palliative treatment only. His raspy breathing soon filled the ward, especially during nights. As the days went by, I began to dread going on duty. Mr. Stafford's eyes pleading for help were more than I could bear. There was simply nothing anyone could do for him; he was slowly choking to death. Finally his breathing became so deficient that abnormal levels of carbon dioxide built up in his bloodstream. He became confused and more desperate for air. We put him in a bed with siderails. Eventually, he became like a clawing animal, his hoarse roars interrupting his labored, wheezing respirations. It affected the whole ward but no one could offer any help. Then finally, one night, as I was pouring medications in the corner of the ward, I suddenly realized something was different. The ward was silent.

"He's gone," I thought. "Poor man, what a relief."

I picked up the phone and paged the house intern. Then I pushed two screens around Mr. Stafford's bed, an indication he had expired.

Life went on and we settled into a quiet routine again.

One evening, I passed out medications after dinner. Mr. Farrell's bed was empty so I kept his medication on the cart. He must be talking outside, I figured. I reached the patients on the veranda. They had a radio going softly, newspapers were strewn about and there was even a card game in progress.

"Seen Mr. Farrell?" I asked.

"Sure haven't, saw him at dinner though."

"Tell him I need him when he comes by."

"Have you checked the bathroom?" one patient asked.

"Yes, I did. He's not there either."

Visiting hours came and went. I had the usual urine samples to test and paperwork to be done. After eight, I noticed Mr. Farrell's bed was still empty. Strange, he could have gone for a walk but not outside the confines of the ward. I called the house orderly and security guard. They searched the premises and reported back to me at 8:30 - no sign of Mr. Farrell anywhere. Alarmed, I called my supervisor who notified the house physician. He came, asked questions and made some notes on the chart. I had never lost a patient this way! Then the phone rang and I quickly answered it. "Ward 2, Nurse Hoffmann speaking."

There was a woman on the other end, she sounded confused.

"I'm Mrs. Farrell," she said, "say, my husband just came home in a cab. He is still in his hospital gown. I didn't know he was discharged."

Neither did we. Turned out Mr. Farrell just decided he didn't need to stay in the hospital any longer, walked out to the front gate, hailed a cab and went home.

My initial determination to "see what would happen" in this four-year training had been effectively buried under tons of work, classes and activities. And now, four years of blood, sweat and tears were rapidly coming to a close. Unbelievable. They had been incredible years, full of youthful energy and resiliency which had allowed us to learn, absorb, play, laugh, cry, care and grow up as mature adults. Reminiscing one evening in the nurses' lounge, we talked about the two patients with Typhoid Fever we had cared for in Ward 2. They both recovered. Two others with Tetanus in Ward 14 were not so fortunate. Had we had respirators in those days, things would have been different.

"Remember that patient in Ward 10 after a gasterectomy?" Robin, another classmate reminisced. "He was an alcoholic and we didn't know it. Two days after surgery, he got out of bed, IV and Levine tube (stomach tube) and all. He bolted through the window and jumped to the ground. Since he was on the second floor, he would have died but he hit the little roof over the door below him. He jumped off there to the ground and started running to the front entrance on Macquarie Street. All he had on was his hospital gown. The guard apprehended him, strapped him on a gurney and brought him back to his bed. We medicated and restrained him and thought he'd busted all his stitches. But he didn't. He healed perfectly and was discharged the following week."

"I'll never forget my first night in Ward 8," I mused. "Male Urology. All these catheters that had to be irrigated every two hours. It was so dark, I couldn't see a thing with that little torch. A lot of patients were bleeding and those catheters kept plugging up. The sterilizer was very slow and it took forever to boil."

"Remember that young man in Ward 1, the skin ward? The one with Pemphigus who was on these huge doses of Cortisone? He must have been in and out of there for four years. I wonder what happened to him?"

"I liked that place, though," someone else remarked, "most patients were ambulatory, hardly anyone ever died there."

"That's true," someone else piped in, "but they did not get well, either."

"What about the Eye Hospital? Remember standing there in surgery, shining a flashlight into an eyeball for hours. Move one fraction of an inch and you're dead. My arms got so tired, I finally tied a bandage to my belt in the back, brought the other up over my shoulder and tied it to my wrist. This took some of the pressure off of my arm."

"The only thing I remember from the Eye Hospital was my first shave." Rose remembered. "You know after those detached retina surgeries, they had both eyes covered and couldn't move or do anything for themselves? Well, the first patient I had to shave didn't trust me very much. 'Have you ever shaved anyone before?' he asked. I said 'Sure, many,' then went ahead and shaved him. When I was done he said 'I can tell that you have had a lot of experience, Nurse.'"

"Remember when Queen Elizabeth and Prince Philip visited Sydney? We were on Ward 3 in front of the hospital. When they passed, Philip looked right up to our balcony and waved at us."

"When I get out of here, I will never train for anything else," was a common line from our class of '57. Obstetrics? Another year? You must be crazy. Hospital finals and State Board exams were coming close. We all studied hard. Hospital exams came first. At least, we all knew each other as we sweated through long days of oral, practical and theory days. We all passed. A few weeks later came State Boards, held at a nearby University. Over five hundred graduates from all over the state of New South Wales sat in rows at small tables in a cavernous state room. Multiple choice tests were unknown in those days. When I finally finished, I felt sorry for the people who had to wade through these stacks of test papers to grade them. Weeks of anxious waiting followed.

Finally, the results came in. I had been an average student throughout my training and would be happy with an overall pass. Grades were not mentioned on diplomas, I reminded myself. Imagine my surprise when an assistant Tutor Sister called me in her office one day to make the startling announcement that I was one of the top ten in the State Finals. I was the only one from Sydney Hospital. To justify her straight A students and to be sure this wouldn't go to my head, she quickly added: "Well, these tests are not always graded accurately, you know."

Graduation ceremonies were special. We wore a veil with our student uniform. Matron smiled as she handed us our Certificates. Parents and other relatives crowded the auditorium. The press was there. Betsy and I, together with a German girl, Rose Holzer, were the first New Australians ever to graduate from Sydney Hospital. We were interviewed on TV and radio. Public speaking was not our best side. Few people had TV sets in those days and the radio broadcast was full of static. But the newspapers published our class group picture and so did the New South Wales Nurses' Journal, *The Lamp*. We were now Sisters, Single Certificate Sisters. We could work anywhere except OB or Psych hospitals. Who cared about that. Not us.

We finished four years of hard labor. That's all that mattered. It wasn't until many years later that I began to fully realize how extremely unique and valuable those four years of training at Sydney Hospital had been.

Chapter 6

BABIES IN BRISBANE

"I'm going to visit my brother, Bill, in Brisbane," Betsy said a few weeks after our graduation. "Want to come along? It'll be a nice vacation."

Brisbane was six hundred miles north of Sydney, a large semi-tropical city in the state of Queensland. It sounded like a good idea so we worked out details and prepared for our departure. The climate in Sydney was mild, high 80s in the summer (October through March) and in the 60s during the winter (April through September). Getting used to upside down seasons had taken some time. Now, we were going north where it would be warmer, as opposed to traveling south, to Melbourne for instance, where it was much colder.

We took a train from Sydney's railroad station and for the next twelve hours enjoyed the interesting, although rather dry Australian countryside. The train slowly passed through vast plains of prairieland with an abundance of drooping Gum trees (Aussie for Eucalyptus) with their typical peeling bark, and an occasional huge flock of sheep. Fascinated, we watched a few, well-trained sheepdogs control a vast sea of woolly bleating creatures, moving along the countryside like an enormous living carpet. One or two men on horseback, typical Australians with their wide-rimmed hats, were quietly overseeing the slow-moving mass, giving occasional, brief commands to the agile, obedient dogs.

We passed the large, industrial coastal city of New Castle, made stops in smaller country towns like Maitland, Kempsey, Crafton, Lismore and finally, towards evening, arrived in Beaudesert, a small farm community forty miles south of Brisbane. Bill, Betsy's brother, his Australian wife, Gloria, and their little boy, Billy, were waiting for us. It was a dark night and we didn't see much of the countryside as we drove to the tiny town where they lived. Their modest, wooden home was roomy but unfinished with bare walls and floors. Travel weary, we chatted some, then unpacked and crawled into bed. At four in the morning, Betsy and I, who shared a room, were awakened by blaring country music. It came from a small portable radio in the kitchen next to our bedroom. Bill and Gloria were up, getting ready for their daily chores. After they left, we got up, turned the radio off and snoozed again. Later, around seven, we woke up as a flood of bright sunshine streamed through the curtainless windows.

Next to their home was another, fairly large, older house, where the farmer and his family lived. Bill and Gloria worked for them. The farm was small and surrounded by flat fields and paddocks (meadows) with an occasional gum tree here and there. There were pigs, horses and chickens. Gloria was a good hostess and taught us to ride their small pony. We fed the pigs, canoed through a pond in the back and generally had a restful time.

After a week, we decided to explore Brisbane and rode a tram into town. Brisbane, like Beaudesert, was much warmer than Sydney. It was close to the coast and built on hilly terrain. Downtown, although not as big as Sydney, consisted of several busy streets lined with six to eight story buildings and many shops and offices. City Hall, the equivalent of Sydney's Town Hall, an impressive sandstone building, towered in the center of Brisbane. It was surrounded by massive pillars. There were no municipal offices in these city halls just a large auditorium and meeting halls. Gently waving palmtrees lined many a street in Brisbane and we noticed an abundance of bananas, mangos, coconuts and other tropical fruit for sale which we did not find in Sydney. We had heard about the large Brisbane General Hospital and decided to take a look.

Hopping on one of the many city trams, we got off on a wide, busy road. In front of us towered several large, interconnected, six-story brick buildings. Next to them, built in the shape of a cross, was another four-story structure, Brisbane Women's Hospital. This was flanked by a large, modern two-story building, complete with lawns and tennis courts, (a very popular Australian pastime) for the nursing staff of the Women's Hospital. Avoiding the Women's Hospital, we found the office at Brisbane General and talked to someone at the staffing department. Yes, there were several openings, one of them in the Emergency Room for a single certificate RN. We could start any time. I was still not interested in midwifery, another full 12 months of hard work and study, neither was Betsy. I did need a job, however, and I liked Brisbane. Also, the challenge of a new city and a different environment appealed to me. Finally, Betsy decided she'd rather go back to Sydney and get a job closer to home while I accepted the ER job at the General Hospital.

A few days later, I joined several other new employees in the Nursing office. After some paperwork, physicals and orientation, we were directed up a very steep hill in back of the hospital to the Nurses' Quarters. Out of breath, we reached a large multi-story building. On the first floor, we entered a small hallway, lined on either side with about fifteen doors. The last one on the right was mine. I noticed with dismay that the walls separating these rooms were only about eight feet high, while the ceiling was at least ten feet above me. No privacy, I thought. It turned out to be worse; there was no darkness, either. If even one nurse had her light on, all the other rooms were lit up as well. Unable to sleep for several nights, I asked for another room which had become available in yet another building on this high hill.

The Emergency Room at Brisbane General was a bustling place. An average of eight hundred patients passed through its many divisions and cubicles each day. They ranged from people needing prescription glasses, to heart attacks and accident victims. I worked under Sister Burke, an older, rather placid woman in charge of the nursing staff and Elaine Richards, a pleasant brunette who was also a recent graduate. There were two major areas in the ER, medical and surgical. My first assignment was surgical. Ambulances screeched in and out all day long. One day, they walked in a man with his hand bandaged and covered with a towel.

"I wanted him to lay down on a stretcher," the driver confided in me, "but he insisted he was OK and could walk."

"What happened to him?" I inquired, pad and pencil in hand.

"He was working with a chain saw and noticed something on the floor. He bent over and picked up his own four fingers he had just chopped off right above the knuckles. It happened so fast he didn't even feel it."

The doctor had ushered the man into X-ray; Surgery and Admitting had already been notified.

"Why don't you sit with him," he asked me.

I entered the cubicle where I saw a large, outdoor type man in his thirties sitting on the side of the examination table. One hand held the other, still wrapped in a towel.

"Hello," I ventured. "How are you feeling?"

"Fine," he said.

"You're not hurting?"

"No."

"Why don't you lay down?" I sugggested.

"No, that's OK," he insisted."I'm fine."

I knew he was close to shock and had not quite apprehended what happened. Unable to persuade him to lay down, I stayed and made some small talk, watching him carefully. Suddenly, I saw it coming, the blood drained from his face, he turned deathly pale, then, drenched in sudden perspiration, he keeled over.

Quickly, I called for an orderly, hoisted him on a cart, elevated his legs and lowered his head. His bloodpressure, which had been normal when he walked in, had now bottomed out. Good thing he had an IV going. Soon, he was admitted and taken to surgery. Techniques for sewing on severed fingers were not too advanced then and, as far as I can remember, no attempt was made to reconstruct his fingers to his hand.

One day, after climbing the ever present Mount Everest to the Nurses Quarters, I passed an open door and heard two nurses talking. One of them had a Dutch accent. I introduced myself and met Chris, a delightful blond, blue eyed nurse, from Amsterdam. She worked in the Operating Room and had left Holland about two years ago.

We became fast friends; she liked swimming and classical music and on our days off, we began to check out the happenings at City Hall. There were excellent concerts by the Brisbane Symphony Orchestra and many outstanding soloists from Europe and the States. We also discovered the marvelous beach at Surfers' Paradise, a small beach resort an hour south of Brisbane. Closer yet, in the suburb of Sunny Brook we found "The Oasis" a combination of gardens and swimming pools which became our frequent hangout.

We often talked about midwifery.

"If you don't take your middy now," Chris warned me, "you will never forgive yourself. It's part of nursing. You'll never be an all-around nurse if you don't know anything about obstetrics."

I knew she was right. Besides, the ER was an interesting place to work but eventually I'd want to move and do something else.

"It's just next door," Chris reminded me, "and you don't have to walk up this cardiac hill every day. The quarters at Women's Hospital are super."

Finally convinced, I went next door to the Women's Hospital and filled out an application. Conditions were much the same as Sydney Hospital. A forty-four hour workweek, three weeks of school then eight-hour days on the floors with specialized classes by physicians scheduled in between. Board, lodging and uniforms were free and a small salary was paid in cash every fortnight. The next class, I was told, would start in three months. That sounded just fine. I wrote home and asked Mom to mail me the rest of my things. The matter was settled and I felt rather good about it.

Although Chris liked her new life in Brisbane, she was also homesick, something I had observed frequently in people from Amsterdam. The old, picturesque capital of Holland, with its close, unique atmosphere, accents and lifestyles, seemed to have a strong hold on its people. Few of them were able to break those ties and settle permanently beyond her boundaries. Eventually, Chris returned to Holland while I waited out my time in the ever busy ER.

David Palmer was a middle aged, efficient orderly in Minor Surgery, part of the ER. I liked him and often spent my tea breaks in his little surgery domain.

"David," I said one day, "it really bothers me to see so many people come back here time and time again for the same chronic ailments.

Especially back problems. We give them a shot or pills or a linament but nothing seems to help."

"I know what you mean," said David, busy wrapping his instruments for sterilization.

"You know," he lowered his voice, although no one could hear us, "I know someone in town I often refer them to."

"Who's that?" I asked, interested.

"His name is Dave Whiting," David continued in a low voice, "he gets everyone well."

"But how?" I persisted. "Is he a doctor?"

"No, not really. I don't know what he does, but many patients with chronic ailments we can't do anything for, he has helped. We never see them again here."

"Where's his office?" I asked.

"I don't know," he said,"I don't even know him. I just know of him, that's all."

He picked up a heavy phone book, found an address and wrote it down on a slip of paper. Then he handed it to me.

"I'm going to see that man," I said, "and see what exactly it is he does."

The following week, I took a tram downtown, found the busy, commercial section the street was located in and looked for the number. When I found it, instead of a door, I faced a steep, wooden stairway leading to the first floor. On one of the lower steps I read: David Whiting, Chiropractor.

Where had I heard that word before? Suddenly I remembered: My mother! Last year she had severe low back pain for several months. Unable to help her, a local doctor in Collaroy had sent her to a man named Martin who, oddly enough, had an office on Martin Place in Sydney. He was a Chiropractor. She had seen him just a few times and her back problems were over. All he did, she said, was manipulate her neck. I had listened with only half an ear as Betsy and I were busy planning for our trip to Queensland. Now here it was again, that word, chiropractor.

Intrigued, I climbed the stairway. At the first landing there were several doors, one of them had Whiting's name on it. I entered it and found myself in a small, plain waiting room. One man was reading a newspaper. There was no receptionist so I sat down and observed the room. On the wall was a Diploma from the Los Angeles College of Chiropractic in Glendale, California USA conferring the title Doctor of Chiropractic on David Stanley Whiting. Another door opened and an elderly woman walked out. Behind her a tall, slightly greying, gentle-looking man, ushered in the next patient.

"I'll be right with you." he said to me, then disappeared. Ten minutes later he returned.

"Come in," his soft spoken voice was reassuring, "what can I do for you?"

I told him the purpose of my visit. He was surprised and confirmed that he didn't know David Palmer, the orderly at the Emergency Room.

"What exactly do you do?" I wanted to know. "David says you cure everybody."

He laughed. "No, not really," he said, "I don't prescribe medicine or do surgery. I just manipulate people's backs and give them specific physical therapy."

"How long was your training?" I wanted to know.

"Four years," he said, then gave me some specifics on the many subjects covered during this course.

"Well," I finally said,"I just wanted to know who you are and what you do. Any chance of me watching you treat some of your patients?"

"Of course," he said. "That'll be fine."

We set a time for my next visit which, eventually, was followed by several others. I closely observed him, fascinated, as he twisted and manipulated muscles and backs. His large, yet gentle hands seemed to know the contours and secrets of every bone and joint and muscle. Eventually, I referred several patients to him.

Time went by fast and before I knew it my time in ER was over. I had become rather attached to that little world of its own with it dramas and tragedies. I would miss Elaine and Mrs. Burke, her little office next to the special chairs where wheezing asthmatics were treated with Ephedrine and Aminophylline, the corner where infected wounds were taken care of, the large Hold area where patients were separated into various categories and Dr. Merriott, the pleasant, energetic young doctor in charge who taught the ever present group of interns while examining and treating the endless procession of patients passing through his office each day. I would even miss the ambulance drivers I had come to know so well.

Little did I know that the next year would be one of the happiest in my life. The atmosphere at Brisbane Women's Hospital, or BWH, was different from Sydney Hospital. Here, all students had already graduated from general nursing and the strict protocol and military strictness was replaced by a much more relaxed attitude between staff and students. Our uniforms were nice, simple, short-sleeved, white dresses with buttons in front. We could wear our RN veil but pinned back.

The course started with another Tutor Class. There were thirty-five of us. For the next three weeks an energetic, young, and exceptionally good tutor guided us through a maze of delivery techniques. I had no idea a baby had to go through so many motions and movements and twists to pass from the womb through the birth canal to the outside world.

"It's the only way," Sister explained, "for the head to get through the small pelvic opening which separates the abdominal from the pelvic cavity."

"If the head comes down first," she explained, "the crown, called the occiput, can be posterior or anterior, further subdivided into right or left. Thus is can be a ROA, LOA, ROP or LOP. The most common and easiest is LOA."

"That's only the beginning," she continued, "other possible presentations are transverse, brow, shoulder or breech, each with the same possible subdivisions."

"It's very important that we know the exact position of the baby before and during labor," Sister explained. "We do this by palpation. The mother needs to be laying down on her back. Place both hands on her abdomen like this," she demonstrated, "then press down till you feel the head. It should be in the lower abdomen but it can also be just under the ribcage, in which case you have a breech presentation."

"At any rate," she continued, "you need to find two poles - a head and a bottom. If ever you feel three poles you may have twins in there."

Fetal heart tones came next. Instead of a stethoscope, we used a little metal device, shaped like an ice-cream cone with a round metal plate at its pointed end. This end had a hole in it. After the baby's position had been determined, this metal device was placed over what we hoped was the baby's back. We then bent over and put our ear to the other end and listened. A tiny heartbeat could be heard very clearly, IF we were in the right position.

"How do you know if what you are hearing is the heartbeat and not the cordbeat?" Sister asked. We didn't know.

"Try both sides of the abdomen," Sister suggested. "The cord can be anywhere but the only place you can hear the heartbeat is from the baby's back. You can't get to the chest, they're curled up and there are arms and legs in the way."

"It's important to count the heartbeats. If you hear another beat in a different location, it can be the cord, but it can also be a second baby. If there are two there will be a difference in heart rate of anywhere between eight and twelve beats per minute. Also, if we are dealing with twins, you should feel three poles, either two heads and one bottom or two bottoms and one head."

Next came an intricate teaching on the various techniques of measuring the progress of labor; i.e. dilation of the cervix, thinning of the rim, descent or station of the head, etc.

"You will get more and more experience as you go along," Sister encouraged us. "It may seem difficult at first but practice makes perfect." She smiled, "it's not as hard as you think."

Each month, nine hundred babies took their first breath at BWH. That's about thirty a day or ten per shift. Or, since there were two major delivery areas, five per eight hour shift for each area. That is to say, IF they would arrive in neatly spaced intervals. However, we soon discovered, this was seldom the case.

"Before you graduate," Sister warned us, "you need to deliver at least twenty-five babies. You will be transferred every six months but you will have two stints in the delivery suites. I am warning you, however, that the medical students also need their quotas so you will have competition. Other areas you work in will be Post-Partum (newly delivered mothers), Nursery, Premature Nursery, Milk kitchen, High Risk Pre-admits, Out-patients and Surgery."

After tutor school, we were scattered to the different delivery floors. Each floor had several four-bed rooms. These were special beds for both labor and delivery. Curtains could be drawn between the beds but they were open at other times so patients could keep each other company. A small bottle of Trylene, a temporary mild anesthetic, was kept handy for patients in hard labor. A small mask was attached to the bottle. Patients were instructed to put this mask over their face and breathe deeply during hard contractions. My first few days in Delivery, I listened to fetal heart tones, palpated positions, tested urine samples for protein and sugar and washed out tons of bloody sheets before sending it to the Laundry. I also observed dozens of deliveries.

Each patient was assigned a student nurse. The student was responsible for admission paper work, vital signs, enema, urine sample, fetal position, heart rate and progress of labor. Usually, the student had one Delivery Room with four patients in her charge. She was not entirely alone, though. Other students would assist her and the Delivery Supervisor came by for frequent checks. When a patient was fully dilated and ready to deliver, drapes were drawn around the bed, a cart and crib pulled close. Several observers, medical and nursing students, the Nursing Supervisor and sometimes a Resident or Physician, would gather around the bed. The patient was now turned on her side, one leg elevated in a stirrup, the other drawn up. The lower end of the bed was detached and removed.

I will never forget watching my first delivery. The mother was having her first baby. When she was ready for delivery, the student assigned to her donned a gown, gloves and mask and positioned herself behind the patient. Bending over her, she put one hand over the lower abdomen, the other over the rectum. She now had the little head, which was partially visible, under complete control between both hands. Now was the time to watch the perineum, the area just in front of the rectum. It should stretch but not tear. This phase took a while.

Eventually, during a contraction, using both hands, the baby's head was gently exposed to the world. Someone nearby suctioned the mouth.

"Feel for a cord around the neck," Sister instructed.

The nurse stepped to the foot of the bed and felt for a cord. I knew that if it was wrapped around the neck, she would try and loosen it. But luckily it wasn't there. Now, still standing at the foot of the bed, she placed her hands on each side of the little face and waited for the next contraction. When it came, she gently bent the head down to get an elbow born, then up to get the other one out. Now she grasped each shoulder and the rest of the body emerged together with a flood of messy water, cleansing the birth canal.

"Suction again!"

Baby was now held upside down by its ankles. It soon let out a protesting wail.

"It's a girl!" Someone announced to the mother.

The cord was milked towards the baby, giving it the benefit of some extra blood, then tied with two ties, covered with a gauze bandage and cut with sharp scissors in between the two ties. The little pink baby was then put on the mother's stomach and suctioned again. Mom could now take a first look at her new offspring. Another student took the baby, wrapped it and took it to be weighed. The mother was turned on her back and both legs put in stirrups. One hand of the delivery student was placed on the upper abdomen.

"When the placenta separates, the fundus (upper part of the uterus) will rise," Sister had explained in class. "When that happens slightly push on the fundus till the placenta (or afterbirth) is delivered."

"You NEVER pull on the cord," she had warned us.

The student waited for the placenta to separate. When it did, she pushed gently on the fundus and there it was, like a funny looking round thick purple pancake with a dangling cord in the center. It was carefully examined to see if all parts were there. Then the fundus was rubbed rather vigorously to help it contract and stop the bleeding site from which the placenta had just separated. Now I knew why Mom had lost so much blood after the birth of my sister, Helen. This accomplished, the foot of the bed was reattached, stirrups removed, patient washed, protected with pads, given a cup of tea and, after some further observation and massaging of the fundus, discharged to a Postpartum Ward.

After observing dozens of these routine deliveries, the day finally came for me to do the honors. Confident, I scrubbed and gowned. This was easy, I thought. I've seen so many, I know the routine by heart. But as I stood behind my first patient, bending over her and feeling that little unborn head between my cupped hands, things suddenly looked different.

"Take it easy," Sister admonished. "You're doing fine."

When the head was delivered I noticed everything was slippery.

What if I drop it?! I panicked. I felt clumsy, a klutz with two left hands. No cord around the neck! Thank goodness.

Standing at the foot of the bed now and holding the wet, slippery head with both hands, I tried to move it down. It didn't budge.

"A little harder, Nurse." Sister's calm voice was reassuring. Suddenly a shoulder popped into view.

"Now upwards. Put your fingers under the axilla (armpits). That's good. OK, there it is. It's a boy!"

He immediately let out a healthy howl, probably in protest to my firm grasp on his slick, wet body.

Capable hands suctioned his mouth, wiped the eyes and wrapped him in a receiving blanket. I waited for the placenta which cooperated and was delivered smoothly.

Wow! What a relief that was over. It looked so simple from a safe distance. The next delivery, however, was a little less awkward and eventually those little slippery bodies were quite easy to handle as delivering babies eventually became a daily routine.

One day I admitted Mrs. Wolff, a private patient. Most patients at BWH were so-called public admits; i.e., they would be under the medical care of the hospital staff. In Australia, all hospital care at public hospitals was free. Sydney Hospital, Brisbane General and the Women's Hospital were public facilities. All citizens belonged to a state medical insurance program with small deductions automatically taken from their paychecks. This took care of all hospital and doctors' expenses. However, they were under the care of the hospital house staff. Some patients, however, preferred their own private physician. We did all the initial checking and when delivery was imminent, called the patient's doctor.

"How many children do you have?" I asked my new patient.

"Three," she said, "all girls. I hope this is a boy."

"Looks like it is going to be a big one," I observed.

"Yes, it's a lively one too," she admitted.

After the usual checks, I got to the palpation part. Was that a head or a bottom? I changed position and tried again, still not sure. Let's try the hearttones, I thought. They were loud and clear in the left lower abdomen. I counted a firm, regular heartbeat of 144 then moved my little fetal stethoscope over to the right side and listened again. Another clear heartbeat. That must be the cord. I carefully counted 136 beats per minute. One hundred and thirty six? That can't be! Let's try again. Concentrating, I intendly stared at my watch, counting carefully. The difference was still there. Could she have twins? Again I palpated but wasn't sure I felt two or three poles.

"Excuse me for a moment," I said to Mrs. Wolff.

I found my supervisor and told her of my findings. She came and checked the patient herself then called Mrs. Wolff's doctor.

"She may have twins, doctor," I heard her say.

He laughed. Impossible. He had checked her regularly. How was her labor coming along? OK, he'd be there in an hour.

"Don't say anything to her, nurse," she warned me.

Her labor progressed and when fully dilated her doctor was there. Without much trouble, he delivered a healthy baby, around six pounds.

"It's a girl, pet!" he announced.

"Oh well," Mrs. Wolff said, "as long as it is healthy."

"Sure looks like it." The baby was suctioned, wrapped and taken to be weighed. Doctor waited for the placenta. It didn't come. He poked around a little and finally felt inside. Suddenly, he took a sharp breath and said, "Did you say you wanted a boy?"

"Why yes, doctor. Why do you ask?"

"Well, let's see what we can do here." He gently pushed on her abdomen. Slowly another tiny scalp became visible. A little head popped out followed by the shoulders and a body. It screamed.

"A boy!" he said triumphantly, "you got your boy!"

Uncomprehending, the patient stared at the doctor, the nurses and finally at the squirming baby on her stomach.

"What do you mean, I have a boy," she whispered, wide eyed, "you just told me I had a girl."

"That's right," he smiled, "you have one of each."

"TWO! Oh no!" her eyes opened wide, "we're only ready for one!"

"Well, you'd better get things ready for two, my dear." The doctor removed two placentas, checked the cervix for tears and the fundus for firmness. Everything was in order. He stood up and stripped off his gown, gloves and mask.

"Sorry, pet," he said, "I sure missed that second one. But you said you wanted a boy," he continued with a twinkle in his eye, "and you got him."

Six weeks later, I was moved to a Postpartum floor. Mine was a huge ward, partitioned off into six sections, three to the right and three to the left with a wide lane in the center. Each section had six beds so there were thirty-six patients in our charge. Attached to the floor was a nursery where the babies were cared for and taken to the mothers for feedings. Babies were assigned to nurseries according to their weight. There was a Nursery for big babies (eight pounds and over), medium weight nurseries (four to nine pounds) and one large premature nursery where babies stayed after mothers were discharged, waiting, sometimes for months, to reach a certain weight. My first ward was for mothers with medium weight babies, the most common category. It was a happy place to work. No one was sick, everyone contented with their new babies and relieved that labor and delivery were over. Patients could walk around, take showers and visit with each other. One day, a new admit was wheeled in. I looked at her chart: Mrs. Greet van Ommeren. That sounded Dutch. I settled her in bed, noticed her accent and soon we continued our conversation in Dutch. She was in her early thirties and had just delivered her first baby, a son. When I put a screen around her to check her, she suddenly burst into tears.

"What's the matter?" I asked, surprised.

No answer. More tears.

"Please, tell me," I urged soflty, "why are you crying?"

"There's something wrong with the baby," she finally sobbed. "They only showed me his head. He was all wrapped up and I heard them whispering outside."

I tried to calm her down and settled her in bed. Then I checked her records and found that, indeed, something was wrong - the baby was born with clubfeet.

Later, the doctor came in and wanted to see both the patient and her husband. When he arrived, he took them aside and explained in detail what the options and prognosis would involve. Actually, he was rather optimistic. The little feet needed to be put into a special splint right away. Eventually, surgeries would follow, but a complete correction and cure in the future was a good possibility. When I saw the little crooked ankles, bent inward almost at ninety-degree angle, my heart sank. An orthopedic pediatrician had already been notified and had examined the baby. Soon, his first set of splints were put on. Greet and Leo van Ommeren and I became very close, drawn together by our nationalities and the baby's disability. They were fairly new to Australia and had not made many friends. I often visited them and babysat little Lex so they could have some time out together. He was a good baby and made rapid medical progress. Greet and Leo also loved classical music and we would often sit quietly together in their typically Dutch living room, deeply moved by Beethoven's violin concerto or inspired by his magnificent symphonies.

In my quest for spiritual fulfillment, I had joined a philosophical group. They provided an abundance of literature extolling ancient Egyptian wisdom as well as promoting a blend of Eastern religions. I was intrigued and studied their material diligently. There were also monthly meetings, heavily structured with special steps, positions, repeated vowels and incense. Afterwards, we had "supper," an informal time of fellowship. It was there I met yet another Dutch family, the Dammerboers. They hailed from Indonesia, had two daughters and lived in a cozy suburban home. We became friends and I enjoyed many a delicious Rysttafel meal at their Dutch/Indonesian home. Their oldest daughter, Ilse, sang in Brisbane's Municipal choir.

"Why don't you join?" she asked me one day.

"Me? I can't sing." I laughed.

"I bet you can," she urged. "Why don't you try it out?"

I went along for the next rehearsal at the huge City Hall auditorium. Christmas was coming and Handel's Messiah was on the program. Besides the Hallelujah chorus, I was unfamiliar with this great, classical masterpiece. Ilse sang alto, so did I. I stood close to her and kept my eyes focussed on both the conductor and my music while also listening to the voices next to me. It was hard but I did enjoy it and finally seemed to get the hang of it. After three more rehearsals, I took a simple test and was officially admitted to the choir. I became familiar with the "Messiah" and enjoyed the magnificent, yet intricate musical patterns, the various solos and the use of the many different instruments of the orchestra. The words, taken directly from the Bible, sounded suitable for the score but did not move me as much as the music did.

In January, I was put on night duty for six weeks, eleven to seven a.m., eleven nights on, three nights off. I was assigned to the Premature Nursery with another student, Margaret Brooks. There were forty-five cribs with tiny babies, all under four pounds. One of us was in charge of changing diapers, the other did tube feedings. The infants were too small to have enough strength to suck from a bottle so a tiny tube was inserted through the mouth into their stomachs and the prescribed amount of specially prepared, warm formula slowly poured into a small funnel at the end of the feeding tube. It was a simple procedure which was repeated every three hours. It took just about three hours to feed or change forty-five little creatures. After a short break, we would start all over again. The other team partner would change diapers, take a short break and start changing again. Simple enough although rather monotonous. Trouble was my 5'10" frame had to bend over quite a bit to reach the low cribs. After three hours of changing or feeding, I could hardly straighten up.

Margaret, on the other hand, was short and found the nightly chores much easier. Sympathizing with my problem, she often urged me to lay down in an empty room during my supper breaks.

"I'll be here," she urged, "if the supervisor makes rounds I'll cover for you."

Grateful, I would stretch out my weary back and limbs for half an hour or so and be ready to bend over for another three hour stretch.

I liked Margaret. She was an excellent nurse, very meticulous and great to work with. She was engaged to a fellow named Handley Shakespeare. Handley was in Bible college. After his graduation and Margaret's midwifery course, they planned to be married and go overseas as missionaries. I understood that to mean they would help underprivileged people with health education and social problems.

Margaret frequently talked about her church and often invited me to attend. Even though I liked her, I had no desire to go to her church. Somehow her church seemed restrictive to me. I wanted to be part of everyone's religion, broadminded, universal. I felt that Margaret, who said she was a Baptist, had automatically shut herself off from other world religions as well as other denominations, Catholics, Methodists, Lutherans, Presbyterians, Church of England (Episcopalians), etc.

But Margaret persisted. To get her off my back, I promised I would meet her one night for a midweek "Endeavor" service. I didn't like that word although I had no idea what kind of an endeavor this could be. It was her day off which she spent at home but she had given me directions on how to get to the church. Still reluctant, I finally took a tram down to a rather rundown area of Brisbane. Then a funny thing happened.

The tram fare was a few shillings. I sat down and when the attendant came by I handed him a ten pound bill. That's all I had. But the man had no change and ordered me off the tram since, he said, I could not pay the fare.

"I CAN pay the fare," I retorted, "YOU don't have the change."

"I don't have to have change for ten pounds," he insisted. "you have to get off at the next stop."

Furious, I got off. I didn't want to go to this church in the first place; I didn't like this seedy part of town and now I had to walk ten blocks on this dark, deserted street alone past all these rowdy pubs. I couldn't go home; the next tram probably wouldn't take my ten pound bill, either, and going into a dark, noisy bar to ask for change was out of the question. There was nothing left but to get to that church as fast as possible. Out of breath and sweaty, I finally arrived. Margaret was waiting for me at the door of the large brick building sandwiched in between storefronts and warehouses. She beamed!

"I'm so glad you made it," she smiled. "We're meeting downstairs in the fellowship hall first. Let's go."

She led me down a flight of stairs to a large room. There were about twenty-five young people sitting on chairs forming a circle. I was introduced, there was some sharing, followed by prayers. I felt highly uncomfortable, didn't really hear what anyone said and wished, for the umpteenth time, that I had stayed home. My panic increased when I realized that everyone, one by one, prayed out loud for something or other. I knew that soon it would be my turn. I had never prayed out loud before and wasn't about to start now. Cold sweat gathered in my palms. Oh, that the floor would open up and swallow me. Margaret sat quietly on my right. Then the girl on my left started to pray. I froze, my heart pounded furiously, both my hands and feet were icy cold. The girl finally finished. There was a very short pause then, to my utter relief, Margaret started to pray. I was off the hook. I could have hugged her but didn't, of course, for my awkwardness greatly embarassed me. After all, I was the broadminded one here, certainly not to be intimidated by a bunch of simple people I hardly knew.

When the prayers ended, we all moved upstairs to the main sanctuary. It filled up as folks from other rooms joined as well. After some singing, a friendly young pastor delivered a short message. His text was from the Gospel of John, chapter three, "You must be born again." Still feeling out of place and waiting to get out of there, I halfheartedly listened to his words. They were certainly not for me. Of course I was born again! After all, I believed in God very deeply and sincerely. Finally, the service was over. Everyone got up, gathered their things, chatted and shook hands with the pastor at the door. When my turn came, Margaret introduced me. The young pastor smiled.

"Nice meeting you, Aubrey!" he beamed. Then, holding my hand and looking me straight in the eye, he probed, "and are YOU born again?"

I met his steady gaze without a blink.

"Oh yes!" I said firmly.

He hesitated.

"Well, that's fine!" he said at last, letting go of my hand, "so glad you could come. Hope we'll see you again."

"Thank you," I smiled, thinking, "Not if I can help it" and quickly joined Margaret whose parents were giving us a ride back to the hospital.

A few days later, another strange thing happened. Margaret and I visited an invalid aunt of hers whose home was right next to the hospital. When I walked into the kitchen to get a drink of water I over-heard the aunt say: "Is Aubrey a Christian, Margaret?"

Amused, I waited for Margaret's confirmation. Of course I was Christian. I believed in God, didn't I? Imagine my surprise when I heard Margaret's immediate reply: "No, she isn't."

Her voice was soft, almost sad but without hesitation.

The nerve! I fumed. Who does she think she is to judge me? What does she mean I'm not a Christian! Unfortunately I couldn't say any-thing as the remark was not meant for my ears. I remained silent, never went back to Margaret's church but maintained a good working relationship with Margaret herself.

To my great relief, our six weeks of night duty finally came to an end. I never learned to sleep well during the day under a bright, blue sky and warm sunshine in spite of blinds and heavy curtains in my room. My next assignment was the Pre-admit Ward where women with problems and high risk pregnancies were admitted before their due date. Most of them were pre-ecclamptics, a condition in certain pregnant women characterized by high blood pressure, albuminuria (protein in the urine) and edema (swelling of the legs and ankles). It can endanger the life of the unborn infant and, if unchecked or untreated, the mother may go into convulsions with great risk to both her and the baby's life.

I will never forget Mrs. Love, one of my first patients in this ward. She was forty-three and pregnant with her first child. For years, she had suffered from a condition known as Bell's Palsy which left part of her face paralyzed. She spoke with difficulty and was a rather placid and sluggish woman. Yet both she and her husband were looking forward with child-like anticipation to the birth of their first baby. But Mrs. Love was pre-ecclamptic. Only in her sixth month of pregnancy the al-bumen in her urine was 4+, the highest level, her legs swollen with pit-ting edema, her blood pressure a dangerously high 190/110. She was put on strict bedrest, a salt free diet, diuretics and other medication.

As the weeks went by, her tests and vital signs remained stable. Even though they were too high, at least they were not increasing. The baby's fetal heart tones were strong and regular. She said she felt lots of movement. Things seemed fairly well under control.

Then, one day, Mrs. Love's blood pressure began to come down, her edema was a little less, the albumen in her urine only 3+. I was unable to hear a fetal heart and called the charge nurse to double check. She thought she could hear a faint beat but wasn't sure. All our patients in this ward were under constant doctor's care. The Resident, making rounds the next day, spent a long time listening to Mrs. Love's ab-domen. Finally, he made a note on her chart, stating he was unable to feel fetal movement or hear any heart tones. Mrs. Love insisted she was still feeling life.

As the days moved on, her BP continued to drop till finally it was a normal 120/80, her urine became free of albumen, her edema vanished. Fetal heart tones were silent. We all knew what had happened - the baby had died! Mrs. Love maintained she still felt life. We were sure it was either her imagination or gas.

"What will happen next?" I asked the Resident one day.

"She will deliver spontaneously," he replied. "We don't have to do anything. When a baby dies in the womb the uterus will eventually begin to contract and the fetus will be expelled."

Mrs. Love was now in her seventh month so we could be in for a long wait. But as the days went by her BP slowly began to rise again, a trace of albumen was found in her urine and a slight edema returned. Everyone was stumped. Nobody could hear any fetal heart beats or feel any movement except Mrs. Love who, with her crooked little, childlike smile, would optimistically declare that the baby was still kicking around.

Eventually, now in her eighth month, all her previous pre-ecclamptic symptoms returned in full force. We waited anxiously for her to go into labor. One day she did. We quickly wheeled her from the floor to Labor and Delivery where I had to leave her and return to the ward. When my shift ended, we still had not heard anything. I hoped she and her husband would be prepared for what seemed to be inevitable - a dead baby. The next day when I came on duty, I didn't have to ask anyone what happened. The night nurse met me with a grin.

"Guess what happened to Mrs. Love?"

"What happened?" I urged.

"She delivered live twins!"

"What?! I don't believe it." I said, incredulous.

"Well, you'd better believe it for she did. Two boys. However," she continued sofly, "they were very small and one of them died. The other one is doing fine and in the Premie Nursery."

Later on my break, I visited Mrs. Love in one of the Postpartum Wards. She was beaming.

"Yes, I'm sorry one of them died," she confided, "but we were only expecting one baby anyway so it wasn't that difficult."

"I know nobody believed me," she smiled, almost apologetically, "but I just knew I felt life all along."

She was right, of course. This, we all decided, was one for the books.

My next transfer was to the Milk Kitchen, a small place were the premie mothers brought in their daily milk supply. Often, their tiny babies would stay in the nursery for weeks or even months. One baby I remember weighed one pound eight ounces at birth. He had five big brothers and sisters who initially were not very interested in another addition to the family. But as the family peeked through the Premie Nursery window day after day and week after week, they began to love that little tyke who quickly developed a personality all his own. When he was six months old, he finally went home when he reached the magic weight of four and a half pounds. By then, he had become the family hero. Anyway, the milk kitchen staff would receive these little bottles of milk, expressed by the mothers at home and brought in twice a day. We blended them all together, sterilized and homogenized the mixture and then fed it to our premies.

They all thrived. We would also mix a formula from regular cow's milk, called M4 which was bottled and channeled to mothers in other wards who, for one reason or another, were unable to breast feed their babies. I also did a stint in surgery where the Ceasarian Sections (called Ceasars) were done. They were few and far between and we only assisted with these.

More complicated and time consuming were the Rh exchange transfusions done on certain babies with mothers with Rh Negative blood. For hours, I would assist and watch the doctor fill and empty syringes full of blood, pushing it in through one bloodvessel of the umbilical cord and withdrawing it out the other. Most of these babies eventually died in spite of the exchange transfusions.

Meanwhile, I continued to see Dave Whiting, the Chiropractor, from time to time. I was still fasciniated by his simple yet effective treatments and loved to watch him work on his patients. He was a humble man, pleased that he could help people feel better. One day, he asked me to wait in his small waiting room.

"This patient is a little fussy," he confided, "she does not want anyone watching."

I clearly remember sitting there, staring at an old picture on the wall. Midwifery training was coming to an end, graduation just around the corner. I would be a Double Certificate Nurse, able to work in almost any hospital or nursing job I fancied. But was that what I wanted? I definitely liked nursing but often felt stymied by the lack of responsibility and the little initiative we were allowed to exercise. We couldn't even give an aspirin or a laxative to a patient without the OK from a doctor, often an inexperienced, young intern. I wanted to be more independent.

There was Bush Nursing, of course, going far into a sparcely populated farming community and living among these people, treating anything and everything that comes along. However, that sounded a little too advanced for a new grad. Suddenly, the thought hit me. Why not become a Chiropractor? I would be my own boss, get people well and still live in civilization. Why not? Excited, I waiting for Whiting to finish. When he did I came straight to the point.

"What would you think of someone like me to be a Chiropractor?" I asked. His kind face lit up.

"An excellent idea," he beamed.

"Where would I have to go and how long would it take?" I ventured.

"You'll have to go to the States. There are several schools there. It takes four years."

"America! Four years? You mean I can't stay here in Australia to study Chiropractic?"

"No, not yet," he affirmed, "I'm sure in the future we will have our own colleges, but that will take a while."

"But I would really encourage you to look into this, Aubrey," he stressed, "with your nursing background you have a definite advantage."

America? Leaving Australia? What would my folks have to say about that? By working twenty-two days straight, I had accumulated six days off. A few weeks after my talk with Whiting, I flew home for the first time in almost a year. It was wonderful to be back. My folks had bought a small home in Narrabeen, next to Collaroy, close to a pretty lake. One day after dinner, we were sitting together in the living room.

"Remember that Chiropractor I told you about in Brisbane?" I began.

"Yes," Dad said, "interesting he let you watch him treat his patients."

"I'm still feeling so well," Mom said, "after years of back trouble it's great to be pain free."

"Do you know how long it takes to become a Chiropractor?" I asked.

"No, how long?" Dad asked.

"Four years."

"That's a long time."

"Yea, I've been thinking about looking into it myself," I confessed.

"You have? Well, that's sounds like a good idea."

"You think so?"

"Sure, with your nursing background and all, that must be an advantage."

"Yes, I guess it is. There's one thing though..." I paused.

"What's that?" they both looked at me now, sensing I was about to say something important.

"I have to go to America to study." I looked from one to the other.

Dad's face lit up, "That's great!" he said, "what an opportunity."

"I'll be gone for four years," I reminded them, relieved they did not object to the idea.

"We'll come and visit you." Mom smiled.

"Why don't you go and meet Dr. Martin, the doctor who treated me?" she continued, "he may be able to give you some more information."

The next day, I was in his office. Martin was a large and energetic man, younger than Whiting. He had a roomy, modern office.

"You want to be a Chiropractor?" he beamed, "great idea, we need more of them in this country."

"Where did you go to school?" I asked.

"Palmer College in Davenport, Iowa. Here, let me show you some pictures."

Enthused, I went home and wrote both colleges, in Los Angeles and Davenport. I also asked if there were other students there from Australia I could correspond with. My six days off passed quickly and soon I flew back to Brisbane where final exams were around the corner. We hardly left the nurses quarters, cramming in our rooms and nurses lounges. For breaks, we would buy a bunch of papayas (called pawpaws), cut them in half, scoop out the seeds, then fill them with ice cream and top it off with instant coffee powder. A delicious treat.

I heard from the States. Both schools mailed me catalogs, curriculums and admission details. I also heard from a nurse from Australia who was a student at Palmer and a young man from New Zealand who was enrolled at Los Angeles. Both Colleges sounded good but the climate in Los Angeles seemed unbeatable, especially when compared to the weather in Iowa. I contacted the Immigration Department. Yes, I could get a student visa but I needed lots of cash to pay for tuition and living expenses as I would not be allowed to work. That put a kink in my plans. As soon as I graduated, I had to get a full-time job and save every penny for at least two years.

In the meantime, another important event was looming up. I had signed up for naturalization classes. By now, I felt so completely at home in my new country, loved the people and had mastered the language, that I wanted to make it official and become an Australian citizen. I went for several interviews, filled out reams of papers, got fingerprinted and signed my name to countless documents. There was to be an official ceremony at City Hall.

When that day arrived, I sat on the main floor with about six hundred other "New Australians" from dozens of countries, mostly European. Flags, representing each country, were displayed on the stage - an impressive, colorful sight. I also discovered the red, white and blue one from Holland. There was music and there were speeches. Finally, raising our right hand, we were sworn in as Australian subjects. The strains of the national anthem, "God save the Queen," began. All flags were slowly lowered till they were gone from sight. Then the Union Jack and Australian flags were raised. When the anthem finished, only these two flags were visible. It was a strange and emotional moment. In a sense, I felt more like a citizen of the world than a citizen of just one country. Yet, I knew this was now my home. It felt good. There were no regrets.

Final exams at BWH came and went. We all passed, unpinned our veils, were photographed, listened to speeches by hospital officials and received our Midwifery Diploma at yet another official ceremony. This had been a good year. I was going to miss my fellow students, especially Margaret. She and Handley had set their wedding date and were still planning to go to some faraway mission field. Dad drove up in his new little Austin all the way from Narrabeen to take me and my formidable amount of luggage home. Just before we left, Margaret came by my room to say goodbye.

"Here's a little gift," she said, handing me a small, wrapped package.

"Thanks," I said, "thanks for everything, Margaret. I really enjoyed working with you."

"Same here," Margaret smiled. "Let's keep in touch."

After she left, I opened her gift. It was a Bible. I sighed and quickly packed it with the rest of my books.

Chapter 7

MOONAN FLAT

The six-hundred-mile trip south from Brisbane to Sydney in the little Austin was a slow but pleasant event. The two lane road, a rather fragile connection between these two major cities, was full of surprises. The first one came after about two hundred miles. During a long stretch of lonely gum trees drooping in the vast, hilly, dry plains, a massive flock of sheep slowly drifted across the road keeping a growing line of cars and trucks at bay. The barking, snapping sheepdogs somehow kept the bleating mass together under the steady, almost nonchalant supervision of the few ranchers on horseback.

The next day, heavy rains left some stretches of our road totally submerged making for interesting driving, almost boating at times. When we finally reached Hornsby, one of Sydney's northeastern suburbs, we were suddenly enveloped in a deluge of rain. It came down in such heavy sheets that visibility was zero. Dad decided to park the car till the worst was over. The curb where he stopped was rather high. Soon rivers of angry, brown waters swished under our wheels and almost reached the doors. We had to find another parking place but where and how? Just as the car was about to be swept along in the raging stream, the downpour suddenly stopped and pretty soon the roads were passable again. An hour later we were home in Narrabeen.

I wasted no time looking for jobs. There were some good opportunities but pay was modest. It would take me several years to save enough to satisfy the U.S. Immigration Department. Several people suggested I look into bush nursing.

"You'll make good money and be independent," was the argument.

I decided to investigate and found the office of the New South Wales Bush Nursing Association (BNA) in downtown Sydney.

"Yes, we have several openings," said the director, a kind, middle-aged nurse with the unbelievable name of Miss Roach. "One of them is in Moonan Flat, a small place near Scone, which is one hundred miles inland from Newcastle."

"It's part of the Upper Hunter River District," she continued. "The area is about a hundred square miles and has a population of about one hundred families, mostly farmers. There is a Committee of local people who are responsible to raise funds for your salary and medical needs. They built a nice cottage with a dispensary for you to live in. The pay is thirty pounds per month."

"That sounds great," I said, "but I am a new grad with very little practical experience."

She smiled. "The last three bush nurses all married local men," she said. "They still live near Moonan Flat and are more than willing to help or advise you."

"What about doctors or the nearest hospital?" I wanted to know.

"There are several doctors and a hospital in Scone," she said, "just forty miles down the road. You can call them any time or take patients down there."

Somewhat relieved, I filled out an application but said I would like to think about it before making a final decision.

"That'll be fine," Miss Roach said. "I will write to the local Committee and tell them about your application. I'll let you know when I hear from them."

Back home I did some figuring. It was January of 1959, the middle of summer, with clear, blue skies and a balmy breeze ornamenting the ever-inviting beaches. If I saved arduously for one year, I could have enough money for the U.S. The college had a fall, spring and an optional summer semester. Perhaps, if I took a month off to get some rest and prepare for this new bush nursing venture then start in Moonan Flat in March, I could leave after a year, take a boat to California and get to Los Angeles by May of 1960. Excited, I wrote the Registrar at the Los Angeles College of Chiropractic (LACC) and tentatively registered for the 1960 summer semester.

I managed a quick trip by train to Katoomba, a lovely recreational area in the Blue Mountains about fifty miles west of Sydney which boasted the famous Three Sisters, a three-pronged mountain peak landmark. The Waratahs, a magnificent proteus and Australia's national flower, were in full bloom. There was also an abundance of blooming wattle (acacias) and flowering gums (eucalyptus), bright red desert pea flowers and many other typical Australian flora. The vast Blue Mountains had a distinct bluish-grey hue which stretched all the way to the far horizon. According to some, this was due to the presence of the Eucalyptus oil in the gum trees. It was a delightful, quiet and restful interlude.

Miss Roach wrote to say the Bush Nurses Committee had accepted my application. The days went by fast and soon I was packing my bags again and boarding the train headed for New Castle a hundred miles north of us. There I changed trains and turned northwest and inland. Slowly, we passed the familiar Australian landscape - hilly, dry terrain, gum trees, sheep, an occasional farm under generally blue skies with some large, white, slow moving clouds. We passed several townships, including Maitland, Singleton, Musswelbrook, Aberdeen and finally, after several hours, pulled into Scone where I had to get off. As I gathered my bags on the almost empty platform, I spotted an elderly couple, Mr. and Mrs. Hindmarch, who were supposed to pick me up.

"Welcome to Scone," Mr. Hindmarch, a pleasant retired farmer, beamed. "Let me carry your bags."

"I'm so glad you are here, Sister," Mrs. Hindmarch, a sweet grey-haired lady smiled. "We've been without a nurse for almost a year."

As we stowed my luggage in the large four-door sedan just outside the railroad station, I looked around.

"This," said Mr. Hindmarch with a sweep of his arm, "is the city of Scone! Just one street actually, but to us it is town."

Indeed, there was one street, paved and dusty with an occasional building here and there displaying various signs of merchandise.

"Here is the hospital," he pointed out as we drove by. "There is a general section and next to it two midwives run a small maternity hospital. There are four doctors here in Scone," he concluded proudly. "They're all good and very friendly and helpful. I'm sure you will meet them all before long."

We had left Scone behind and entered a fairly straight paved road marked by a sign: Moonan Flat. An occasional farmhouse was visible here and there. The hilly terrain looked friendly and pretty with the usual variety of gum trees. Rabbits were hopping helterskelter in front of us.

"They're real pests," Mr. Hindmarch remarked. "There are thousands of them; they eat everything, dig under fences, multiply incredibly fast and have no natural enemies."

I remembered this from high school. The rabbit is not a native Australian animal. An enterprising passenger brought two over from England. Some clever person foresaw the possible danger and sounded a warning which was ignored. Now Australia has millions of these woolly creatures which have become a major plague.

The paved straight road came to an abrupt end and continued as a winding dirt trail with sharp curves and an increasing number of deep potholes. We swerved from one side of the road to the other and passed an occasional truck. There were no other farms or homes visible now.

"I hope you will like your new home. We just painted it inside and out. Your water tanks are pretty full so you should have no shortage and we piled up a good supply of wood underneath the cottage for your stove and fireplace."

"We want you to have tea (dinner) with us tonight," Mrs. Hindmarch continued. "My sister who lives with us is an excellent cook. Would that be all right?"

"I'd be delighted," I said, grateful for their warm hospitality.

We continued our hazardous ride, avoiding potholes for another thirty miles or so. Finally, the road widened and we made a sharp left turn. On my right was a rather dilapidated general store with a single petrol (gasoline) pump in front of it. A haphazard array of boxes, scrap iron and corrugated metal sheds were scattered about. Scrawny chickens, skinny, barking dogs and a litter of kittens completed the scene. A few children played in the dirt at the side of the store. An old man sat in front of it balancing on a tilting, wooden bench, doing nothing in particular. To the left of the store partly hidden behind blooming foliage and tall gum trees, I spotted a fairly large, brick building. A slightly lopsided, faded sign proclaimed this to be a "HOTEL." Opposite on my left were four one-story, simple wooden homes.

"This is one of our general stores," Mr. Hindmarch announced, pointing to the gas pump and a faded toothpaste sign on the door. "Mrs. Barnes and her husband run it. Next door at the hotel live the McGregors. They have three kids and run the pub as well as the hotel."

"And the homes?" I ventured.

"Oh," he said, "several families live there. The men are mostly sheep shearers. They're gone for months during shearing season when they travel from station (sheep farm) to station. The rest of the time they are home making sure the pub doesn't go out of business." He laughed.

"I'm sure you will meet all of them soon. They're good blokes."

We continued. Ahead of me the road dipped down into a low, one-lane bridge crossing a small, swift river. Alongside it was a high, dangling, narrow suspension bridge for pedestrians.

"This is the Hunter river," my host explained. "After the rains, this bridge usually is under water or covered with branches and debris. You will have to walk across the suspension bridge to get to the store."

"How do you get across with supplies?" I asked.

"On horseback, that's the only way. Do you ride a horse?" he suddenly asked me.

"No, I don't."

"Want to learn?"

"Not really. Why?"

"Well, what if someone needs you to come to their home when the river is up?" he queried.

I had never thought of that. I just assumed everyone would come to me in their times of distress.

"I don't know," I finally said.

"Well, most of them have four-wheel drive jeeps," Mrs. Hindmarch piped in, "they ought to be able to come and get you. Besides, we haven't had any floods for a while."

We crossed the narrow bridge and the road made an upward curve again. Ahead of me, I saw a variety of scattered homes and buildings each surrounded by shrubbery and gum trees.

"There's another general store," Mrs. Hindmarch pointed to a small, shaky building on the left, "but they don't have much to offer as a rule. Next to it is the Post Office."

The latter was an even tinier structure, covered with fading brown paint and surrounded by a dilapidated, wooden walkway.

"Miss Hay is our postmaster," she continued, "she also runs the telephone switchboard. She's Chinese."

"That road leads to the Community Hall and the Catholic church," my guides continued, "there are more homes there, mostly sheep shearers, truck drivers and retired farmers."

Ahead of us the road seemed to come to an end. On our left, we passed yet another brown wooden home framed by several sheds and piles of wood.

"That's the police station," I was told. "Bruce and Pat Hanson live there. They have four little ones. You'll like Pat," she continued, "she's nice and also is your neighbor."

The road curved and we passed a dirt, fenced-in tennis court. Then in front of me, almost next to the court, neatly perched on a small hill, stood a lovely, freshly-painted white homestead flanked by two large, corrugated water tanks. A sturdy, low fence surrounded the entire building. Several large gum trees shaded the backyard which sharply inclined down to the quietly murmuring Hunter river below. Behind the river was a flat stretch of ground, ploughed and planted with something green. In the distance, I noticed a small cluster of buildings nestled amid another grove of trees. Mr. Hindmarch followed my gaze.

"That's the school," he pointed out. "The Icorns live there. Ivan Icorn teaches about fifty kids all in one classroom. He may ask you to teach some First Aid principles."

"And this, Sister," he said triumphantly, pulling up in front of the neat white building, "is your new home!"

It was a nice, balmy day. Stiffly, I got out of the car and took a deep breath. The air was clear with a trace of farm smells. Slowly, I looked around. So this was it - my home for the next twelve months. Mr. Hindmarch opened the boot (trunk) of his car and lugged my suitcases to the front door. I noticed that the entire building like so many others in Australia, was built on several sturdy concrete blocks, elevating the entire home several feet above the ground. Underneath were several piles of neatly stacked wood. Three wooden steps led to the front door.

We opened the door and stood in a small hallway with a door on either side. The left door opened into a bright, fair-sized room lined with cupboards, several counters, small sterilizer and a row of cannisters. There was also an examination table under two large windows. Behind the other door was a small hospital room complete with bed, nightstand and bedside table. Ahead of this small hallway was a built-in veranda separating the clinic part from the living quarters. Here, to my delight, was also a small bathroom with a real toilet rather than the usual outhouse. There was also electricity throughout the house. The living quarters included a bathroom with sink and tub, a bedroom and a small, cozy living room with fireplace adjacent to a large kitchen. The kitchen was also the dining room, complete with a kerosine-operated refrigerator and a massive black cast iron stove which burned wood. From the back door in the kitchen, I noticed another very small shed next to the clotheslines. This turned out to be the laundry room complete with two sinks and a copper, a large metal built-in tub over a brick fireplace. No wonder there was so much wood under the house!

The Hindmarches left me alone to unpack. Later they came back and picked me up for tea. Their homestead, a couple of miles down the road, was old but well kept and comfortable. Elaine, a young widow and Mrs. Hindmarch's sister, proved indeed to be an excellent cook who handled the wood stove like a real pro. We had leg of lamb with pumpkin and baked potatoes and bread and butter on the side, fresh fruit pie and tea for desert. Everything was homegrown or homemade. Although I enjoyed my warm welcome to Moonan Flat, I felt rather intimidated by this new, rather primitive lifestyle and realized my cooking capabilities were lagging far behind my nursing skills. In fact, the latter did not seem very adequate, either, in this new, non-institutional environment.

After a good night's sleep, I settled in, unpacked my things and went on a discovery tour through the treatment room/dispensary and the little hospital room. In the hallway, I noticed an ancient-looking telephone. I picked up the worn, black horn and quickly turned a little, creaky handle. Soon a high pitched, Oriental voice crackled:

"Yes, Sister?"

"Oh, hello," I said. "I'm just trying this thing out. Are you Miss Hay?"

"Yes, I am. You know how to work phone? You ring when you need to make a call and I connect you, OK?"

"Thank you. By the way, what time and how often does the mail come?"

"Every day except weekends, usually around one. You have to pick up your own mail. You come in and I show you where."

I thanked her and hung up. There was a knock and I realized some-one was at the front door.

"Hello, Sister, my name is Daphne Barwick. I am the BNA secretary."

In front of me stood a plain, wispy little woman in her early sixties. I invited her into the treatment room and she efficiently explained how to order supplies and medicine.

"I hope you will like it here," she said. "If you need medical advice, there are several former bush nurses here who will be happy to help you. Margaret Miller is from England. She lived here with her mother. Now that she is married, their home is just about a mile from here. Judy White is another nurse. She was here with her little four-year-old daughter, Zoe. They're about six miles from here now. I'm sure she will stop by soon."

"By the way," she continued, "that little building over there, next to the police station, is our community church. Every Sunday a Church of England pastor comes by and we have a service. You're welcome to join us."

I thanked her and found out later that she was also the church or-ganist. The ancient little organ was grossly out of tune and had to be vigorously pumped to produce any sound at all. Yet somehow, it seemed quite appropriate and adequate just the way it was.

That evening, I decided to try out the bathtub. The water in the small tank just above the faucets had to be heated by a wood fire (what else?). Stuffing some paper, kindling wood and logs in the small open-ing, I carefully lit a fire and waited for half an hour. I have never been a Girl Scout, I thought, and here I am supposed to know all about fires. The water tank felt nice and hot. Anticipating a long, hot bubble bath, I expectantly opened the faucet all the way. It coughed, sputtered and coughed again, followed by some gurgling noises. Hissing steam started to escape from the water tank at various strange angles. Finally, after a huge sneeze, the faucet ejected a sudden stream of warm water. It was, however, black and full of soot. I slowly realized that the pipes had rusted through and the water running through them was quenching the fire and freely mixing the ashes with my bath water. Exhausted and disillusioned, I took a cold spit bath at the sink and went to bed. A few days later, the contraption was fixed and from then on functioned fairly well.

"When you have a baby to deliver," Miss Roach had cautioned me back in Sydney, "try and get the mother to the hospital in Scone so you won't be tied down at the BNA center with a mother and a baby."

I remembered that a few days after my arrival when a local farmer called to announce that his eighteen-year-old daughter was having labor pains. She had not been seen by anyone so there was no medical history.

"Please bring her in as soon as possible," I told him through Miss Hays' listening ears at the post office telephone exchange.

The farmer, a simple, kind man soon arrived with a young, healthy and very pregnant girl. He explained that his daughter was unmarried; the father was a transient farmhand. Both he and his wife had agreed to raise the child rather than give it up for adoption.

I examined Joan. Her vital signs were normal and she was in mild, early labor. It would take quite a while before this baby would be born.

"We'll take her into town," I announced. "There is plenty of time."

I called Miss Hay to say I would be gone for a couple of hours, called the midwives in Scone to announce our arrival, packed an emergency bag and got in the back of the car with Joan. Her Dad took the wheel.

Joan's pains were about ten minutes apart when we left and not very strong.

I enjoyed the scenic route which just a week before, I had seen for the first time. The potholes were still there and so were the crazy corners.

"I'm having another pain," Joan groaned.

I put my hand on her abdomen and counted. Goodness, I thought, that feels like a second stage contraction. Two minutes later she yelled:

"Oh no, there's another one! This one's real bad."

It sure was a long, strong contraction followed almost immediately by yet another one. It's the potholes I suddenly realized. This bumpy ride is speeding up her labor!

"Better step on it," I said to her Dad, trying not to sound panicky.

How in the world could I deliver a baby on the backseat of this car when there was hardly enough room for the two of us to sit? I kept my eye on her. She was in hard labor now. Well, at least this is her first baby, I thought; they usually take longer.

"How long before we're there?" I asked the father.

"About twenty miles," he yelled, his foot heavy on the gas pedal, "can't go any faster."

"That's all right! Take it easy." I cautioned.

"Oh, I feel lots of pressure!" Joan yelled. "Please help me, the baby is coming!"

"Take some deep breaths, Joan," I urged. "Don't hold your breath when you have a pain. Keep breathing normally!"

We arrived on the straight paved section of the road leading into Scone. The Dad let out all the stops and the old car suddenly lurched forward, throwing us off balance in the back.

We reached the outskirts of town in a cloud of dust. Flying round the corners on two wheels, the car finally came to a screeching halt in front of the little maternity hospital. The nurse was waiting with a wheelchair and whisked her patient into the delivery room. Her dad and I wearily sank into a chair and gratefully accepted a cup of tea. I heaved a huge sigh of relief. Ten minutes later the nurse returned.

"It's a boy," she said, "born the moment she hit the delivery table."

Well, at least I had learned a new and effective way to speed up slow labor. Hours later, I returned to Moonan Flat, tired and ready for a hot meal.

In the past, meals had always appeared at the hospital or at home at appropriate times. How they were prepared had never concerned me too much. In fact, my lack of cooking abilities had become quite a joke at home. Once, on my day off from Sydney Hospital when we still lived at our flat in Collaroy, I wanted to wash some undergarments. Since we did not have hot water, I decided the best way to get them really clean was to put everything in a big pot and boil it on the stove. Unfortunately, I forgot about it. When Dad came home hours later, he entered a smoke-filled kitchen. He turned the gas off, lifted the lid from the pan and dryly said to Mom:

"Guess what we're having for dinner? Fried bra! Aubrey must be home."

As students, cramming for tests, we would often concoct all kinds of sandwiches, fruit salads and experiment with new coffee or tea brands. Part of our training at Sydney Hospital even included a course in Cooking for Invalids which meant whipping up a variety of bland soups and custards. But meat, potatoes and vegetables? That was quite a different matter and now, suddenly, it had become a major undertaking. First of all, I realized, there had a to be a hot stove. Ah, what magic to simply turn a knob and have instant heat. How do you light a fire that will not go out? My venture with the bathtub heater fresh in mind, I gingerly opened a little door on one side of the stove and stuffed it with paper, kindling wood and some small logs. Soon, it was transformed into a glowing red fire. Above it, on top of the stove, were several metal rings that could be removed for more direct heat. So far, so good.

Since we had never had an oven at home, my mother either boiled or fried all our meals. Boiling potatoes seemed easy enough. Peel them, get the eyes out, boil water, add a little salt and let them cook. Test them with a fork once in a while to see whether they are done, then drain the water off, let them sit a minute, shake the pan to get them fluffy and voila, the potatoes are done. Cooking vegetables should be similar - boil until done. A small frying pan should take care of two lamb chops. Twenty minutes later everything was on the stove.

Then the doorbell rang. It was dinnertime. Who could that be at this hour? On the doorstep stood a young, hefty farmer. One hand was wrapped in a towel.

"Sorry to bother you at this hour, Sister," he began, "I was opening a can of sardines and cut my hand."

"Come in," I said, "let me take a look."

I ushered him into the dispensary, sat him down and removed the towel. On the side of his hand was a deep, gaping cut.

"Can you move your fingers?" I asked.

Yes, he could move them all.

I lightly scratched a pin over his hand.

"Can you feel this?"

"Yes, I can."

Satisfied, I realized there was no nerve or tendon damage but the cut was deep and needed to be stitched. The only thing I knew about stitches was how to remove them. However, I had often watched and assisted doctors suturing every conceivable part of the human anatomy. What should I do?

"Why don't you drive into town and get the doctor to stitch this up for you?" I ventured.

"Oh no, Sister, I don't have time. Can't you do it?"

"Well," I hesitated, "I'll need to sterilize some instruments. Why don't you lay down?"

"No, thanks, I'm fine," he insisted.

Well, here goes, I thought. What shall we use? I found several sharp, curved suture needles, some catgut and forceps. Luckily, my little electric sterilizer worked quickly. In the meantime, I seated my patient beside the examination table and cleaned and draped his hand.

"I need to give you some local anesthetic," I said efficiently, as though this was a daily routine. I clearly remembered assisting doctors in minor surgeries and knew what solution of Xylocaine to use. Injecting this into the man's hand was not so simple, though. His skin was extremely tough.

"You sure you don't want to lay down?" I asked again, wishing he would so that he couldn't watch me so closely.

"No, I'm fine. Just carry on," he insisted, trying to act tough.

Well, I thought, I can be tough too. I turned to the sink, scrubbed my hands and put rubber gloves on. Then, after threading the needle, I tried to thrust it through one edge of the cut on his hand. It would not budge. The skin was too thick. What in the world am I doing here? I wondered, feeling beads of perspiration on my forehead. This is not going to work. I felt totally clumsy, inadequate, unprepared.

To make matters worse, the young man suddenly turned deathly pale and keeled over on the floor. Then he started to throw up. Horrified, I just stood there, the stubborn suture needle still in my gloved hand.

Forget that cut, I said to myself, and get this guy off the floor.

But how? He weighed at least fifteen stones (210 lbs). Luckily, the man did not pass out completely. He was just numb, sick and very embarrassed. I threw some towels on the floor, covering the mess he made, put a cloth with cold water on his forehead and stuffed a pillow under his head.

"Take it easy," I said, my professionalism returning, "you'll be all right. Just stay there for a few minutes."

He didn't object.

I'm going to butterfly that hand, I thought, and splint it.

"Listen carefully," I said to my patient on the floor, "I'm not going to stitch your hand. I'll bandage it but you can't use it for at least a week." Relieved, he was willing to promise anything. The color returned to his face and he sat up again. I cleaned his hand once again and put two thin strips of tape over the cut, holding the edges firmly together. This was known as a butterfly. Then I placed his hand in a splint and bandaged it in such a way he could not move it and put his arm in a sling tied at the shoulder.

"Can you drive with one hand?" I asked.

"No problem," he said, his bravado returning.

"OK, I'll give you a Tetanus shot and I'll need to see you again in one week. And remember," I stressed again, "don't use your hand."

Back to his normal self, he smiled and left. Relieved, I cleaned up the mess.

"Well my dear," I said to myself, rather unnerved, "you wanted to be independent. You got your wish!"

Had I bitten off too much in accepting this job? Was I really prepared for it? Hunger pains stopped my reverie. Suddenly I remembered: The stove! The fire! My dinner! I rushed back to the kitchen. The fire was out. Even the embers had lost their glow, the potatoes were hard, the meat still raw. It was eight o'clock. Dejected, I opened the refrigerator and fixed a cheese and tomato sandwich. There was an apple for desert.

"Hi, I'm Judy White, the former bush nurse."

I saw a young, vivacious, smiling brunette on my doorstep the next day.

"Please come in," I said, relieved it was not another patient. "I've been wanting to meet you."

We sat down at the kitchen table and I plugged in the hot water pot for a cup of tea.

"How are you doing?" Judy asked with a smile.

I related the incident with my last patient. She laughed.

"I really learned fast how to butterfly cuts myself."

"How long were you here? What all did you run into?" I was full of questions.

"Well," she said, taking a sip of her tea, "I was here for a year and ran into all kinds of things. Right after I got here, there was a mumps epidemic. Adults really get sick with this, you know. I made daily house calls to a great number of families. I had to bath them, cook, clean, do everything for some of the older folks."

Mumps, that was only a textbook word for me. Helen and I never had the mumps and nobody was ever hospitalized with the mumps during my training. In fact, when I did my time in the pediatrics ward in Sydney, one kid developed a barking cough, the likes of which I had never heard before. Turned out it was whooping cough, a sound I was unfamiliar with at the time but will never forget.

"Had a lot of croup too," Judy continued.

"Croup? What do you do for that?" Another textbook word. Judy smiled.

"You'd never believe it," she said, "I had no idea what to do for croup. Lots of kids have it here, they're desperate for air and wheeze like an asthmatic but with a loud, raspy sound."

"Someone told me about an old folk remedy," she continued, "it works!"

"What is it?" I was eager to learn.

"Take a spoonful of sugar and add a few drops of kerosine on it. Swallow it and the congestion will be broken up in minutes."

"You're kidding." I was incredulous. "Isn't kerosine a poison?"

"Yes, if you drink lots of it. But one of my patients was siphoning kerosine from one tank to another and accidentally swallowed several mouthfuls. I called the doctor but the stuff never hurt him."

I still looked doubtful.

"If you don't like the kerosine," she said, "drench a towel with Methylated Spirits (Rubbing Alcohol) and wrap it around the kid's neck. That will do the trick also. The fumes will break up the congestion."

We talked for hours and I received a new education.

"Thanks so much for coming, Judy," I said as I finally let her out, "please come back sometimes."

"Why don't you come over for tea," she invited. "How about next Saturday? I'll pick you up at six."

"Thanks, that'll be great!"

Life in Moonan Flat settled down into something of a routine. I had never lived alone and found it difficult at times not to have people, patients, friends or staff around. Of course, there were many new things to learn. Laundry was one of them. The big copper sink in the back needed a roaring fire underneath it to get the water hot. Washing sheets and clothes by hand was certainly a new experience. Keeping a fire going long enough to wash a load of laundry proved to be another challenge. The river in back of the sloping backyard was a wonderful place to swim but out of reach of the phone and rather isolated. If something happened to me, nobody would ever know.

The old tennis court just down the road was often used by local housewives, most of them expert players. Tennis had never been my thing but I was encouraged to try it, anyway, and got to know some more people in the process. Several families asked me over for a meal or a cup of tea.

The community hall, I discovered, had an old piano I could practice on. At home, my faithful HiFi record player bought in Brisbane gave me many hours of pleasure. I discovered I could check out records by mail from various libraries. They also mailed books. A small radio kept me in touch with the rest of the world.

I had also brought a small portable typewriter to Moonan Flat and to kill some long hours on rainy days, I began to relate detailed stories about my new life as a Bush Nurse to Doe. Yes, all through the years, I had kept in touch with my old pal from Blaricum. She was now married and living near Antwerp in Belgium. One day she wrote:

"I received your last, long letter just as I was going for a doctor's appointment. I started to read it in the waiting room but your stories were so hilarious, I couldn't help laughing. Particularly funny was the one about Miss Roach's visit. I finally had to stop reading. Everyone was staring at me, I was laughing so loud. Next time, I'll wait till I am totally alone before reading any of your letters."

I was glad somebody laughed at my stories. Actually at the time, they weren't funny at all. Take Miss Roach's visit. I'll never forget that fateful day. I had been in Moonan Flat for six months.

The fenced-in yard had been relieved of hundreds of rocks and weeds, borders and flower beds had been constructed and a nursery in Scone had provided an abundance of seeds and small plants. I worked that barren yard for hours on end. Finally, my labors and broken fingernails paid off. There was an abundance of snapdragons, pansies and daisies, especially against the fence in the front yard. I was proud of my accomplishments and inspected each seedling and plant first thing every morning.

Imagine my chagrin when, one sunny dawn, my eyes beheld rows and rows of short, green stumps, carefully chomped off by the sheriff's horse which he had left overnight in his paddock next to my garden. Only a few beds too far for the horse to reach over the fence, were left intact. Furious, I stomped over to Bruce's little office and gave him a piece of my mind. Undisturbed, he listened to my ravings, shrugged his shoulders and drawled,

"That's what happens when you live in the country."

In that depressed state of mind, I saw the mail truck coming to the post office. There was a letter for me from Miss Roach, the head of the BNA in Sydney. She said she was coming over for a weekend visit in four weeks.

"Oh, no," I groaned, "My garden is gone, I can't keep a fire going or cook a decent meal and now Miss Roach is coming on an inspection tour. What am I to do?"

A brilliant idea suddenly struck me. Betsy! I'll invite her, too. Betsy was the oldest of nine kids, surely she knew how to cook. Besides, she needed a break, having completed her midwifery training in Sydney. Excited, I wrote to her immediately.

"It's beautiful here, Betsy," I said in my letter, "you wouldn't believe it. Totally different from Beaudesert. You'll love it. Why don't you take a week or so off and come over? You need a break, you know."

She took the bait and arrived on the mail truck two weeks later. I settled her on the veranda in a spare bed and showed her around. Then I told her about Miss Roach's imminent visit.

"Can you cook dinner?" I asked her, "please!?"

Surprised, Betsy's innocent blue eyes focussed on mine.

"I can't cook," she finally said, "didn't you know that?"

"You have eight brothers and sisters and you don't know how to cook?" I asked, my voice rising.

"My mother or sisters always cook," she said. "I've lived in hospitals and nurses' quarters for years. Honestly," her soft voice was very serious, "I don't know a thing about cooking. But I'll be glad to help."

"Well, that'll be plan B. Let's go for it," I finally opted.

We carefully put together a tasteful, yet simple menu.

"If you keep her company around dinner time, I will concentrate on the cooking," I proposed.

And so, it was agreed. Miss Roach arrived in good form. She was serious and efficient yet friendly and a little surprised to see Betsy although that was not against BNA rules. We pored over policies, procedures, finances and record keeping. She seemed satisfied with my overall performance. I put her up for the night in the little front room with the high hospital bed. Around mid-afternoon, I got busy birthing a fire in a kitchen stove. It worked. Removing the heavy metal rings, I placed several pots and a frying pan over the bright, healthy leaping flames. So far, so good. We set the table, complete with the customary bread and butter plates, tea pot, cups, condiments and salt and pepper. Then the phone rang. A mother had a child with fever.

"Bring her right over," I heard myself say.

The child had tonsillitis and needed a penicillin shot. The syringes needed to be sterilized which took a while. I counted out some pills for her to take home, waited for the glass syringe to cool off, gave the shot under strong protest of the feverish child then calmed down mother and youngster who were both in tears by now and finally ushered them out the front door. Betsy was still keeping Miss Roach occupied in the living room.

I rushed back to the kitchen. Some of the fire was still burning, a little lopsided, most of it was reduced to cooling embers. Carefully, I poked around the contents of the pots with a fork. Most of the potatoes were still hard, others boiled to a pulp, a few just right. The rest of the food was in similar condition. Traditionally, dinners are all arranged on individual plates in Australia before being served. At that moment, I was very grateful for that custom. I served the best food on Miss Roach's plate then heaped the soupy, overcooked mess on mine which left Betsy with the hard and almost raw items.

Carefullly arranging the plates on the dinner table, I gave it one last look and called the two hungry guests from the living room into the kitchen. Miss Roach was delighted and ate every morsel. Betsy bravely chomped on her sturdy dinner fare while I just imagined I was back at Invalid Cooking Class, soft and easy for toothless people. Just perfect.

Miss Roach departed, followed a few days later by Betsy. We had a good time but Betsy could not imagine how anyone could live in such isolation under such primitive conditions. I agreed but somehow was getting used to it. Besides, one year could not last forever. My worst problem was still the stove.

"You people are raised with wood stoves," I told Daphne Barwick when she came by to pick up my supply orders, "I wasn't and I find it very difficult to operate."

Daphne was sympathetic and promised to talk about it with the Committee. The following week Mr. Hindmarch's car pulled up at my front door. He opened the 'boot' and walked up to the house with a large box. Inside was a small, electric oven with a hot plate on top. What a luxury! I dared not mention I had never used an oven, either. The hot plate was large enough for three small pots. Just what the doctor ordered. I was delighted and decided life was worth living after all.

A few days later, just after dark, the doorbell rang. It was a middle-aged couple from a distant village. They had driven through several rivers and crossed a steep mountain to get to Moonan Flat.

"I feel fine," the woman said after they sat down in the treatment room, "but ever since we had supper I can't keep anything down."

"You mean you are throwing up?" I asked.

"Not really, but when I swallow, it won't stay down."

"What did you eat for supper?" I wanted to know.

"Steak and vegetables. I feel like something got stuck in my stomach, right here," she pointed to a spot just below her rib cage.

"Perhaps you swallowed a large piece of meat?" I ventured.

"Yes, I think that's what it is. That's what it feels like, anyway."

"Well, if that's the case, I can't help you," I replied, "you need to go into Scone and see a doctor. They have special instruments to get that piece of meat out."

"Well, we've come this far," the husband said, "we may as well drive a little further."

I called the hospital in Scone. The doctor agreed with my diagnosis and set up for a esophagoscopy, a procedure designed to remove an object lodged in the throat.

"Let me know what happens," I asked before they left.

They didn't have to. A few days later the doctor called.

"We got her to surgery," he related, "but I could not get hold of that piece of meat. It was really stuck at the end of her esophagus. Finally, I called Newcastle hospital and they agreed to give it a try."

"Good grief, that's over a hundred miles," I said.

"Right," he agreed. "They drove all night and arrived there in the morning. Guess what happened then? As they walked up the hospital steps, she suddenly felt that piece of meat slide into her stomach." He laughed.

"How could that happen?" I said, amazed.

"Well, some of the acid in her stomach must have digested part of it," he said, "just enough to make it small enough to pass from the esophagus into the stomach."

"Well, I guess they'll never forget that ride," I laughed.

Not so simple was another call a few days later at bedtime from yet another faraway, elderly couple.

"My husband is having a nose bleed," the wife said.

I heard Miss Hay's breathing as she listened in on the conversation at the exchange. I questioned the wife and found out he'd had nose bleeds before and also high blood pressure.

"Put some cotton or gauze in his nose," I instructed her, "have him lay down and put ice on his nose. If it does not stop call me back."

I went back to bed. At one o'clock, the phone rang again.

"Sorry, to bother you again, Sister," there was concern but no panic in her voice, "but it hasn't stopped."

"Is there any way you can get here?" I asked, tying my bathrobe and rubbing sleep from my eyes.

"Yes, I guess so," she said, "our son could drive us over. He has a jeep. The rivers are high here and there's lots of mud on the road. It'll take an hour probably."

"OK, see you then." I said. She hung up.

"Miss Hay?" I knew she was listening.

"Yes, Sister?"

"Get me the hospital, please."

I got a doctor out of bed and consulted with him.

"Pack the nose with gauze, soak the gauze with adrenaline first," was his advice. "Pack it tightly, keep ice on his nose and keep his head down. It'll stop."

An hour later, the doorbell rang and three people stood in the dark night, one of them holding a towel to his face. I carried out the doctor's orders (never thought I'd be so happy to HAVE doctor's orders) but two hours later, the man was still bleeding. The bleeding simply changed to a steady postnasal drip which he spit into a rapidly filling basin. Should I call the doctor again? I debated. There seemed little else to do. I cranked the phone again for Miss Hay.

"Hospital again, please."

"What's his pressure?" the doctor asked.

"One eighty over one hundred, pulse a hundred and ten."

"Better bring him in, Sis. Keep his nose packed. Keep ice on it, too."

I heard Miss Hay heave a sigh of relief. She was going to get some sleep after all. We all filed into the car and made it safely to Scone.

Avoiding potholes in the dark was a new experience. I was grateful to have such calm, unpanicky company. Living in isolation as they did had probably prepared them to take things in their stride. It took another day in the hospital to get the man's bleeding under control. When it finally stopped, his blood pressure was also considerably lower! Perhaps nature had done him a favor, after all.

I finally met Margaret, the other former bush nurse. She had brought her mother and two huge dogs from the old country, England. Having dogs in her house had caused quite a stir among the population, she said over a cup of tea at her cozy cottage. Dogs were strictly outside creatures around here. I liked her. She was tall and skinny, in her early forties, with a distinctly non-Australian English accent. Her husband, Bob, was called a "mixed farmer", she explained, tending both sheep and some cattle while growing corn and other produce on the side.

"What do you think about farming in Australia?" I asked.

"I never knew there were so many natural pests in this country," she exclaimed. "There are foxes who eat newborn lambs if we don't get to them first or crows who will pick out their eyes."

"See those parrots?" She pointed to some tall bean stalks with a dozen or so of the prettiest, bright pink, little parrots I have ever seen.

"They love corn," Margaret said, "they have an unbelievable appetite. Then, there are the rabbits, millions of them, who burrow under any fence and eat absolutely everything - to say nothing about the kangaroos."

"What about the kangaroos?" I questioned her. "The other night when I made a house call, one was hopping along beside our car. It was huge."

"Notice the fences along the road?" Margaret continued, "that's for the cattle. But when the road passes over a creek, the fences narrow down on the road. That's when those kangaroos get too close to your car. They can easily push it off the road. They also trample your crops."

"Can you eat the meat?" I said, remembering the kangaroo tail soup at Sydney's swanky restaurants.

"Let me show you," Margaret said.

We got up and walked over to a grassy area behind a shed. An empty gasoline barrel stood on a large, rough, wood fire. Huge hunks of meat were simmering in it. I recognized a kangaroo hind leg.

"Look," Margaret said. She got a butcher knife and cut the meat.

Large, dead worms and eggs were clearly visible.

"Yuck!" I said, "are they all like that?"

"Yes, that's why they only eat the tails."

"What happened to this one?" I wanted to know.

"Got caught in a fence."

"What do you do with the meat?"

"Feed it to the dogs. After it's boiled it's all right."

"When do you shear the sheep?" I said, changing the subject.

"In about a month. Care to watch?"

"Sure would."

"It's fascinating," Margaret said, "you'll never believe how fast those blokes are. I must say," she said apologizing, "I do like it here, you know. It's just so different from England. There are so many new things to get used to."

"Yes," I said, "I can sure relate to that."

The following Sunday afternoon the phone rang. Perhaps it's Helen, I thought, walking to the hallway to answer it. Helen was a long distance telephone operator in Sydney now and often called on weekends. It was wonderful to hear a familiar voice and catch up on the news in civilization. Miss Hay was peeved about these calls since we spoke Dutch and she couldn't understand what we were talking about. She felt that, after all, she was entitled to the news, too.

"Hello! BNA." I cheerfully smiled into the receiver on the wall.

"Sister?" It was an unfamiliar male voice.

It was definitely not Helen. The smile disappeared.

"Yes, can I help you?"

"Sorry to call you on Sunday. Name is Davies, we're just beyond the schoolhouse in Moonan Brook. I have this cow," he hesitated, "she's got a stopped up udder. Just talked to the vet in Scone. He suggested I ask you to give her a penicillin injection. Would you mind?"

A cow? Give a cow a shot? On Sunday?

"Uh..., I don't know," I stammered, "I have never treated a cow before."

"She's well tied down, Sister. Can't move. It won't take long and I'll be right there holding her."

Well, I thought, why not? Try everything once, right?

"What's the vet's number?"

He gave it to me and hung up. Miss Hay connected me right away. I could hear her think, "Wonder how she's going to handle that one."

"Yes, hello Sister," came a cheerful voice from Scone. "Thanks so much for helping me out with that cow."

"What do you want me to do?"

"Well, if you don't mind, get a large, firm catheter and try to get it into the udder. It's infected and the milk by now has curdled. It can't come out and is putting pressure on the udder. It's pretty painful."

"What about the rest of the udder?"

"Oh, that's probably fine. The four compartments of the udder are completely separated by membranes."

"What if I can't get the catheter in or the curdled milk out?"

"Eventually that quarter of the udder will atrophy and shrivel up. See what you can do, please, but don't worry if it does not work. Give her ten million units of penicillin."

"Doctor?" I queried timidly.

"Yes?"

"Where do you give a cow a shot of penicillin?"

He laughed. "Try her neck, Sis. Thanks a lot and good luck."

I called Davies. He arrived fifteen minutes later in his Landrover jeep. I packed several large intramusclar needles, the largest syringe I could find and several firm catheters with a 50 cc irrigation syringe.

We arrived at the farm where I found the cow firmly tied in between two wooden poles. Greatly intimidated, I sat down on the little wooden stool under her big belly.

Only once before had I been in this position. It was with Betsy's brother Billy in Beaudesert. After Gloria had milked the cows which was done by machine, the udders had to be "stripped" or completely emptied. This was done by hand. It had looked very easy and Gloria patiently showed us how it was done. I tried but was so awestruck by the enormity of the size of the huge belly I sat under, I pulled and squeezed but produced no milk.

Now, here I sat again under this large wall of flesh. I spotted the inflamed udder and carefully palpated its contents. I had to actually lean into her hide to do so. My patient immediately objected to this examination. She furiously stomped her feet, shook her head and accurately hit her tail right into my face. Davies tipped his wide-rimmed, old hat back and steadied the cow.

"Go on, Sister," he yelled. "I got her! She can't hurt you!

Gathering my fragmented scraps of courage, I boldly pushed the catheter into the swollen udder, expecting (and almost receiving) another tail lash. I ducked this time and it only hit my hair. I worked that red, swollen udder with both hands, trying to break up the infection but the holes in the catheter were too small.

Meanwhile, the cow used one of her last trumps. She raised her tail again but this time emptied her huge bladder, a brisk and heavy waterfall, right near my face. Why had I come here in uniform? my befuddled brain asked. I needed overalls and boots. I had no sooner considered this question when my patient triumphantly raised her tail again, this time giving me the rare opportunity to splash me thoroughly with the source of those wonderfully pungent and familiar farm scents. I was overwhelmed in the most literal sense of the word.

"Sorry, pal," I said to Davies, "can't get any milk out this way."

Slowly, in a daze, I extricated myself from my low position on the stool. I dared not look at my bright blue uniform or shoes.

"I'll give her the penicillin. That's all I can do."

I mixed the powdered penicillin with 20cc of saline. The stuff often clogged the needle so it had to be given fast. Approaching my patient's neck, I wondered about alcohol sponges. Do you wipe a hide before giving a shot? May as well. Ready? Shoot! I jabbed the large needle into the black hide in front of me. At least that's what I intended to do. Instead, at the point of impact the needle stopped dead then ricocheted and bent in a sharp ninety-degree angle. Stunned, I realized what cowhide is used for: shoes, strong leather shoes. Ever tried to stick a needle in the sole of a shoe? How stupid of me.

Undaunted, I hooked my second and last needle to the syringe. There's only one way to do this, baby, I thought. You're not going to like it but that's tough. Just as tough as your hide. I lightly touched the point of the needle on her hide, then increasing the pressure, twisted it to the right and to the left. It worked! The tip barreled through. Oh, let it not clog! It didn't. Do you pull back for blood? Not this time, I decided, and quickly emptied the syringe into the lowing animal. Relieved, I packed my soggy belongings and jumped into the Jeep. Davies was very grateful and apologized for the mess. I had one wish left: A hot bath! Immediately!

Time moved on. I had now been a bush nurse in Moonan Flat for seven months. Things had sort of fallen into a pattern and daily routines were established. I got to know many wonderful and interesting people.

One young man had a roving, romantic eye fixed on this available bush nurse but living in Moonan Flat on a farm and spending most of my days behind a wood stove was not exactly what I had in mind for my future and I successfully brushed him off. Most families in my district were simple, honest, hard-working folks.

Especially wonderful were Ivan Icorn, the schoolteacher, and his wife, Doris. I could see the little one-room schoolhouse and the Icorn's home from my backyard. Ivan efficiently taught a roomful of kids, thirty-five of them in fact, ranging in age from five to fifteen. Those who went on to high school in Scone did well. I gave some simple First Aid classes to this mixed group, the little ones in front, wide-eyed and toothless, the older ones, some of them almost adults, quietly watching from the back.

Doris, a bright, petite and pretty lady was an excellent cook and hostess. I spent some delightful and interesting evenings at their home. We discussed a wide range of topics, from cooking to politics. Doris, I learned, had been raised on a peanut farm. I had no idea where peanuts came from until she told me all about it. The Icorns were childless and were thinking of adopting.

"You already have thirty-five kids," I laughed, "why do you want more?"

Ten miles further down the road, in Moonan Brook, was another little one-room schoolhouse. This one only boasted twelve pupils. In Ellerston, forty miles and four hundred potholes further down the road was the third and last district school. Once a year, all the schools gathered for an annual sports event at Belltrees, a large farm with plenty of flat ground for games. During the grand "March Past," the highlight of the event, each school dressed in identical sports outfits and, preceded by a school flag bearer, proudly marched past the wildly applauding audience. The entire population gathered for this event which ended with a huge cookout.

I knew the Committee had difficulty raising my support. One day when Daphne made her routine visit I said,

"Why don't we organize a benefit concert?"

She looked a little alarmed.

"What do you mean, Sister?"

"Well, we have the community hall and there's nothing much going on there except for an occasional movie or party. I'm sure we can get a program together with the schoolkids singing something. Others can do some skits, a dance or whatever. We could announce it throughout the district even in Scone and sell tickets. The Committee ladies could serve refreshments and all the proceeds would go to the BNA."

She still looked doubtful.

"It's never been done before." she said, a familiar line I had heard many times before.

"Talk about it to the other Committee members," I encouraged her, "I'll take care of the entire program and publicity. All the men have to do is get the hall set up and the ladies can serve refreshments."

I didn't hear anything for a while and decided to give them some time to digest this strange idea.

August, the middle of winter, was cold and wet in Moonan Flat. I kept my fireplace lit all day and watched some snow cover the ground in between rain and thunderstorms. A little electric heater kept the dispensary room fairly warm. One late afternoon, I got call from a mother in Ellerston. Her three-year-old daughter Sharon was "croupy."

"Could you please come?" she begged.

"I don't have a car," I began, "and the rivers are up, anyway. I don't have a horse, either."

I asked her to describe the symptoms of the little one. It sounded like croup but what could I do even if I was able to make a house call?

"Do you have a steamer?" I asked.

"Yes, we do, we've added some eucalyptus oil and some other medicine we had but nothing seems to help. She can hardly get any air and her breathing scares me."

What else is there to do for croup? I racked my brain. Suddenly, I remembered Judy's advice about the kerosine and sugar. Did I dare try that radical home remedy? I hesitated. Perhaps the rubbing alcohol would work.

"My husband can come and get you," the frantic mother begged. "He has a good car. It got through the rivers today. Please!?"

"I'll come," I promised, "but I'll tell you what you can do in the meantime. Do you have some rubbing alcohol?"

"Yes, I think so."

"OK, take it and pour lots of it on a washcloth or tea towel. Put it around Sharon's neck and keep it there."

She promised she would. I went back to my warm living room, ate some supper and checked my emergency bag. Almost an hour later, I saw a mud-spattered car laboring towards the Center with Sharon's Dad and her grandfather. It was dark by now and the roads slippery and dangerous. These men knew the terrain, their home turf after all, and they successfully maneuvered through puddles, mudslides and potholes till we safely arrived in Ellerton. I entered the brightly lit, warm living room where several women were seated. One of them stood up and welcomed me.

"Thanks for coming, Sister," she said.

"Where is the patient?" I asked.

"She's asleep," she said, a little sheepishly.

"Asleep? I thought you told me..."

"Yes, she could hardly breathe when I called you but I did what you said and a few minutes later she started to breathe normally again and fell asleep. By then my husband had already left to fetch you."

I took a look at the sleeping child with rosy pink cheeks, her little chest moving up and down without a wheeze, heartbeat steady.

"Well," I said at last, "she certainly seems to be fine now."

"Would you please have some tea?" she offered.

"Of course, I'd love to."

I silently thanked Judy for her excellent advice. What in the world would I have done without this effective home remedy?

My "concert" idea was being mulled over by the Committee members who had mixed feelings. I eloquently presented the positive aspects such an endeavor would have including fun, community spirit, increased awareness of BNA needs, support and added income. They smiled uneasily. Finally, just to get me off their backs, they reluctantly agreed, making it very clear that they didn't think it would work or that many folks would show up. That was all I needed to hear. Eager and full of unspent energy, I went to work. Ivan promised to get the kids involved with song and dance numbers. I got together with some local couples and persuaded them to try some skits I dug up from our family gatherings in Holland. The idea was totally new to them but I didn't give them too much opportunity to refuse, naming all the other folks who would be involved also. For the grand finale, I had a male ballet in mind. Dressing hairy men up in short frilly skirts, stuffed bras, make-up and wigs, then having them dance in unison to some brisk polka music had always been a tremendous hit in the past. I knew Moonan Flat would not be an exception. But how to get these shy, Australian country farmers to consent to something so utterly outrageous?

The most important principle was to avoid telling them too much at one time. I needed seven men including one to be the main ballerina who would be lifted high in the air by the other six as the music climaxed to an end. I listed seven candidates, then approached each one, careful to mention the names of all the others. Surprised and rather amused, they all consented to give it a try. I was making progress! We started with rehearsals in the Community Hall. It was hilarious. They were totally uncoordinated which would only add to their success.

Meanwhile, I got busy on publicity. I made some colorful posters which proclaimed: "AT LAST... FAMOUS ARTISTS FROM ALL

OVER THE DISTRICT JOIN IN A GRAND CONCERT AT THE S.M. HALL MOONAN FLAT ON SATURDAY, SEPTEMBER 26, 1959 AT 7:45 PM SHARP. Supper after. Proceeds B.N.A." I added some crude drawings of a surprised, bearded hillbilly farmer and a ballerina. These were pinned to doors and windows of shops, banks and post offices all over the Upper Hunter District. The Scone Advocate newspaper printed a press release I mailed them: *On Saturday, September 26, 1959, a variety concert will be given at the S.M. Hall, Moonan Flat, in aid of the Upper Hunter Bush Nursing Association. Preparations for this show commenced about three months ago and in spite of floods and holidays, rehearsals continued, sometimes under very difficult circumstances. The "famous artists" presenting this concert are not only from Moonan Flat but come from as far as Pages Creek, Ellerston, Moonan Brook, etc. and include young Moonan students, ballerinas, musicians, detectives, artists, surgeons and many others.*

The night before the concert, we had a final dress rehearsal. It went well and I was excited. So were all the participants including the stage hands. The next afternoon, I went over to the hall again for a final inspection. Some of the Committee members promised to be there to set up the chairs. In spite of lively rehearsals and all the publicity, they had remained skeptical about the whole adventure. Now, I saw to my dismay that there were only a few chairs set up.

"That's all you'll need, Sister," a Committee member said. "About fifty or so."

"What will you do if more show up?" I asked, rather chagrined.

"We have plenty more but don't worry, we won't need them."

No matter what I said, they would not be persuaded to set up more seats. At seven that night, I returned to the hall. The show would not start for another forty-five minutes but the hall was already full - all seats taken. Trucks, pick-ups and jeeps were arriving in a steady stream from different directions. The surprised Committee members were shaken into action and busily hauled wooden benches from the shed into the back of the hall. I smiled and went backstage to calm down thirty-five excited kids ready for their opening number, a story about a farmer in Arkansas with a leaking roof.

At showtime, the hall was filled with a hundred and twenty people including a reporter from the Scone Advocate. Ivan opened the evening then I took over as MC and introduced the Moonan Flat School choir. They did great! They also did a short skit originally developed by my Uncle Henk from Bussum. There were wild whistles and there was prolonged applause. The skits went over equally well. I was proud of my "actors." During intermission, we gathered in a small section behind stage to get the ballerinas ready. They looked hilarious, totally clumsy and ridiculous but loving every minute of it.

"Whatever you do," I instructed them for the last time, "don't laugh!"

The intermission over, we continued with some musical numbers and another skit. Then finally, it was time for the grand finale. The house lights went out and the men quietly took their place on the stage, standing neatly in a row, tippy-toed, feet together, arms raised. The hall quieted. Then the opening chords of a lively Strauss Polka broke the silence. At the same time, the lights went on and the dancers, raising their right knee in unison, hopped along the stage. There was instant pandemonium! Ignoring the roars and whistles, the hairy dancers continued their steps, waving arms right and left, forming circles and lines, finally raising their ballerina high into the air, pointing one raised arm at her, completely serious. They were magnificent and brought down the house. Peals of laughter, applause, whistling and stomping feet left no doubt they were a smash hit! The entire cast got a standing ovation. Everyone, including the Committee members, beamed! The evening had been a huge success. Ticket sales covered three months of BNA expenses and for years to come, folks at Moonan Flat would have something to talk about.

My life went on about like it had been. Just before Christmas, I asked for a week off to attend Helen's wedding. She was going to tie the knot with Tom, a Dutch fellow she had known for some time. They had a lovely wedding in Collaroy and I persuaded my folks to come back with me to Moonan Flat for a visit. I also met Kaye Campbell at the wedding, one of my former Sydney Hospital classmates. She, too, spent some time in Moonan Flat at my invitation. In between these visits, I continued to find things to do around the Center. Sometimes days went by without any calls or patients, other times a steady stream of folks appeared at my doorstep. I read volumes of books, many of them dealing with world religions and philosophies and diligently studied lessons about spiritual truths and ancient masters, the reality of visible and invisible worlds and many issues dealing with life and death. Strains of Bach and Beethoven from borrowed library records often filled the silence at the Center. I was able to purchase Bach's entire St. Matthew's Passion performed in Amsterdam in 1939 by the famous Concertgebouw Orchestra and conducted by Willem Mengelberg. It was a collector's item and kept me going especially on long, rainy days.

True to her word, Margaret called me when their sheep were going to be shorn. I came over one afternoon to see the most amazing spectacle. Five shearers worked side by side in the shearing shed. Each would grab a huge woolly sheep and turn it on its back. Going to work with their electric clippers, they peeled off a fleece as though it were a coat. The whole coat of wool came off in one piece in about three minutes. Shivering and greatly reduced in size, the pathetically bleating creatures were then immediately "dipped": herded through a deep ditch filled with an antiseptic solution. The fleeces reminded me of the war years in Holland when this kind of unbleached, untreated wool was the only yarn available. Many women had even reinstated spinning wheels in their homes and spun their own yarn. And now, here I was, right at the source of the finest wool in the world in its most natural form.

One day, early in January, Mom called.

"I met this lady from Mona Vale," she said, "she has a seventeen-year-old daughter, Diana, who lost a lot of weight. She's down to 6 1/2 stones (91 lbs.) and has gone through an emotionally difficult time. The doctor recommended she go away somewhere quiet for a while to recoup and gain some weight back. I told her Mom about you and Moonan Flat. She was very excited and asked me to please see if you could take Diana for a couple of months. All her expenses will be covered."

"Well, I need to talk that over with the Committee," I said, "I'll let you know."

The Committee didn't mind as long as it did not interfere with my availability to the community and so a few weeks later, Diana arrived brought to Moonan Flat by her parents. She was a pretty brunette teenager with large brown eyes and a sharp mind. Her frame was skinny, almost transparent, but her appetite improved in the fresh country air in spite of my inadequate cooking skills. Nursing fascinated her and she was constantly asking questions.

"Oh, how I would love to see a baby born!" she said one day.

"I don't deliver babies here if I can help it," I explained, "most of them go to the hospital in Scone."

However, during the next week, I got a visit from Mrs. Wilson, a pleasant, plump woman who lived close to the Community Hall. Her husband was a truck driver.

"You know Lynn Allen is having another baby," she announced after Diana served us a cup of tea.

"Yes, I noticed," I said. "She lives right over the hill behind the church, close to Old Blue, doesn't she?" Old Blue was the local drunk, harmless, poor and toothless.

"That's right," Mrs. Wilson said, "Lynn has four children, all born close together. Her husband is gone most the time and does not support her but she's a very good mother and housekeeper. Her kids always look nice and clean."

"Yes," I said, "there's always a load of clean laundry on her lines."

"Right," Mrs. Wilson agreed. Then coming to the point, she continued, "I wonder if you could deliver the baby here, Sister. She can stay at my home afterwards so you can check her, still you won't be tied down here at the Center. Some of our friends will take care of her other kids."

Diana's eyes opened wide.

"Please!" she said to me, "will you do that? I'll help you! I'll do anything you say! I won't get in the way, I promise!"

"Well," I hesitated, "it's against BNA rules since she won't be an emergency. But if you can take her right after delivery, I guess that'll be all right. I need to clear it with the Committee, though."

The Committee OK'd it and I had Lynn come in for an appointment. She was a nondescript, plain woman, polite but numbed by a life of abuse and neglect amidst one pregnancy after another. I felt sorry for her but admired her courage and efficiency for keeping her humble home and children in such good shape. She was about seven months pregnant, had not had any checkups but appeared in good health. Her previous pregnancies had been uneventful.

"I usually have a very short labor," she said.

"When's your due date?" I asked.

"Early February, I think."

"I want to see you once a week," I said. "If you have any pain or if your water breaks, I want to see you right away. Call or get a ride, OK?"

She promised she would. Diana was ecstatic.

"Can I watch?" she asked again.

I hesitated. A seventeen-year-old watching a delivery? What if she fainted or cried or got sick?

"Please!? I promise I'll be OK. Can I do anything?"

"OK, you can watch," I said finally. "You don't have to do anything but I am going to walk you through the whole procedure beforehand, step by step, so you know exactly what is happening and why. We're going to get the hospital room ready, have everything we need sterilized and set up since we don't know when she will deliver."

We went through the entire routine several times. Secretly, I had all kinds of questions - not about Diana but about myself. I realized I had never delivered a baby all by myself. There had always been people around me to hand me the basins, receiving blankets, cord ties, scissors and other things. Of course, I could have all this ready by the bed. Could I trust Diana as my assistant? I decided not to count on her. I planned a strategy, mentally going through the motions. It had better be an easy delivery, I thought. After all the preliminaries were completed, there was nothing else to do but wait.

Two months later, Diana had gained almost 20 lbs. Her sunken cheeks were pink and glowing, her rib cage not so prominent. Even her hair had an added luster to it. January came to an end. February entered with bright, sunny, summer days. It was 1960, a leap year.

Lynn faithfully came to see me once a week. Everything checked out just fine. The lazy summer days came and went. One afternoon, Barbara Shepherd called. I had met her and her husband, Gorden, at a school function some months ago. They were a friendly couple in their thirties with two children. We became friends and often spent time together shopping or just relaxing at their farm on weekends. Gorden was a strapping farmer, raising steers on a fairly large ranch several miles beyond Ellerton. He had also been one of the ballerinas at the concert.

"Aubrey," Barbara said, "Gorden was hurt by a steer. He hit him in the hand with a horn. It's bleeding pretty badly. We're on our way to see you. Just wanted to call to make sure you're there."

"Put a pressure bandage on, Barb," I said, "I'll be here."

Within an hour they pulled up at the Center.

"Hi Gorden, been steer wrestling?" I asked, removing the home made bandage. He didn't smile.

"I don't want any needles," he stated grimly.

"Well, let's see what we have here," I humored him, "can you move your fingers?"

I saw a mangled, bloody hand but as I carefully began to clean the area, it didn't seem too extensive an injury after all. The steer had hit him hard, causing irregular, ragged cuts over the entire back of his hand. He moved all his fingers well and squeezed my hand with vigor. There was no tendon or muscle damage either. Great!

"You're lucky," I said, "could have been much worse. Just need a few stitches, that's all. You'd better go to Scone for that."

"I don't want any stitches," Gorden said, quite determined, "or shots."

"But you need a tetanus shot," I stated matter-of-factly, "and a penicillin shot, too."

"I told you, Sis," his voice rising, "no needles! No shots!"

Exasperated, I looked at Barbara. She shrugged her shoulders.

"He's always hated needles," was all she could say. "Sorry, I can't help you."

We continued to argue till I realized it was just no use, he was not about to go to Scone or get any shots. What could I do?

"Can't you just bandage it?" he wanted to know.

"Yes, I can," I replied, "but I can't guarantee it will heal well."

I remembered my first patient, keeling over with half a stitch in his hand, getting sick on my clean floor. The butterfly dressing I had finally resorted to had done the trick and his hand healed beautifully.

"OK, Gorden," I made up my mind, "I'll try and fix it without stitches but you're a big baby and I won't guarantee anything! Besides, you won't be able to use your hand at all for anything for at least a week to ten days. Not at all! Understand?"

"No problem," he promised, "as long as you don't give me..."

"...any needles," I finished it for him. "Here, sit down over here."

Gorden was a hairy man, even his hands were covered with long, black hair. I shaved the injured area, cleaned it carefully and put some antibiotic ointment on. Several thin strips of butterfly tape held the ragged edges of skin together. A dressing and bandage covering his whole hand came next. Then I added an arm splint which covered his lower arm, wrist and hand. His fingers bent over the edge. An ace bandage followed to keep the splint in place, then an arm sling to keep the whole arm immobilized. For the first time, Gorden smiled. Satisfied, he went home. A week later, Barbara called.

"How's Gorden doing?"

"Aubrey," she said, "you won't believe this! I am exhausted!"

"Why?" I asked, surprised.

"He took your advice literally. He won't do anything! I have to feed him, dress him, bathe him, even take him to the bathroom. He's driving me nuts!"

I laughed. He was taking my threats seriously.

"We can't come in till next week," she continued, "the car broke down."

"That's fine," I said, "but he can't move his hand till I have seen it."

"Well, I'm getting used to it," Barbara sighed. "See you next week."

Gorden looked rested and Barbara quite tuckered out when they returned. I removed the sling, ace bandage, splint, gauze bandage and finally the dressing on the back of his hand. Clean, pink skin greeted me, healed perfectly with hardly a scar.

"Good boy!" I told him, "you can start moving your hand again."

Gorden's arm was still in the same position as when I removed the splint and the bandages, wrist extended, fingers sharply bent.

"Gorden," I repeated, "you can move your hand again!"

He did not move. Just sat there and stared at his hand.

"What's the matter, Gorden?" Barbara said.

"I can't move!" Gorden stammered, "I'm paralyzed!"

I held his hand and moved each finger back and forth.

"Do you feel this?" I asked.

"Yes," he said.

"Good, you'll have to move your fingers with your other hand now. You've been so completely immobile for two weeks, the muscles are stiff, that's all. Here," I found a small rubber ball, "take this home and squeeze it till your strength comes back. Move your wrist too."

Still staring at his "paralyzed" hand, Gorden finally left with a greatly relieved wife. Four weeks later, I saw him again just before my departure from Moonan Flat. There were no signs of infection. The hair on his hand had grown back, his grip was as firm as before the injury and for scars there were some tiny, thin, white lines. He did not show any signs of tetanus, either.

"See, I was right," he beamed, "I didn't need any shots or stitches after all!"

It was now the end of February. Lynn still wobbled around, carrying an active baby that wasn't eager to be born. She was overdue. I consulted with a Scone physician who advised to do nothing but wait and observe. On February 29, I heard a soft knock on the front door before time to get up. Sleepy, I grabbed my bathrobe and opened the door. It was Lynn. She was alone and on foot.

"Sorry to bother you, Sister," she began, "I don't have any pains yet or anything else, but I do feel some pressure so since you said to come..."

"Please come in, Lynn." I was wide awake now. "Let me check you."

Diana had heard the knock on the door also and quickly joined me, still in pajamas and bathrobe.

"I'll check her first," I said to her, "then we'll get dressed and make some tea."

I threw a sheet on the bed and readied Lynn for an exam. As I looked for some gloves, I suddenly noticed a little head, ready to pop out. Oh no! I gasped. She's fully dilated! Ready to deliver!

"No time for tea, Diana," I yelled. Or to get dressed or to get gloves, I added to myself.

The baby practically birthed itself. I grabbed it with both hands and without another moment's hesitation, junior made a smooth entrance into the world. He let out a healthy yell as I held him upside down in my bare hands still clad in my bathrobe, hair in rows of large rollers. Diana watched the whole thing from her place near the window. She was awestruck, speechless, her eyes big as saucers. I cut the cord, wrapped the baby and put him in the little bassinet. Then I asked Diana to make some tea.

"That was wonderful!" she beamed, finally finding her voice, "that was absolutely marvelous! Oh, I will never, ever forget this!"

"Neither will I," I thought.

After this grand finale, my time in Moonan Flat was rapidly coming to an end. It had been a good year, trying and lonely at times, frustrating and funny at others but all in all well worth the effort. I had come to love these simple country folks. Friendly, honest and hard working, they always had time to help a neighbor, fix a truck, cook a meal or have a beer at the pub to discuss their harvest or the latest price of wool. Even the sheriff and I had become friends. Bruce's wife, Pat, had heart palpitations at times, something that scared her badly. The doctor in Scone assured me there was nothing I could do for her except give her a sedative, which I did. However, keeping her company proved to be the best treatment.

When word got out I was going to California, several folks just did not believe me. I may as well have said I was going to the moon. Going to Newcastle or Sydney, that was possible, even the old country, England, but California? Who would want to go that far? Diana had left a few weeks earlier, determined to go into nurses' training. She was back to her normal weight and had a healthy outlook on life. Some Dutch friends of my folks, Rien and Dini Boortman, were due for a vacation and came with their little son, Jeffrey, to pick me up. The Boortmans stayed a few days to relax in the quietness of the Upper Hunter country. I had packed my belongings, closed accounts with Daphne and finally retired for the last night at the BNA. The Boortmans occupied the little hospital room and the spare bed on the veranda.

During the night, a very pregnant lady knocked at the door. Would you believe she was Dutch? Her Australian husband was taking her into Scone but she did not think she could make it. I was able to check her and called the doctor.

"I can't possibly deliver her," I told him, "I'm leaving tomorrow, everything is packed."

He told me to give her a mild sedative and send her over. She refused the shot - another patient deathly afraid of needles. I had prided myself on the fact that many of my patients were still holding their breath to feel that prick when the injection was already over. Some who were sleeping, never even woke up when I gave them a shot. Kids kept smiling (some of them, at least) not knowing a needle had been jabbed into them. I revealed these skills in detail to my reluctant patient but all to no avail. No shots! Period!

"Well, then you better make it to town fast. I can't help you," I finally declared.

"Will you come with us? Please?" they begged.

Why should I ruin my last night with another wild ride into town? Did I really have to? Yes, of course, I had to. I had known it all along, got dressed again and squeezed into the small truck with my familiar emergency bag. We made it safely to Scone. The baby was born an hour later. David, the new father, took me back home to the Center. It was nearly morning when we got there.

A few hours later, I closed the door of the BNA Center behind me for the last time. Yes, it had been a good year but now it was time to move on. Uncle Sam was beckoning.

HOLLAND

Mom and Dad skating in Holland, 1929. Notice the long, wooden Dutch skates strapped under their shoes.

"I don't want to play with that guy!" I cried in my sandbox. "He doesn't know how to talk!"

Our home in Blaricum, Holland.

Later we became friends. Mickey, Helen and I take
a stroll down our street, the Dwarslaan (1938).

Helen and friend on the greengrocer cart,
a local vendor who came by twice a week.

When school was still in session during the early war years, we posed for
a picture (1941). Here is our third and fourth grade classes in Blaricum.
I'm sixth from the left, center row with big bows in my hair.

Doe, the stage director (left), me and
Mickey take a break during playtime.

Typical Dutch farm, this one in Blaricum. Farmer's living quarters in
front with the cows in back during the cold, winter months.

In 1945, we were liberated by the Canadians. Two of them, Whitey and Tubby, became family friends. Dad, in uniform, had joined the Underground.

During the severe winter of 1944, icy roads became our skating rink.

During the lean years of World War II, all trees were cut down and used for fuel to keep us warm. Here Dad and friend are busy with a handsaw.

A few weeks before the war ended, the home of our neighbor was torched by Dutch Nazis.

AUSTRALIA

Sailing into Sydney's majestic harbor
was an unforgettable experience in 1952.

Our first home in Collaroy was a one-bedroom flat, upstairs,
close to the beach. The outhouse was in the back.

INDONESIA

At the well in Depok, our source of water. From left to right: Mom, Baboe (cleaning lady), cook, Anna, me, *kabon* (errand boy/gardener) and Helen.

Above: View from the bridge over the *kali* (river) just outside Depok.

Above: Our veranda in Depok where the flying ant invasions took place. Left to right: Uncle Auke, Helen, Dad, Hans (Dutch MP), me and Henk Koevoet (also Dutch MP), former neighbor in Holland.

Left: Helen in a *betja* in Djakarta. It proved to be too small for two Dutch women.

Forlorn, Dad shared his lunch with the pigeons at Sydney's Botanical Garden.

We fell in love with the beaches, the people and the weather. Collaroy Beach with olympic-size saltwater pool in front.

Sydney Hospital on Macquarie Street, my home for four years.

Right: The busy second-year nursing student in the "Pan Room".

We finally graduated in 1957. Sister Rodmell, our tutor, far right. Betsy fourth from left (back row) next to me (third). Note the mattresses on the veranda of the second floor. We lugged these on our shoulders every time a patient was discharged.

1958. Another graduation. Meet the new midwives. My friend Margaret, second row, far right. Me, as usual, in the back, second from left.

Brisbane's impressive City Hall where I sang in the Municipal Choir and became an Australian citizen.

At "Casualty" (ER), Brisbane General Hospital. Two ambulance drivers deliver a patient.

My pride and joy! "Sister Hoffmann" shows off her very own garden. Small building in back is the Police Office. After the garden grew to perfection, the policeman's horse ate it all!

BNA Supervisor, Miss Roach, during a short visit in front of my Bush Nursing Station in Moonan Flat. She almost did not get any supper.

Ivan Icorn, teacher of one-room Moonan Flat School with thirty-five kids ages five to fifteen.

A huge flock of sheep drifts across the road.
All traffic comes to a halt.

The bridge over Hunter River was flooded after rain.
The only way across was on foot or horseback.

Betsy visited during Miss Roach's visit. Here she sits near the water tank
on the side of the BNA bulding. Our only source of water was rain which
was a scarce commodity.

CALIFORNIA

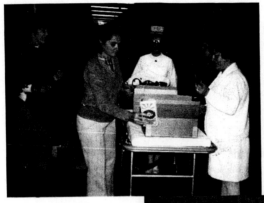

Our first offical act as an HCF group - distributingBibles at our Hospital. Right to left: Jean Clary, RN; Bette Hamilton, NA; Regina Cronin, RN; Inez Detwiler, Secretary and Lillian Havens, RN.

Busy Nurse in the Recovery Room in San Clemente, 1972. I exchanged veil and uniform for a scrub gown.

Some of the original HCF group. Left to right: Lupe, at whose home we had our first outreach meeting; Regina Cronin, RN; Carol Lee, Ward Clerk and Linda Francis, NA, who first told me about HCF.

Helen, now a Psychiatric technician, often helps out at HCF seminars and conferences.

Sandy, home on leave from the Air Force, loves to visit his grandparents.

Below: Delegates from all over the world came together for an International Staff Conference in Holland.

NATIONS ARE WAITING - a challenge for all.

SPECIAL FRIENDS

Our first National Conference was held in Tulsa, 1980. Left to right: Rev. Ken Ragoonath, Trinidad; Brother Andrew, Holland; Margaret and Bill Malcomson from Pittsburgh.

Above: Francis Grim and his wife Erasmia, founder of the Internat'l Hospital Christian Fellowship.

Joni Eareckson-Tada featured speaker at our National Conference San Diego.

Corrie ten Boom was made an Honorary HCF Member.

Chapter 8

CALIFORNIA

It was wonderful to be back in civilization again. I had missed the beach with its stiff ocean breeze, crashing white, foamy surf, its marching lifeguards and far, clear horizons, the pigeons and screeching seagulls, various scents of suntan oil and the many brightly colored beach umbrellas on the soft, white sand. My visits to these sandy shores were limited, however. There were many things to be done. Appointments with the U.S. consul in Sydney, boat passage through Cooks' travel, passport application, college entrance formalities, housing arrangements, lists of things to bring and pack to say nothing of the many goodbye visits to friends and colleagues. And then one bright April day in 1960, just before my 27th birthday, we crossed the gangplank of the P&O luxury liner, "SS Orsova", moored just underneath Sydney's Harbor Bridge, very close to where we had arrived from Holland eight years before.

Again, Henk and Bets Zwart and their two children were there to see me off. So were Mom, Dad and Helen, of course. Helen and Tom had given me a camera so I could send pictures back from all the exotic and faraway places I would see. I had practiced taking slides of familiar places in Sydney so my own memories of Australia would remain fresh in mind as well. My cabin was comfortable. No passengers in the hold on this cruiser. Instead, the ship seemed filled with happy tourists. Three loud, booming whistles announced the "Orsova's" imminent departure, time for all visitors to get off. Hugs and handshakes, followed by wild arm waving from the quay. The band played and confetti streamers snapped one by one as the huge ship slowly edged away. The familiar Sydney Harbor Bridge now towered in front of me. I took several shots of it as we gathered speed and headed for the ocean. The bridge became smaller and smaller till we finally rounded the harbor heads and everything familiar faded from sight. The finality of my departure began to sink in. With mixed feelings of adventure, sadness, anxiety and anticipation, I found a comfortable desk chair and stared at the blue expanse of the quiet Tasman Sea. Another ocean, another ship, another destination. What would await me at the other end of this trip? Little did I know.

We were headed east and slightly south for Auckland, capital of New Zealand, where we arrived two days later. Sightseeing tours on comfortable busses with excellent guides were at our service. I had heard much about the beauty of New Zealand and was not disappointed. The island was lush and green, mountainous with magnificent coastal views. We even visited some beautiful botanical gardens where I saw my first real live kiwi, New Zealand's famous wingless bird. Dressed in colorful costumes, a group of native New Zealanders, the Maoris, came on board during the evening for a special performance of their lively, graceful dances. The following day, we left Auckland and headed north, leaving the Tasman Sea and entering the quiet Pacific for the Fiji islands. Three days later, we entered the harbor of Suva, Fiji's capital, a lazy, laid back, palm-filled island full of happy brown skinned people with large crops of black curly hair. Another tour bus took us sightseeing around the island and dropped us off at a large hotel. A pig wrapped in banana leaves, surrounded by smoldering charcoal, was cooking in a deep pit on the grounds in back of the hotel for our dinner. The area was marked by some fierce-looking totem poles.

After Fiji, we continued our trek north on the quiet vastness of the blue Pacific. On Tuesday, April 29, we crossed the equator, home of Father Neptune. The next day it was Tuesday, April 29 again, making for an unusual, eight-day week. Honolulu was to be our next port of call. Back in Holland, Hawaii had been a magical name, synonymous with grass skirts, hula girls, guitars, palm trees, sun-drenched beaches and deep blue oceans. As none of this was even remotedly synonymous with Dutch culture or customs, everything associated with Hawaii had always been more a magical concept than a real place. As teenagers, we even idolized Dutch musicians playing Hawaiian music. Gazing at blond, blue eyed singers sporting large flowers behind one ear and leis around their shapely necks, backed by fair-skinned guitar players in bright-colored shirts, was the closest we ever hoped to come to the magic of Hawaii. If my friends had guessed that I would actually set foot on this legendary island, it would have caused quite a stir. Too bad no one, including myself, knew it at the time. But here it was actually happening, the magic of Hawaii was waiting for us right at the harbor. A Hawaiian band, hula girls and lots of leis, one for each passenger, in fact. The weather was balmy with bright skies, blue and clear. There were waving palm trees just like the pictures. Somehow, though, because of my long absence from Holland and time spent on Java and Australia, the magic was diluted. There were surprises, however, but of a different kind: the huge American cars, people driving on the right side of the road, American accents and dollar signs instead of pounds. An Australian girl I met on board and I took a bus and toured the whole island. We saw endless fields of pineapples, gorgeous views from high vantage points with vast, green vistas flanked by towering volcanoes in the distance. Memories flooded back as we passed through Pearl Harbor. We tippy-toed on shoeless feet through mysterious temples and impressive churches, passed Chinaman's Hat Island and eventually returned to Waikiki Beach. After Sydney's matchless beaches, I was a little disappointed to see my dream island not quite as heavenly and perfect as it had been in my childhood imagination. But the hula girls, dancers and music brought back the magic again. These people were the real thing! Amazing! They actually existed, swaying in real grass skirts under real palm trees with real Hibiscus flowers behind their ears.

All too soon we had to leave our enchanted island and continued northward. After several days, the coast of Washington appeared in the distance followed by the Lion's Gate and rainy Vancouver in Canada. Another bus tour through sunken gardens, suspension bridges, totem poles and beautiful suburbs and it was time to move on again. Now, we were going south and *I left my heart in San Francisco* was a popular song on board. The next day, it became a reality as we passed Alcatraz Island and the Golden Gate Bridge. I wanted to visit San Jose where the headquarters were located for that spiritual, mystical organization I had belonged to for so many years. Imagine meeting these people who had such a tremendous access to ancient wisdom and knowledge. I took a bus from San Francisco. In San Jose, I found the elaborate building complex and was cordially welcomed by an elderly man assigned to be my host. He showed me around the Egyptian-like buildings and even arranged a short visit with the president. Though highly impressed with the facilities, I was nevertheless quite disillusioned by the people I met. They were so very ordinary, spoke of mundane, everyday things and never even mentioned mystical or spiritual concepts. I don't know what I had expected but after this visit, my enthusiasm and awe for the whole organization and what they represented took quite a blow.

Back in San Francisco, it was time to leave again. Los Angeles, our final destination, was just a few days away bringing a most pleasant, three-week boat trip to an end. San Pedro, LA's sprawling harbor, filled with arriving and departing vessels of all kinds and descriptions, loomed ahead. A tugboat pulled the "Orsova" to its designated pier where a small crowd was waiting, scanning the decks for familiar faces. I was supposed to meet Ron Watson, a New Zealand student at LACC but didn't know what he looked like. However, as soon as we had disembarked, a dark haired, rather short young man with a disarming smile, walked right up to me and said:

"Are you Aubrey? Welcome to California."

Ron was a good letter writer and had supplied me with all kinds of interesting and useful information about my new country. Now he even had taken time off to pick me up.

"Hello Ron," I said, "nice to finally meet you. I sure appreciate your coming here to pick me up."

"Oh, that's all right," he shrugged, "sorry my car is so old."

Fancy apologizing for a car, I thought. I had never owned one so any vehicle that worked would have been a prized possession, no matter what it looked like or how old it was.

We left San Pedro and soon entered a busy freeway leading to Glendale, a fairly large, busy suburb in the foothills of the San Gabriel mountains where the College was located.

"I have rented a room for you in a hotel next to the College," Ron explained. "It's not much but it will give you a chance to look for an apartment yourself. There are quite a few available all over town."

We stopped by a friendly, two-story, ivy-covered building, taking up the better part of the whole block.

"This is it," he said, "that's the LA College of Chiropractic over there and here is your hotel."

He stopped in front of an old, white building, the Forum Hotel and lugged my suitcases up a flight of stairs. It was small but comfortable and adequate. Grateful, I thanked him again. He had to go to work, he explained but told me where I could find the Registrar at the college the next day.

I unpacked, ate a light dinner, took a hot bath and studied the College's curriculum again. The course consisted of 5,200 hours or 160 units. There were fall, spring and an optional summer semester. By taking a full load of classes for all available semesters, the entire course could be completed in three years. That's what I wanted to do. Most students took off to work during the summer which kept enrollment for these semesters down to small classes. Subjects included some familiar ones from my days in nursing training like anatomy, physiology, pathology and public health. Others were new such as chemistry - organic, inorganic and bio, detailed studies in neurology, X-ray, histology (study of tissue), physcial therapy and manipulation. Later, there was an externship in the adjacent out-patient clinic during our senior year. Would I really be able to get through all that? My eyes were heavy and I dozed off dreaming about miles of nameless muscles, nerves and bloodvessels.

"And where are you from, Aubrey?"

Our class had gathered around the catering truck during break. My new classmates, 15 in all, seemed friendly and interested in my strange accent.

"Australia," I said, "Sydney, Australia."

This caused quite a stir and more fellows came closer to observe this unusual student.

"How old are you?" asked one.

"Are you married?" another wanted to know.

"No, I'm not married."

"Then you WERE married," someone insisted.

"No, I never have been married." I said.

This seemed to come as a surprise to them. Twenty-seven and never been married must be a phenomenon, I thought. I wonder why?

There was only one other female student in my class, the others were all men varying in age from twenty to forty. They were very open and friendly. They were also polite, opening doors, offering seats, helping with coats and other little chivalries I was not used to. I was amazed at the friendly service in restaurants and stores. Even automobile drivers were different, more careful, less easily provoked. The often-asked question as to where I was from bothered me, however, and I resolved to get rid of my telltale Australian accent. One gallant student took me to a drive-in restaurant, a new experience. Fancy being served in your car right through the window. Another one cruised me through Hollywood, Vine Street, Grauman's Chinese Theatre and Sunset Boulevard. Imagine, me in Hollywood! Not that it was anywhere near as glamorous as I had imagined but the thrill was nevertheless quite real.

Every day, Monday through Friday, we were in class until two in the afternoon. Subjects were well presented, interesting and not too difficult. Whiley had been right, my nurses' training had been very helpful. A week after my arrival, I found a nice little furnished apartment within walking distance of the College and moved in. The cost of living, I discovered, was much higher than estimated. My savings would not be adequate to get me through the entire three years. I applied for, and received, a part-time work permit, obtained a social security number and asked a student for a ride to the nearby Glendale Memorial Hospital.

"Do you have a California nurse's license?" was the first question I was asked. "No, I don't. What do I do to get one?"

A long list of requirements followed, transfer of transcripts to the Board of Nursing in Sacramento was number one.

"While you're waiting for that," the friendly nursing supervisor said, "you can apply for a temporary license. You get that almost immediately but it's only valid for three months."

She hired me part-time for the graveyard shift and gave me a tour through the hospital. I was in for some very big surprises. Surprise number one - you buy your own uniforms, (anything will do as long as it is white), your own cap (the one from your particular training hospital) and you pay for your own meals. Other surprises - nobody wears veils, nobody is called Sister, nobody lives in, most student nurses are married, nurse's training includes psych and OB and only takes two to three years and, most surprising of all, student nurses pay a high tuition for their training, they don't work full-time like we did. They spent more time in classrooms than at patients' bedsides.

I was scheduled to work four days a week in a small, five-bed, Intensive Care unit, a new concept in those days. There were, as yet, no cardiac monitors, respirators, crash carts or other sophisticated equipment surrounding each patient. We could not only see our patients but also reach them and converse with most of them. The PM headnurse, Lottie Conroy, introduced me to my colleague and co-worker, Marilyn McGuire, a petite, friendly dark haired gal.

"Nice meeting you," I said, trying to sound like an American.

"Where are you from?" she smiled.

"Take a guess."

"It doesn't sound like anything I ever heard before," she pondered, "maybe England?"

I helped her out of the woods and she wanted to know all about nursing in Australia. We worked well together and I liked her. My vocabulary needed lots of adjustments, however. One day a physician came in and examined a patient. It was rather dark where he was standing so I grabbed a flashlight and asked him: "Would you like a torch, doctor?"

He looked up in amazement, laughed and said, "No, just a flashlight will do, thank you." I heard Marilyn snicker behind my back.

"What was so funny?" I asked her after the doctor left.

"We call them flashlights," she explained, "torches are something else."

One Monday at LACC during break time, I overheard the following conversation.

"How was your weekend?"

"We had a ball!"

"How was yours?"

"For the birds."

What kind of a ball? I wondered. Basketball, baseball, football? What kind of birds? If it had another meaning, what was it? Good or bad? Most confusing was the almost imperceptible difference between two, short gutteral sounds everyone used, meaning either YES or NO. It seemed perfectly clear to everyone except me.

"Nod your head - yes or no?" I would demand over and over again.

Finally, after about six months, my accent was diminishing and my vocabulary had adjusted. I received notice from the Nursing Board that my high school diploma was not acceptable as it was from a Third World country. I had to take a high school equivalency test in Los Angeles.

"How am I going to study for that?" I asked the College registrar.

"You don't have to study for it," she said, "it's all multiple choice anyway."

"What's multiple choice?" I wanted to know.

She explained. Incredible! They give you four answers and you choose the right one? Who has ever heard of that? Encouraged, I got myself to a huge examination hall in downtown L.A. and made little crosses in little squares for three days. It wasn't quite as easy as I had imagined, though. American history hadn't been taught in much detail in Indonesia and the ever present mysteries of English math still hadn't been completely decoded by my metric-oriented brain. When the results were mailed to me, I stared at rows and rows of figures on three pages of densely printed material. I returned to the College registrar. Passing grades at College were 75. I noticed some 80's and 90's but also low 70s.

"Did I pass or not?" I asked bewildered.

She glanced at the columns and smiled.

"Yes, you passed," she said.

"How can you tell?" I wanted to know.

"You're above the national average," she explained. "you did well on all tests, except math but your overall grade is 73."

"What's the national average?" I wanted to know.

"33," she said. "So you see, you did well."

Relieved, I mailed the results to the Nursing Board in Sacramento. Now they were ready for my transcripts from Sydney and Brisbane.

Several months later, I received notice that the transcripts were received but I was short on Psych hours and needed to take a three month course. A list of accredited colleges was enclosed. I extended my temporary license, took a leave of absence from my job at Memorial Hospital, dropped some classes at LACC and enrolled at Glendale Hospital and Sanitarium, an excellent new teaching hospital. By now I was used to the fact that I couldn't see all my patients all at once. There were no wards, just private and semiprivate rooms. Electric beds were a marvelous invention, TV and telephones in each room an amazing luxury.

Three months of intensive training later, I submitted my needed Psych hours to the Nurses' Board expecting a favorable response. Not yet, however. It was discovered that my student visa didn't qualify me for California licensure. That seemed to be the end of the line. Discouraged, I renewed my temporary license once more so I could stay at Memorial Hospital.

Classes at LACC continued. Ron, my New Zealand friend, went to night classes so I didn't see him very much. He was engaged to a nurse, he told me and would graduate soon. He hoped to return to New Zealand although his bride-to-be preferred to stay in the States. One of my classmates, a tall, deep-voiced young man a few years my senior, began to spent a lot of time with me. At first, it was just during school hours and study times. Then, we went out for lunch or coffee. He often took me to work. I was flattered and charmed by all this attention and convinced he was getting serious. My balloon was rudely deflated, however, when during breaktime one day, a female student came up to him and asked innocently, "How's your wife?"

To my immense surprise, he said, "Fine, thank you."

It had never occurred to me that this man could have a wife. Why was he spending time with me if he was married? I asked him. He seemed surprised and said, "Yes, I'm married, but my wife and I don't get along well." He then disclosed that this was his third wife! Hurt and disappointed, I stopped seeing him. It was a hard pill to swallow.

A few days later during a break, Bill, another classmate, was talking about Puerto Rican food. When the bell rang, he invited me over for dinner. I hesitated, then accepted. As soon as I arrived at his apartment, I asked him if he was married.

"No, I'm not." he laughed, "why do you ask?"

"Oh, nothing, just curious," I dodged.

Relieved, I ate a scrumptous, homecooked dinner he cooked up in his little apartment directly across from the College. We laughed a lot that night and the ice was broken. Bill hailed from Juana Diaz, a little place on the south coast of the island of Puerto Rico, a U.S. Territory in the Caribbean Ocean. He had spent many years in New York. Although fluent in Spanish, he still had a definite New York accent. Besides cooking, Bill liked to dance and patiently taught me the basics of the cha-cha, samba and other Latin classics. We discovered that the Hollywood Palladium often featured Latin bands. We tried out exotic, plush restaurants. On weekends, we explored the mountains, Lake Arrowhead and Big Bear or headed south for a shopping trip to Tijuana, Mexico.

Working four days a week and taking a full class schedule, my time off was scarce. When final exams came, we crammed together, Bill patiently explaining the secrets of chemistry, a subject he knew well. He often spoke of his mother, a lawyer and judge in Juana Diaz.

"Why don't you come along when I visit Ma?" he said one day,"I'm planning to fly down during next semester break."

A trip to the Caribbean? Sounded exciting. I counted my pennies and inquired about air fares. Delta Airlines flew directly from Los Angeles to San Juan, the capital of Puerto Rico. I decided to go.

We were in Puerto Rico for a week. It was delightful, a sunny, rather mountainous tropical island with miles of sugar cane fields, the latter supporting a thriving rum industry. We drove around the entire island to an old Spanish fort near San Juan in the north built on the white, sparkling beaches of the Atlantic Ocean. Then to the south where the Caribbean Ocean quietly caressed the tropical shores. No tides or beaches here, just a large, lake-like expanse of blue water.

Bill's Mom was a pleasant lady. She spoke English well. Most other people I met did not, however. My Spanish was very limited and the few words I had memorized didn't sound familiar. Puerto Ricans, I discovered, were one of the fastest speaking people in the world. All too soon our short vacation was over and we winged back to smoggy Glendale.

To keep up with my heritage, I checked out a Dutch social club, "Neerlandia," in Los Angeles. Once a month, they organized dances, produced plays and served real Dutch and Indonesian dishes. I met Eric and Ann Hof, a delightful Dutch couple, very active in "Neerlandia". They lived in Eagle Rock, close to Glendale. Eric, a born actor and comedian, approached me one day.

"We're going to do a variety concert," he began, "can you help getting some skits together?"

"I don't have much time but I can coach a male ballet," I began.

He thought that was a super idea. At the next meeting, he corralled seven men to attend rehearsals. It was Moonan Flat all over again - clumsy and uncoordinated those seven pranced across the stage, unbelievably ungracious but in unison just the way it should be. Later, on opening night, their bras, wigs, make-up and frilly skirts clinging to them at various odd angles, they brought the house down. The rest of the show featured more conservative acts which were also greatly appreciated. The whole evening was a huge success and "Neerlandia" continued to blossom under the capable leadership of Eric and Ann Hof.

The years seemed to fly along. We lived through the horrors of President Kennedy's assasination, color TV sets were introduced and we saw a new comedian named Bob Newhart. Classes and exams at LACC accellerated, many hours were spent in the clinic, treating patients, filling out forms, reading X-rays. We practiced adjustment and manipulation techniques on fellow students. State Board exams loomed in the distance. In the midst of all this, I was asked to work a few hours a week at the LACC research office headed by Dr. Henry Higley. A big landmark was the purchase of my first car, a light blue 1945 Ford sedan. A fellow student, Hugh McClure, let me have it for $150. We named it Old Blue. Even though it was old, it was in pretty good shape. Several students coached me behind the wheel as I needed to re-learn my almost forgotten driving skills.

Meanwhile, back in Australia, Mom and Dad had settled into new jobs in Sydney with a Dutch import and export company, booted out of Indonesia. They moved from Narrabeen and had bought a comfortable house in Collaroy. They were also planning their first real vacation in twelve years, a trip around the world lasting a full twelve months. Leaving Sydney by ocean liner, they crossed the Indian Ocean, Red Sea and Suez Canal. In Egypt, they caught a sightseeing tour to the pyramids and even rode a wobbly camel. Then off to Naples where a hospitable Italian family who did not speak a word of English entertained them and showed them around their ancient city. The trip continued by train to Holland. After visiting friends and relatives and reminiscing at memorable places, bike paths, lakes and heather fields, they burrowed in for a freezing winter at one of Mom's older sisters in the sleepy city of Weesp, Mom's birthplace. Severe snowstorms and prolonged sub-zero temperatures paralyzed most of the country for several months. They were stuck, bored and miserable. One day, they received a letter from me. It said: 'Mr. Voils, the College business manager, is going to have surgery. They need a replacement for a couple of months. I said you may be interested.' The prospect of some action in the future was like a ray of light. It kept them going as they completed their involuntary house arrest in Weesp.

In January, they finally left Holland by boat, the "SS New Rotterdam," crossed the Atlantic Ocean and after a rough and choppy crossing sailed by the Statue of Liberty in New York Harbor. Through my part time job at the College, I had contacted an affiliate college in New York and persuaded two students to pick Mom and Dad up, show them around New York and drop them off at Grand Central Station for their train to Chicago. From there, they would cross the U.S. by train to Pasadena, California.

Everything went according to plan. Mom later reported: "Those young men were fabulous! Here we were in a strange country in this huge city. The dock workers were on strike, we had to find our own hand luggage and then go through customs. Without the help of these two efficient students, we would never have made it. After customs, they drove us through New York, pointing out landmarks and offering us something to eat. They acted like professional tour guides and dropped us off in freezing temperatures at that huge Grand Central Station. Then they even sent you a telegram in California: 'Your parents are on their way.' We slept at the Y in Chicago, then boarded another train and began a cross-country trek to the West. It was fantastic! We loved it!"

Finally, they arrived in California. That night, Bill and I attended an LACC Delta Tau Alpha fraternity dinner. I left early to drive Old Blue to Pasadena to pick up the world travelers. I parked the car and waited on the platform. A distant, shrill whistle signalled the arrival of the train. Clanging bells and the closing of nearby railroad crossings followed. Soon, the massive engine passed me and ground to a halt. Doors opened and passengers came pouring out. I scanned the platform but saw no familiar faces. Suitcases and bags were gathered, people hugged and walked off, conductors scanned the cars. Finally, everyone was gone. The platform was empty. What had happened to my parents? I wondered. Did I get the dates mixed up? One conductor maneuvered a wheelchair to the back of the train. Absent-mindedly, I watched him, pondering what to do next. There was a soft tap on my shoulder. I turned around and there was Dad - alone! Where did he come from?

"Hi!" I stammered, "What happened? Where's Mom?"

He pointed to the back where the conductor was returning with his wheelchair. There was someone in it. Was that Mom? I strained my eyes. The platform was pretty dark. Yes, it was Mom! I ran towards her. She managed a weak smile. It was then I noticed her foot, wrapped in a large ace bandage. She was also holding two crutches.

"What in the world happened to you?" I yelled, trying to hug her.

"In New Mexico the train was going very fast and swayed a lot. A heavy, metal ashtray fell over and hit my big toe. I think it's broken."

"Are you in pain?" I wanted to know.

"Not so much now," she said, "it happened yesterday. A doctor came on board and looked at it. He put ice on my foot and told me to get it X-rayed as soon as possible. The railroad company will take care of all medical cost."

We got Mom and her crutches in the car and drove to Glendale where I had rented a comfortable, furnished apartment in a small courtyard, close to the College. Although the grand entrance into California had been marred by the incident, they were nevertheless extremely happy and grateful to be in Glendale. Graduation was around the corner and that was one of the reasons they had come.

The toe, it turned out, was only chipped. A small cast and crutches for three weeks was all that was needed. Santa Fe also offered a liberal settlement for the inconvenience. The day after their arrival was enrollment day at LACC. Dad, brand new to both the U.S. and the College, was in charge. It was a hectic day full of questions, problems and misunderstandings while endless lines of patiently waiting students filled the hallways. Somehow, he survived and sorted things out over the next several days.

Final exams came and went followed by graduation ceremonies "a la USA." For the first time in my life, I donned a cap and gown. We patiently listened to speeches by faculty and State Board officials while proud and cheering family members and friends filled the large auditorium. It was a momentous occasion.

A graduation party followed. Somehow, I had found time to get a long, rambling poem together hitting each student with something peculiar, dumb or funny they had done over the past four years. It broke the tension and we had a hilarious time.

State Board exams followed. They lasted three days and were rough, both the theory and practical parts. Now there was nothing else to do but wait. The time had also finally arrived for me to take Old Blue and show Mom and Dad around this fabulous country of Uncle Sam. I had made elaborate plans. One hot summer evening, around seven in the evening, we left for Las Vegas, our first stop. The car did not have air conditioning but I had borrowed a contraption full of water which hung in the open window. When a cord was pulled, it was supposed to cool the passing hot desert air blowing into the car. However, instead of cool air it sprayed a shower of warm water all over us every time the cord was pulled. Wet and hot but undaunted, we continued our trip through the pitch-dark desert. I had never been to Las Vegas nor had I driven through the desert and I was very curious as to what kind of landscape we were traversing. The hours and miles seemed endless, millions of stars and an occasional passing truck our only company. One truck blew some soot through our open window. A tiny cinder hit my eye. It hurt, I couldn't see and stopped to have Dad take a peek. He couldn't find it. The eye continued to tear and hurt.

"I think we should stop around here for the night," he said, "and not go all the way to Las Vegas."

Mom didn't drive, Dad didn't want to in a strange car in the middle of the night.

"Where in the world can we stay?" I asked. "It's pitch-dark everywhere." We can't stay here, I finally made up my mind, I'll just drive with one eye closed. And so I did.

When we drove into Las Vegas, it was two o'clock. My eye was fine. We found a small hotel with one vacant room. It only had one double bed but was air conditioned. The temperature outside was 110. I blew up a beach airmattress we had brought for just an occasion like this and tried to settle down on the floor. I was not very successful. Moreover, an hour after we occupied the room, the air conditioning quit. Sweating and balancing on my clumsy, uncomfortable mattress, I finally dozed off for a moment but woke up when a rhythmic snoring, in unison, started to vibrate through the room from the bed above me. The closet, I thought, I'll try the closet. I dragged the plastic mattress into the tiny closet space. However, to my dismay, I discovered the door would not close unless I maintained a fetal position. Finally, the coming of the dawn and a cool shower released us from our hot prison. Exhausted, I felt unable to drive that day so we decided to take a bus to Hoover Dam, Lake Mead and the Grand Canyon. A brilliant idea. Perking up in the comfortable, air conditioned bus, we arrived at the North

Rim of the Grand Canyon the next evening. A solid night's sleep followed which totally revived our sagging morale and put us back in our original high spirits. We gazed in awe at the majestic vistas in front of us, enjoyed the Indian dances and thrived on some excellent meals.

Back in Las Vegas, we took a spectacular trip by bus through this glittering city of a million lights and finished the night with a fabulous performance of "Flower Drum Song." I made my peace with Old Blue and the water contraption, loaded our luggage in the trunk and headed northwest. We crossed the desert again, this time by daylight and stopped in Barstow for a cold drink. Continuing north, we passed Bakersfield, then followed route 65 to Porterville, Lindsay and Exeter, the latter at the foot of Sequoia National Forest. Sequoia was our destination for the day. I had never been here either, and found highway 65 to be endless, narrow, hot and full of smoke-belching trucks. Stiff and tired, we continued to move across flat, hot pasturelands.

"Let's not go all the way to Sequoia," Dad suggested. "We can find a place here and continue tomorrow."

"I don't really want to stay here, Dad." I objected, "It's hot and dry and deserted. I hear Sequoia is beautiful and cool. We should be there soon."

We passed through the little town of Exeter. It was almost 120 degrees. "There are some motels over there," Mom pointed out, "why don't we stop and see if they have vacancies?"

"Let's see how far we have to go," I stalled. We passed through the park entrance gate.

"Seventeen miles and you're there," the friendly ranger said as he gave us a map and a receipt for the entrance fee.

"See? That's nothing," I convinced them, "we have done almost four hundred miles today, seventeen more won't hurt."

What I didn't realize was that these seventeen miles would take us from sea level to well over 5,000 feet via a very steep, narrow, winding road.

The first 2,000 feet went well, then Old Blue started to protest. Steam was shooting from under the hood. We stopped and noticed park rangers checking stranded cars. They filled our overheated, empty radiator and advised us to take it easy. We all realized that we had to continue now, no place else to stay on this narrow, winding path. We stopped again to cool the car. Dad stretched his legs and strolled behind some bushes. Suddenly, he stood nose-to-nose with a stately deer, both of them surprised at the encounter. The car cooled down and we slowly continued our steep climb. A small rock high above us continued to get larger as we ascended towards it.

"It's called Morro Rock," Dad announced, studying the map.

"Do you feel the cool air?" Mom asked, sticking a hand out the open window. We had reached the 4,000 feet level and continued to climb. The shrubs made way for trees, the density of the forest increased and soon we passed the first giant red trunks of the stately Sequoia's. Another five or six miles and we pulled into Giant Forest village. Stiffly, we got out of the car. The scene we beheld was totally unexpected. It was as though we had just entered a different world. Cool air soothed our hot skin, gigantic trees towered above and around us. Everything was green, sounds were subdued and seemed insulated by the silent, red giants.

"What a place," Dad sighed.

"So quiet and peaceful and cool," Mom chimed in.

I just stood in silence, glad I had persevered. It had been worth it. We rented a small cabin with two double beds, a woodstove and cute little veranda.

"Let's stay here," Dad suggested, "and skip the rest of the trip."

I smiled, not surprised by his suggestion. Dad loved nature and didn't like to be cooped up in a car.

"Well," I compromised, "why don't we stay a few days and see." We moved in and settled with a cup of coffee on the veranda.

"Did you see that sign 'Don't Feed The Bears'," Mom laughed. "Are there really bears here?"

"Must be," Dad guessed, "or they wouldn't bother with signs."

"Look over there," I cried, "a squirrel!"

"He's pretty bold," Mom noticed, throwing some cookie crumbs around. "Look, they're gone! See that large blue bird on that branch? It's pretty bold too."

"That's a Blue Jay," Dad said knowingly. "We have 'em back home too. Yes, they'll snatch up anything."

We basked in the majestic quietness of the giant Sequoias and slept soundly that night. The next day, we explored meadows and trails and even climbed the endless narrow stairway of Morro Rock. One night, we saw our first bear, a huge creature, foraging on our neighbor's picnic supplies. Later, we discovered these bears were regulars and came through every night. They were bold and smart and able to open anything - containers, jars, bottles, ice chests, tightly shut trashcans, nothing was safe or outside their ultimate reach.

At last, after five days of pure bliss, we decided it was time to continue our trip and leave this hidden paradise. We descended into Fresno, then ascended again, higher and higher till we reached Yosemite Village, a crowded place where we had difficulty finding accommodations.

Yosemite was also a revelation, especially the mammoth rock formations, clear Mirror Lake, the steep El Capitan cliff and the immensely tall waterfalls. We passed our namesake, Mount Hoffmann, at 10,850 feet. The air was thin, chilly and very clear.

Reluctantly, we started our descent to the hot valley below, into the Nevada desert. From there, we drove north to Reno, Carson City and then quickly climbed up again to famous Lake Tahoe, a huge, spectacular lake in the Sierra Nevada mountains. Two days later, we trekked west through Sacramento, California's capital, and later that day entered grape country, the lush Napa Valley, north of San Francisco. We toured some wineries, making the mistake of entering a sampling room on an empty stomach just before lunch but after a couple of hours of fresh air and a hearty meal were able to continue our trip. Going south, we crossed the famous Golden Gate Bridge in San Francisco and stopped at Fisherman's Wharf for a bite to eat.

The final day of our trip proved to be the icing on the cake - unforgettable Highway 1 - carved high above the sea into sheer mountain wall, weaving with the coastal countours, offering spectacular ocean views. We passed picturesque Monterey with its windswept trees, Carmel, Seventeen-Mile Drive, Big Sur, Morrow Bay and eventually the enchanting city of Santa Barbara. Transformed, we returned to mundane, smoggy Glendale. Adjusting to normal life was difficult.

"Wouldn't you like to live here?" I had often asked my folks.

"No, not really," Mom answered, "it's been great here. We've really enjoyed it but we have our roots in Australia, our home and a good job. We're too old to uproot again. Besides," she continued, "I can't wait to see my granddaughter."

Helen and Tom had recently become parents. Sharyn was right on time and healthy. However, after three months Helen took her to a public health facility for a routine checkup. My friend Betsy was working there.

"I think you need to have your doctor check her out," she told Helen, "there's something strange about the way she holds her head."

Helen agreed, so did the doctor. He immediately hospitalized Sharyn with what in a few days became a severe case of meningitis. She became gravely ill and the doctor feared for her life. Finally, after days of waiting, she pulled through but now extensive brain damage was suspected. Weeks passed. Finally, word came that all was well, no brain damage and complete recovery. No wonder my folks wanted to go home. So did I but somehow the American way of life had gotten under my skin. Bill and I had become rather serious and were talking about marriage and setting up a joint practice. Returning to Australia had lost a lot of appeal.

"How about you, Dad," I probed, "would you like to live here?"

He didn't answer for a while then, thoughtfully, almost wistfully, he agreed with Mom.

"I think we're too old to start all over again."

That settled, they gathered their belongings, packed their bags, said their goodbyes and returned to Australia. It had been a long but exciting year for them.

My student visa was about to expire and since I had graduated and was no longer a student, it could not be extended. It was early October, 1963. Bill and I went to the Immigration Department for advice.

"We're planning to get married next Spring," Bill explained.

The official shook his head.

"Sorry, you can't wait that long," he said. "Your visa will expire in two weeks. You can't stay here any longer; you may be deported if you do." He was friendly but serious. We thanked him and left. Back in Glendale, we debated what to do and finally decided on a quiet wedding in Las Vegas the following weekend. Not all that exciting but legal and inexpensive.

So, here I was back in Las Vegas - so soon, so unexpected. After waiting in line for a marriage license at City Hall, we found a little wedding chapel run by an elderly, friendly couple. It was simple but dignified and not quite as routine as I had anticipated. We left with some flowers, a picture of the event, a 7-inch recording of the ceremony and a Marriage Certificate. For our honeymoon, we took a long trip through Mexico, stopping in Mazatlan, Guadelajara, Mexico City and a few days in Acapulco. In Mexico City, we visited the huge, modern University complex. Bill seemed especially interested in the impressive buildings of the medical school.

Back in Glendale, I continued working at Memorial Hospital. I was transferred to a busy surgical floor where I relieved the charge and medicine nurses on their days off. It was a very pleasant and well-run floor with a good, supportive crew of aids and teamleaders. One day, we admitted a patient by the name of Mrs. Melcher. When I made rounds and entered her room, I stood face to face with Doris Day. What a surprise. Easy to talk to, we chatted amiably for a few moments. She was delightful, ordinary, simple and freckled, insisting on wearing a hospital gown like everyone else. I saw on her chart she was admitted for sinus trouble.

"Call me if you need anything," I said and continued my rounds.

Later that afternoon a doctor I didn't know approached the nurse's desk. He was a short, stocky, middle aged man, a little flushed and a little unsteady on his feet.

"I'm Dr. Crain," he said, "I need to see Doris Day. Where is her chart?"

I hesitated. Dr. Crain? Never heard of him. By now I knew most of the doctors. What should I do? He kept standing there, waiting for me to hand him Doris' chart. Did Doris know he was coming? Thinking fast, I decided to give him her chart, take him to her room but not leave them alone. Doris seemed surprised but remained polite. Dr. Crain sat down on her bed, produced some instruments from his pocket and examined her ears, nose and throat. He then made some notes, got up and left the room. At the desk, he wrote a few orders then slowly, he walked to the elevator and left. I grabbed the phone and called Doris' doctors, two well-known gynecologists who had admitted her. While dialing, Doris walked up to the desk.

"Who was that man?" she wanted to know, "he was loaded!"

"Hello, Dr. Ellis?" I said, "this is Surgical East. Did you send a Dr. Crain to see Doris Day?"

"Yes," came the reply, "we did."

"Who is he?" I asked.

"He's an ENT specialist on staff at Memorial. Why?"

"That's impossible," she exclaimed. "I'll be right over."

Within ten minutes they were there, both of them, apologizing to Doris, shaking their heads, unable to believe our stories were true. However, they were unable to get hold of the doctor in question. The afternoon moved on. It was busy and Doris settled down for the night. Just before the shift ended, the phone rang. It was the supervisor.

"You're getting a new admit," she began, "actually, its a medical patient but we have no beds on that floor. He has pneumonia and is running a high fever. He's in X-ray right now and will be right over. Put him in Room 318."

"What's his name?" I asked.

"Crain," came the answer, "he's a doctor here on staff."

"Doctor Crain?" I said, amazed, "the one who saw Doris Day?"

"Yes, that's him. He was sick all day. Doris was his last consultation. He didn't want to disappoint her doctors but he could hardly walk. So he took some medicine to perk him up and made it after all. Soon after he came home, his fever increased and he had difficulty breathing so his wife finally admitted him. The ER doctor says he'll be all right but he needs some fluids, rest and antibiotics."

The mystery was solved. I related the story to the incoming night shift and went home. Two days later when I returned to the floor, Doris was discharged. I never knew if she ever met Dr. Crain again.

By mid-Janaury 1964, the smell of eggs and bacon suddenly made me sick. I suspected it was morning sickness and went to see Dr. David McAnish, an OB doctor at Memorial.

"Yes," he said, "you're about six weeks pregnant. Everything seems fine." Excited, I wasn't sure how Bill would take the news. Ever since our return from Mexico, he had talked about attending medical school. Since he was fluent in Spanish, he could enroll at the University in Mexico City which would be less expensive than a U.S. school. I was not too crazy about the idea but didn't want to dampen his enthusiasm. He returned to Mexico for further information and things seemed to be falling into place. When I told him about our new arrival, he was delighted.

"I think you should stay here in California to have the baby," he advised, "you know all the doctors and the hospital. Then you can join me afterwards." I agreed.

Something else was developing as well. Mom and Dad were back in Sydney, Australia, happily settled in their cozy beach home close to their new granddaughter. However, after several months, I began to detect some interesting phrases in their letters. They missed California, missed the variety of scenery, the faster pace, the American people. I smiled. Our big trip through California and Nevada had made them homesick for the States just as I had hoped it would. One day, Dad resolutely walked into Cook's Travel Bureau and inquired about fares to the States. Then he stopped by the American Consul and inquired about immigration quotas. "Sorry, sir," the consul told him, "the Australian immigration quota for the States is full. There's a long waiting list."

Disappointment spread all over Dad's face. The girl behind the counter shook her head. Then a sudden thought struck her.

"You have an accent," she said, "were you born here?"

"No, we were born in Holland."

"Holland?" she said, "let me check something."

She disappeared, then returned with some papers.

"There is a small quota for Dutch-born citizens," she said with a smile, "but there are not too many applications. You are eligible to apply."

Dad surprised Mom with all this information when he came home. Do we really want to move again? they asked themselves. From my end, I greatly encouraged them to return to California. Now there would be another grandchild to see. They continued to weigh all the pro's and cons then, within six months, the matter was settled, the house sold, jobs terminated, furniture disposed of and papers processed. They would arrive in Los Angeles in July. I rented a small house for them, furnished it and moved in. Bill left for Mexico while I continued working at Memorial Hospital. The Office Manager at LACC never returned after his surgery. Another man was hired but he wasn't happy there. I talked with Dr. Higley again who said he would love to see Dad back at his old job. When they arrived in Los Angeles, trunks and all this time, there was a job, a home and a grandchild lined up for them. Later, the LACC bookstore manager retired and Mom got a job there, too.

In the meantime, my time for delivery was drawing close. The due date, August 26, came and went. Nothing happened. Remembering the potholes in Moonen Flat, Mom, Dad and I took a long hike in Griffith Park. At the top of a hill, quite deserted and far from the parked car, I felt some labor pains.

"Let's go back to the car," I casually suggested.

"Are you all right?" Mom asked, alarmed.

"Sure, I'm fine," I lied, "just a little tired."

I was scheduled to work that day. After we got home, I knew labor was still very mild and could take a long time. I decided not to say anything and go to work. After all, the Delivery floor was just underneath ours so what better place to be? The afternoon passed without much change except some pressure and continued mild contractions. As I was giving report to the night crew, they wanted to know why I stopped so often in midsentence.

"Never mind report," the night nurse finally said, "you better get yourself checked into Delivery."

I did. There was an Australian nurse in Delivery. She confirmed that labor was still in its beginning stages.

"If I were you I'd go home and try and get some sleep," she advised.

I passed this advice on to my folks and we all went to bed. However, nobody slept. My contractions were now getting stronger and kept me awake. I still didn't want to go to the hospital where I knew an enema would be waiting so we all got up and played gin rummy. Around three, I said, "This is ridiculous. Nobody is getting any sleep. I'll go back to the hospital and you go back to bed."

The night nurse was waiting with her enema.

"Try and hold it," she instructed.

"Are you kidding?" I groaned, "with a belly full of baby?"

I survived the ordeal, got a mild emetic for nausea and slept on and off the rest of the night. In the morning, hard labor finally got underway. The head was still high and the water would not break. In the afternoon, my Australian friend came on duty again.

"Are you still here?" she laughed.

Dr. McAnich came by several times. Finally, after office hours, he broke my water and took me to the delivery room. I was exhausted, sleepy and really didn't care what happened by then. Around four, Servando Alfredo finally made his debut, a healthy, screaming, eight pound, eight ounce bundle of joy. Two days later, I was home.

Dad had sent a telegram to Bill. The following week, I received a letter from him. I'm back in Puerto Rico, he wrote, Ma has cancer. She had surgery but it does not look good. Could you and Servando please come as soon as you are able to travel?

Ma sick? She was a picture of health when I saw her just a year ago. Move to Puerto Rico with a newborn? But this was her only grandchild. Should I deprive her of seeing him on her deathbed? Three weeks later, I packed a diaper bag, some clothes and personal things and flew back to Ponce, Puerto Rico. Ma was hospitalized and had round-the-clock private duty nurses. Her face lit up when I put the baby in her arms. I was glad we had come. Five weeks after my arrival Ma died. Bill was devastated. There was an elaborate funeral. Herminia Tormes was a well-loved lady and many came to pay their last respects. When it was all over, Bill left again for Mexico. He was to return to Puerto Rico after Christmas, he said. I stayed home with Servando, or Sandy as we called him, a name that once belonged to a brother of Bill, a brilliant young lawyer, who had died at an early age. I now lived alone in Ma's little cottage. There was no transport, not many neighbors spoke English and my Spanish was still very inadequate. A friend of Bill's, a cheerful chap named Ralph, came by once a week to take me grocery shopping.

Meanwhile, I received some interesting letters from Helen in Australia. It seemed the Yankee bug had gotten to them also. With both her parents and sister in the States, she and Tom had applied and received an immigration visa and were planning to join Mom and Dad in Glendale in a few months. I was delighted and could not wait to see them and little Sharyn who had made a full recovery after her bout with meningitis. In January, Bill returned from Mexico, stayed home a week and then left for San Juan for a reunion. He wanted me and the baby to go back to Mexico with him and get a job at an English-speaking hospital while he attended medical school. I felt I would rather return to Glendale where a good job was waiting and Helen could baby-sit Sandy. In March, I flew back to California. Sandy was seven months old, an active and happy infant, full of mischief with a quick, disarming smile. Helen had rented an apartment for me right next to theirs and baby-sat both kids. I applied for and finally received my permanent California RN licence and resumed my nursing job.

A few months later, Tom got a job offer in Laguna Beach, south of Los Angeles in Orange County. We took a day off, loaded the kids in the car and drove down to explore the area. We immediately fell in love with southern Orange County. Clear air, sunny beaches, a bright blue ocean, what a paradise! In the neighboring town of San Clemente, we leased a large, fully-furnished, three-bedroom home for a year. It was July, 1965. The only hospital around at that time was South Coast Medical Center in South Laguna about eight miles north of San Clemente on Pacific Coast Highway. Perched on a high bluff, its front rooms had a spectacular and unobstructed ocean view. Excited, I dropped in one afternoon and spoke with the supervisor, Leona Perras. Yes, there were job openings but I should see the Directress of Nursing in the morning. I did and she hired me for the PM shift in the newly opened Intensive Care Unit.

Back in Glendale, we packed to move to San Clemente. The day we arrived in San Clemente and moved into our new abode, something strange happened. After my return from Puerto Rico, I had started to smoke. I had been an occasional smoker before but now I was going through a pack a day. I knew it was unhealthy but continued, anyway. The landlady said she'd stop by that day to collect the rent, the first and last month plus a cleaning fee. As we were new in town, we had not opened a bank account and brought cash. When she arrived, Helen and Tom had their share ready but I could not find my portion. I knew I had put it in a "safe" place but now it was so safe, I couldn't find it myself. The house was still a mess. We hadn't unpacked anything and there were boxes and suitcases everywhere. I searched again - purse, billfold, jewelry box, make-up bag, legal papers envelope. Nothing. I found the waiting landlady.

"I'm so sorry," I explained, "I know it's here somewhere but I need some time to find it. Is there any way you could come back?"

"No, I'm sorry," was the firm reply, "we're leaving for the desert today besides, you agreed to pay today." She was right. I decided I needed a quiet place to concentrate and locked myself in one of the bathrooms. Thinking hard, trying to retrace my steps in Glendale as we were packing it occurred to me that I could pray. Why not? I did believe in God, after all. He knows everything even where the money was. Besides, didn't the Bible say "ask and it shall be given?" "Can you tell me where that money is, God." I said silently. No reply. "Please, God, You know where it is. I need to find it right now. Can't you tell me?"

Sitting silently in that bathroom, a strong impression suddenly filled my mind. "If you stop smoking, you'll find the money." What? Stop smoking? That's blackmail! I'll stop when I'm good and ready. Furious, I got up and started my search again, billfold, jewelry box, purse, make-up bag. No luck. Somehow, I knew I was never going to find that money until I quit smoking. How utterly ridiculous.

I stomped back to the bathroom, locked the door, sat down on the stool and fumed: "OK, God, I'll quit smoking. Now where's the money!?"

"How do I know you are really going to quit? Cigarettes are everywhere. What are you going to do with them?"

What was I going to do with them? Destroy them, I guess. I got up, opened the door and began looking again, this time not for the money but for my cigarettes. There was a half-empty pack in my purse, several full boxes in the bedroom and an extra supply in another purse. I found them all immediately. Now what? Flush them down the toilet? Too bulky, it would clog the drain. Throw them in the trash? Too tempting, I could retrieve them again. Finally, I soaked them in the bathroom sink, wrapped them in paper and stashed them in a trash can outside. Helen was keeping the kids quiet and the landlady company. Everyone thought I was searching for the money. In a way I was, but in a very roundabout way. The cigarettes disposed, I sat down on the john again.

"OK, they're gone. Now where is the money?" I demanded. Utter silence. What? Did I go through all this for nothing? How infuriating! I waited another moment. There was nothing, just silence, except for the dim voices from the living room and the sound of a passing car. Angry at my naive gullability, I got up, opened the door and marched into my messy bedroom. Again, for the umptieth time, I opened the jewelry box. No money. But then, almost automatically, I lifted the top tray inside the box. I hadn't done that before. Suddenly I froze. There, as plain as day, in the bottom compartment, was the money. I felt goosebumps all over. From the bathroom I had walked right to the very place where the money was hidden. Had that "conversation" in my head been real and not just a figment of my imagination? How scary! How awesome! In a daze, I rushed back to the living room and handed the landlady her money. She left and we continued to unpack. I didn't explain to anyone how I had found the money. Nobody asked. But from that day on, I didn't take another puff. I didn't dare. Besides, I told myself, I had really wanted to quit, anyway.

Life continued with long sunny days at the beach, busy afternoons at work. I received some disturbing news about Bill in Mexico. Other, previously ignored, factors also came to the front. Forced to sit down and evaluate my marriage situation, I was coming to the perturbing and sad conclusion that our social backgrounds, ambitions and lifestyles were becoming more and more incompatible. What happened? Who failed? Could we change? Bill was due for a visit from Mexico for the summer break. When he came, I confronted him with my misgivings and concerns about our different lifestyles. We talked but there seemed no solutions, only more complicated problems. When he finally returned to Mexico, I was drained. Dejected and heavy-hearted, I found a lawyer and filed for divorce. Then a month later, Helen's husband, Tom, accepted a new job in Pomona, eighty miles inland. In August, when our lease in San Clemente ran out, they'd be moving and I would be homeless.

Chapter 9

A NEW BEGINNING

"What pretty flowers you have!"

The voice came from the other side of the backyard fence. I was cutting a large bouquet of fragrant sweet peas Helen had cultivated against an old chicken coop.

"Thanks, aren't they lovely?" I admitted. I looked up and saw a smiling, wrinkled face framed by white curly hair, peeking over the fence. A large, red garden hat shaded her blue eyes from the bright sun.

"I'm Ruby Mae," she introduced herself. "I'm your neighbor." She pointed to a quaint, Spanish-style home, typical of San Clemente, behind her.

"Hi, I'm Aubrey," I said. "Would you like some flowers? There are so many, we pick them almost every day." I handed her the bunch I had just cut.

"Oh, thanks, I love the smell." She buried her face in the colorful pastel flowers.

"How long have you lived here?" I asked, trying to be neighborly.

"Only about three months," she said. "We used to live in Capistrano Beach on the Palisades but the doctor said I can't drive any more and there are no shops within walking distance there so we had to move. Too bad. I like it here," she added, "but I miss my home. It's the prettiest place on the Palisades."

"Where's the Palisades?" I asked.

"On the bluff just above Pacific Coast Highway."

"I think I know where that is. What did you do with your home?"

"We put it up for sale," Ruby Mae said wistfully. Then a thought struck her. "Are you looking for a place?" she gave me an expectant look.

"Well, we're here on a lease. My sister Helen and I live together. The lease is up in August and Helen is moving to Pomona but I like it here and have a job at South Coast Hospital. I would like to stay but I need a smaller place to live."

"Oh, are you a nurse?"

"Yes, I am. I also have a two-year-old son. I'm thinking of renting a small apartment. I can't really afford a home."

She nodded then changed the subject. We chatted for a while and she thanked me again for the sweet peas.

That night as I drifted off to sleep, I kept hearing Ruby Mae's voice: "It's the prettiest place on the Palisades." Wouldn't it be wonderful to have a home of my own, I mused, a place just for me and Sandy? I had moved seven times in the last three years and I desperately needed something private and stable, something just for me. Would Ruby Mae rent the house? I wondered if it had a backyard. We could have a dog or perhaps a cat. Yes, I was sure that if I asked her, she'd let me rent it.

Determined, I walked over to Ruby Mae's home the next day and rang the bell. There was no answer but I noticed her name on the door. It sounded Polish and I scribbled it on a scrap of paper. Back home, I opened the local phone book. There it was! Now I had an address. I got into my car and drove south to Capistrano Beach. All the streets in this sleepy, seaside village were short and full of curves. Finally I found a cozy, early American home with wood shingles on the roof, an abundance of pink geraniums in front and a large FOR SALE sign in the window. There was no one home but the key was available from a neighbor across the street. Before getting it, I walked around the side and opened a small gate to the backyard. There I found myself standing under an enormous pine tree. Its cone-laden branches spread out over the roof and backyard. A soft breeze rustled through its long, green needles, producing that typical pine tree sound I remembered so well from our forests in Holland. Birds were twittering in the many thick branches. Two small, grey doves softly cooed on the roof. Other trees, a fig tree and two large eucalyptus (real Australian gum trees) stood in the far corner. A large Wattle, another Australian friend, towered in the center, completing a huge green canopy which covered the entire backyard. A checkerboard of sun and shade spots danced on the ground below.

Oh, what a piece of heaven! I thought. What a sanctuary. Spellbound, I didn't move, holding my breath, afraid the magic of this hidden paradise would vanish. This was too good to be true. Oh, wouldn't it be wonderful to live here? Would there be any possibility I could...? Oh, I do hope she will rent it, I mused. Why not? She has to. I'll be the best renter she ever had. I broke the magic moment, crossed the street and met Sue, a bubbly mother of two. She gladly gave me the key and let me explore the inside of my dream house. I found a cozy living room with fireplace, wood-paneled kitchen, two bedrooms downstairs and, to my surprise, an upstairs bedroom right under the roof, complete with slanted ceiling, a sink and a large closet. The house was partly furnished with a couch, coffee table and two beds. There were drapes and carpets in every room. Delighted, I returned the key to Sue, drove back to San Clemente and knocked on Ruby Mae's door again. This time she was home.

"I love your house!" I exploded as soon as she opened the door.

"My house?" she queried. "How did you find it?"

I told her. Surprised, she smiled.

"Sit down," she offered me a comfortable seat. "So you like it, eh? I told you it was the prettiest place on the Palisades."

"You are right. It is. I would love to move in, but," I paused and studied the wrinkles on her little apple cheeks, "I can't afford to buy a house. I'd love to rent it. Would you rent it to me? Please?"

She looked at me silently, studying my eager face. Some children were laughing outside. A dog barked. Finally, she broke the silence,

"No, we have to sell, but let me talk it over with my husband. Perhaps we can work something out where we can give you a loan ourselves and work out a small deposit and monthly payments you can afford. What do you think of that?"

Buy a home? Me? Alone with a small child?

"I don't know. I need some time to think it over," I hesitated.

"Well, we do too," Ruby Mae smiled, "so let's keep in touch."

She got up to let me out. Somewhat relieved, although still apprehensive, I slowly walked back home. I felt that, in some way, my entire future was at stake here. Little did I know that what laid ahead of me far surpassed my present desire for the cozy home or the peaceful backyard.

"You want to buy a home?" Dad said when I visited my folks in Glendale. "Do you know what that means? You can't call the landlord when something needs to be fixed. You are responsible for everything, the entire upkeep, also property taxes, home owners insurance..."

"Yes, I know all that, Dad." I interrupted him, "but I can ask friends to help with repairs. Besides, the house seems to be in good shape. The payments won't be higher than the rent which I'd have to pay somewhere else. And it will give me a tax break. Why don't you and Mom come over and see it?"

The next weekend they drove down from Glendale. I got the key from Sue again and they immediately fell in love with the house, just as I had. Especially the backyard. We also talked with Ruby Mae and her husband, Johnny. They proposed drawing up a contract, then have a lawyer approve it. Before the weekend was over, Dad relented and even offered to help out with the deposit. I couldn't believe my ears. I was about to buy a dream house! Just for Sandy and me. How incredible!

When August 1964 finally arrived, all the papers were signed and loan terms agreed on. Blue Chip stamps were traded in for some

additional furniture, secondhand stores provided the rest. Helen and
Tom and little Sharyn took off for Pomona while Sandy and I took possession of our enchanting new abode. It was everything I had hoped for
- peaceful, quiet, private and close to the beach. Snoopy, a scratchy but
abundantly happy poodle and Yappie, a shy, black cat, joined our
household. I left for work at 2:30 pm each day and came home around
midnight. On my way to work, I dropped Sandy off at a local baby-sitter and picked him up, sound asleep, in the middle of the night. He
never knew how he got from the baby-sitter's to his own bed.

We took long walks on the beach on my days off and I met some
friendly neighbors and generally kept busy with the house and the yard.
Life settled into a routine. Just what I needed. Eight happy months went
by this way. To stimulate my intellect yet stay home with Sandy as
much as possible, I signed up with Famous Writer's School, a tough
and rather expensive two-year correspondence course in writing. Many
long hours were spent on assignments which were critiqued and
returned later with notes and suggestions. It was challenging and satis-
fying; however, halfway through the course, I got the blah's.

I don't know what started it but slowly my days at home became
long and boring and too quiet. I missed the social life of my college
days, the sightseeing trips we used to make, the theater and concerts in
Los Angeles. I need a piano, I thought, that'll help, and perhaps a roommate. Yes, I can rent out the room upstairs. Good idea. I wasted no
time, put an ad in the local paper and pinned some notices on the hospital bulletin board. Pianos, I discovered to my dismay, were very expensive and out of my ballpark altogether. A few people called about the
room. Some women actually came by and looked at it. Nobody was impressed. I didn't like them and they didn't like the room. Disappointed,
I became impatient. Nothing seemed to be working out. What was the
matter with me? Depressed, I had a conversation with God. I met Him
on His own turf.

"It says, *Seek ye first the Kingdom of God, and His righteousness;
and all of these things shall be added unto you*" (Matt.6:3). I complained. "Well, I have been seeking the Kingdom of God all my life, so
I surely qualify for '*all these things*,' so how come I can't find a renter
for my room?"

Days went by but nothing happened. Nobody called, nobody came.
A week later, I prayed again.

"What's the matter, God," I was irritated by now, "why aren't You
adding '*these things*' like you said You would? I want a roommate and
a piano. What else can I do?" My answer was silence again.

However, as the quiet days at home continued, a proposition was
slowly beginning to formulate in my head. It was almost like a
dialogue. It went something like this:

" I know you believe in Me," said the Voice that was more like a thought, "and I appreciate that. But I want more than that. I want your whole life. Everything."

"My whole life?" I argued, "no way! Too risky. I may end up in Africa as a missionary." Somehow that seemed the worst thing that could happen to anyone. "Leaving this home and California? Never!" The matter was settled, God could stay where He was, safely in the distance. When I needed him, I would ask for direction, otherwise, I'd do fine on my own.

But the long and empty days continued and, almost in spite of myself, I found my mind dwelling on this strange proposition again and again. If I give my life to God, I pondered, He can do anything with me He wants. I will have no control. I can't make any decisions without His approval. Do I really want that? No, I don't!

Would He give me clear directions? Would He want me to do things I didn't want to do? Or couldn't do? On the other hand, what had I accomplished by myself so far? Not much. I was a divorcee in her early thirties, forced to keep a full-time job and raise a child alone. What was there to lose? Perhaps, who knows... if I gave my life to God I would get a roommate and a piano instead of going to Africa.

The struggle continued. Another August came and went, completing a full year in Capistrano. Sandy was growing up to be an active, healthy youngster. The issue of God became more pressing. I felt I had to do something. Slowly, over a period of several days, a decision took shape in my mind. Yes, I would do it. I would take the risk and give my life to God. But I wouldn't tell anyone. It would be kind of an experiment. After all, this whole idea could be just a figment of my imagination. One crisp fall evening in October of 1968, after retiring for the night, I took the plunge. Somehow, I felt like standing on the edge of a cliff on a very dark night. I was ready to jump but had no idea where I would land. How far down was the bottom? Was there a bottom? Would someone catch me?

"OK God," I said silently in my mind, "I do give my life to You. Everything. Do with me as You please. I'm all Yours."

I was very serious and meant every word although part of me kept saying, "You're crazy. What a risk!"

"Too late," I answered myself sternly. "It's done."

I turned over and went to sleep.

Just before dawn, I had a short but vivid dream. Perhaps it was a vision, I don't know. At any rate, I found myself sitting in a large convertible on the passenger side. A man in his thirties, dressed in a suit, was driving. We couldn't go very fast for around us on every side were hundreds of people, shoulder to shoulder, packed together. They were laughing and waving and obviously celebrating something very important. It briefly reminded me of the scene in Dallas just before the tragic assassination of president Kennedy. But this was different. There was no danger in the air, only joy and laughter and a happy celebration. But why? Mystified, I turned to my driver and asked, "What's the occasion?"

He seemed surprised I asked such an obvious question. He turned and looked at me. Then, with a smile he said, "It's because of you!"

Immediately, I woke up. Surprised, I repeated his strange statement. What did he mean? Me? Were thousands of people celebrating because of me? How could that be? What had I done? The whole scene was still sharp in my mind but made no sense. Suddenly, out of the recesses of my mind, a long-forgotten Scripture came to the front: "There will be more joy in heaven over one sinner who repents..." Where had I heard that? Maybe in Sunday School. Were these people celebrating because I had given my life to God? How awesome! I sat up in bed and rubbed the sleep from my eyes. Was that a dream? Yes, in a sense it was yet somehow I knew it was also a reflection of reality. Somewhere that decision I had made last night was heard, noted and recorded. It resulted in a big celebration. Amazing! Excited, I jumped out of bed, showered and dressed. I felt lighthearted and had a strong sense of anticipation. Humming, I got Sandy's breakfast ready. "There will be joy in heaven..., joy in heaven." Wow! That was incredible! (Luke 15:7 NIV)

A few days later, Barbara McDonald, a fellow nurse, and I took a coffee break. I liked Barb. She had been a teacher and was assigned to orient me when I first joined the staff. I could tell she had something exciting to share.

"Guess what happened to me yesterday?" she began after we filled our cups and found a table.

"What happened?"

"This elderly cousin of mine died and left me a baby grand piano. I've always wanted one but could never afford it."

"How neat!" I said. "Do you have room for it?"

"Well, yes," she said, "but I have to get rid of my upright piano."

"Oh, really?" my ears suddenly pricked up, "I've been looking for one for over a year."

"You're kidding? I didn't know you played the piano!" Barbara said.

"Well, I'm not very good, but I like to play just for my own amusement. How much do you want for it?" I held my breath.

Barbara looked at me. She knew I was struggling alone to raise a child and keep up house and car payments.

Finally, she said, "What about a hundred dollars?"

I could have screamed.

"I'll take it!" I almost shouted "if I can pay you a little each month."

"No problem," Barbara said good-heartedly, "I'll give you the bench also."

"Can you get it to my house?" I still couldn't believe my ears.

"Yes, we have a pick-up. My husband and son can bring it over next Saturday. By the way, it's in excellent shape. We've only had it for two years and it was brand new when we bought it."

"Barb, you're an angel. Oh, I'm so happy! Thank you, thank you!"

That Saturday, I had my very own piano. "*All these things*" were being added. Oh, how wonderful life was. "*There shall be joy in heaven... joy in heaven.*" Well, there was joy in my heart also. "*Joy in heaven over one sinner who repents.*"

But wait a minute, I now questioned myself, I didn't repent. I had given my life to God, yes, but I did not repent. After all, I certainly was not a sinner. Sinners are thieves and robbers and murderers. My record with the law was clean. I had never been in trouble with the authorities. Besides, sin and repentance were religious terms, used by those simple and narrow-minded church people I had met in the past. But if I had nothing to repent of, why did it say that there shall be joy in heaven over one sinner who repents? Perhaps I should find out what God's definition of sin was. Maybe it was not the same as mine. How could I find out? I supposed I needed a Bible. Well, I'd never had one before nor did I know anyone who did. Then I remembered Margaret's Bible, the one she gave me when we parted in Brisbane. I had been embarrassed and annoyed about it and had stuffed it under some clothes. What happened to it? Did I bring it to the States? I certainly hadn't seen it. I walked over to the crowded bookshelves in the living room and scanned the many nursing and medical textbooks and volumes on world philosophies and religions. Tucked away in a far corner, I noticed a small, dark blue book and pulled it out.

It was Margaret's Bible!

Delighted and curious, I began to search its finely printed pages. The King James English was unfamiliar and hard to follow at times. Some passages just leaped off the page, others were obscure. I curled up on the couch and began to read, haphazardly here and there, trying to find some definition of sin. It wasn't easy but after several days, a picture emerged. In fact, it was a simple concept once I saw it. Very simple. Basic sin, in God's eyes, was doing your own thing, relying on your own wits and intellect and ignoring Him. In short, a belief in God without a personal commitment to Him was sin. Well, that made sense. In that case, I was guilty and I had to repent. By turning my life over to

God, my sin of independence and "doing my own thing" was taken care of. I had simply switched bosses. I had moved from the driver's seat to the passenger seat. That's why I sat in the passenger seat in that convertible during the recent joyful celebration. Things began to get a little clearer and I continued to read Margaret's Bible. I was grateful now for quiet evenings which allowed me to concentrate on my new studies.

As the days passed, another matter rose in my mind. Was this God speaking again? Was He trying to tell me something else? This new thought soon became a very important question but I had no idea what the answer was. It was solemn and grave and seemed to be of the utmost importance. It was this: "What does the death of My Son on the cross mean to you?"

The words echoed over and over in my head. My first reaction had been: Nothing! Yes, I believed that Jesus was divine and the Son of God, born of a virgin, able to do miracles and deliver great sermons. I believed He was crucified, died and rose again and was taken up to heaven. I had always believed that but what did the death of Jesus on the cross two thousand years ago have to do with me? Nothing, as far as I could see. It was a gruesome historical fact. That's all.

There was no one I could ask. I didn't know any "religious" people and didn't go to church. My last church affiliation had been in Glendale quite some time ago. I had gone to that particular church because they believed all world religions had truth and value. Their favorite motto even came from the Bible: "*Christ in you, the hope of glory.*" The spirit of Christ, they said, was in all of us. I liked that. But there was no affiliate church in this area. Even if there was, I somehow felt that they wouldn't have an answer, either. In all my studies of philosophies and world religions, that subject of Jesus' death on the cross had never been mentioned.

One day during this period, I read an ad about a garage sale. I still needed some furniture and scanned the papers for moving sales. This address was close by so I got in the car, crossed the freeway and stopped in front of a large, ranch style home on one of our many hills. The door was open but no one seemed home. A neighbor saw me.

"You can go in," he said, "she will be right back. There's not much left but you are welcome to look."

Indeed there was not much left, only a very few pieces here and there. A lamp but not what I needed, a blue chair, but I needed a green one and some drapes which were the wrong size. Disappointed, I drove home and did some chores but I could not get that house out of my mind. Maybe the lady had come home by now, I thought. Maybe I overlooked something. But the house was almost empty. I had seen everything that was left. Half an hour later for no particular reason, I got back into the car again and drove up the hill to the empty house.

"Hi," a smiling, pleasant brunette opened the door. "Are you looking for something?

"Yes, I am," I began.

"Come in and help yourself. There is not much left."

I dutifully walked through all the rooms again - wrong size lamp, wrong color chair, wrong size drapes.

"Sorry, I can't help you," she said, sweeping out her dining room.

"Where are you moving to?" I asked her.

"Vista," she said, "what about you? Do you live here?"

I told her a little about myself, the new house and my job at South Coast Hospital. As I was talking, I noticed a large pile of books on the floor. "Are these for sale too?"

"No, they're not. Why, do you like to read these kinds of books?"

"Well, they sound interesting,"

"They are," she said. She put her broom away, looked at me and asked, "Do you go to church?"

"..Uh, no, not really. The church I used to go to does not have one in this area."

"What church was that?" she queried.

I told her. A broad smile covered her face, "Oh really? Yes, I used to go there. No they don't have a church here but you know, there's a place in San Clemente, close to the pier, a large home where they have meetings every Friday. In fact," she emphasized, "there are some medical people who go there. I met a surgical scrub tech there. I believe her name is Muriel."

She was so enthused, I wrote down the address and phone number and promised to check it out soon. Her name was Barbara Gould, she said, and she planned to drive down from Vista some Friday evenings to this house by the pier. We parted. Somehow, I felt I had known her for years. She was so bubbly, so friendly, so real.

A few Fridays later, I found the home, a sprawling, old, Spanish-style mansion overlooking the San Clemente pier. The large living room was filled with people seated on a variety of chairs, couches and even the floor. Some young men were strumming guitars. George, the host, opened with a short prayer and introduced the men who began leading some songs, simple tunes with simple words. I didn't know any of them but they were pretty and easy to learn. Then a speaker was introduced, a man not from the San Clemente area. He opened a big Bible and began to speak, quoting and explaining Scriptures in a very simple way. I was amazed. This was definitely not anything I was used to.

Some things he said I did not agree with but others made a lot of sense. Besides, the people were friendly and they didn't bother me with personal or spiritual questions. They didn't ask me to pray out loud. Others did pray but it was voluntary and spontaneous. Afterwards, Louise, the gracious hostess, served refreshments. I chatted with several people. When I left, they said, "Please come back. We'd love to see you again."

I knew they meant it. Back home, I pondered all I had heard that night including a remark the speaker had made which I did not agree with. He had stated that reincarnation was a fallacy and definitely not biblical.

"What about that, God?" I asked. "Surely he was wrong?"

I received no answer except a strong urge to just put that whole subject on the back burner. "Don't even think about it. In time, you will understand," my new Boss seemed to say.

I returned the next Friday. There was a different teacher that night. In fact, there was a different one every Friday. I also met Muriel, the scrub tech from the Operating Room at South Coast, a petite, friendly brunette and mother of two. I liked her but we worked different shifts and did not see each other much at the hospital. Slowly, the simple Bible sermons I heard week after week began to shed some light on my question about the relevancy of the cross. I also felt a warmth and love among these people that was quite new to me. They really cared and when they prayed it sounded as though God, whom they called Lord, was right there in the room.

One day, my mother sent me a booklet she said I should read. It was called a testimony, a personal story by a pastor of a large church whose beliefs ran along the same lines as my former church affiliations. This pastor, Dr. Ray Jarman, had built the church from scratch, spoke on local radio stations and had a congregation of several thousand. He told about a secretary who insisted he attend a meeting with a bunch of businessmen. To get her off his back, he finally went. During this meeting, for some strange reason, he began to weep. Afterwards, people prayed for him and he had a vision. He found himself standing in a large empty room. A door at the far end opened and in walked Jesus, still bleeding from the cross with pierced hands and a crown of thorns on His brow. He looked down at this pastor with infinite compassion and love and said, "I died for you, Ray."

That eloquent pastor suddenly realized for the first time in his life something he had not known during all the years he had spent behind the pulpit. He was separated from God. Jesus died to bridge that separation but only by accepting this fact and surrendering his life to Christ could he benefit from that transaction. He did surrender and make that commitment that night. Excited, he shared this wonderful revelation with his congregation the next Sunday. The Board and elders were stunned, angry, convinced he had lost his marbles. It must be senility, they decided and promptly retired him from his own church.

"Lord," he cried out, "I just found You and now I have lost my church!" However, word leaked back to the businessmen who were at that meeting. One of them was a pastor who invited him to his church. Now, Dr. Jarman was traveling all over the country, speaking for packed churches and other Christian meetings about his discovery of Jesus.

Amazed, I read this remarkable story. I could relate to it yet it was so contrary to what I had believed all these years. No wonder I couldn't figure out the significance and relevancy of the cross. I never knew that the Bible said we were separated from God, that separation caused death, spiritual death. Only God could bridge that gap and "redeem" us back to Himself. He did that by sending His Son. By dying on the cross, He accomplished what no one else could ever accomplish - a restored fellowship with the Father. Aha! That's where the term "Savior" came from. I had never understood what we needed to be saved from. Now it all became clear - we were saved from ourselves and our self-centered nature that wants to have its own way, be its own boss, live its own life, set its own standards and define its own rights. Now the term "born again" began to make sense. By turning my life over to God, I had actually been born spiritually into a brand new family some of whom were in heaven celebrating and some of whom were here on earth. It didn't really matter which church this "family" attended or where they lived, it only mattered whether they had turned their lives over to Jesus, given Him the driver's seat of their lives, acknowledged Him as their Boss. What a tremendous revelation! So simple yet so difficult. It was free yet it demanded our most prized possession - our independence.

Every major religion, I had studied over the years pointed out ways that we, the human race, could improve ourselves or discipline ourselves in order to get closer to God. The Bible, however, turns that whole concept around and reveals that God is reaching down to us. A humbling thought. That nail-scarred hand has been extended to mankind for all these years. Until we grasp it, we are spiritually dead, a death which will continue after our physical death for all eternity. When we do clasp that hand, however, we will find life and *have it more abundantly,* which will continue into eternity. (John 10:10)

Pastor Ray Jarman's booklet mentioned a church in Anaheim. Up to that time, I had only attended the Friday evening home meetings in San Clemente. Now I decided to check out that church, strapped Sandy into his car seat on Sunday and drove the thirty-five miles to Anaheim. The church seated seven hundred people. There were three services in the morning and two in the evening to accommodate the huge crowds.

I liked it and soaked up the rich teaching, preaching and worship. Like a dry sponge, I couldn't get enough of it and began to look forward to each Sunday. First there was Sunday School, an in-depth time of Bible teaching, prayer and personal ministry followed by a powerful service in the sanctuary with excellent worship, a jubilant choir and a challenging message from the pulpit. Fully charged, I drove home every Sunday. This was the best service yet, I would think every week. It can't get any better.

One Sunday, I spotted a familiar face in the crowd. Her name was Alice, a pretty young mother with large, expressive brown eyes and a ready smile. I tapped her on the shoulder.

"Hi! Didn't we meet last week at pre-school in San Juan Capistrano?" I questioned her.

"Aubrey!" Alice beamed, "fancy seeing you. I didn't know you drove all this way to go to church here."

A special friendship was born which deepened over the years. Soon we met for prayer at my home once a week, later joined by another friend, Marcia. We even volunteered for pre-school Sunday School, which, in retrospect, was a disaster since neither one of us was really geared toward taking care of little fry. Exhausted and frustrated, we decided after a few weeks that perhaps there were other ways to serve the Lord. We joined a choir and sang our hearts out once a month at special evangelistic meetings in Los Angeles.

At the Friday night meetings in San Clemente, I met Ann Christie. She invited me to a sorority, Lambda Sigma Chi (Life Through Christ). Soon, I joined this group of ladies who met once a month in someone's home and was eventually elected to various positions on the Board, climbing the ladder from Sergeant at Arms and Publicity Chairman to Vice President and President. Suddenly, my life was full of action with many challenges and new friends.

One day Mom called from Glendale.

"Do you remember that booklet I sent you by pastor Ray?" she said.

"Of course I remember. How could I forget?"

"Well, we met him last week. He spoke at a local church."

My folks, quite independently from me, had arrived at the same conclusions about their faith as I had. They had quietly surrendered their lives to God and were also growing in their walk with the Lord. Now, we had so much to share we often met in Anaheim after church and compared notes about all the new discoveries we were making. Amazing things continued to happen.

"Dad's asthma is gone," Mom said one day.

For years, Dad had suffered from bronchial asthma triggered by many things such as stress, dust, crowded rooms, humidity or strong perfumes. He always carried an inhaler with some bronchial dilators.

"I haven't used that inhaler for three months now," Dad admitted later, "and I have been in all kinds of crowded rooms and dusty places."

"Praise the Lord," was all I could say, realizing with renewed awe that all aspects of our lives were being touched and changed by a living, loving, personally caring God.

Chapter 10

THE SEEDS ARE GROWING

The sense of anticipation I had felt after my drastic "leap in the dark" and the celebration scene in the convertible never left me. In fact, it became stronger. Somehow, I began to see a plan, well laid out and meticulously executed, for myself and my family. It started way back in Holland. In Sunday School, I had seen glimpses of God's Word through Bible stories and Scriptures and Dad had been led by the Lord, especially throughout the war years and his "hunger trips."

Later in Australia, I had become a nurse because of my inability to speak English well enough to continue in an office career. This led to the idea of studying chiropractic which opened the way to California. A short marriage produced an acute vacuum, a period of frustration and depression. This in turn, provided the right soil for my willingness to take the risk of turning my life over to God. Of course, if I had known more about the nature of God, I would not have felt such apprehension when making this decision. But as it was, I did arrive at that point of surrender and now my life as well as that of my family, was really beginning or actually continuing in a whole new dimension.

Why didn't we make these wonderful discoveries years ago? I'm not sure. I guess the "soil" was not ready yet. Perhaps we were too critical, too caught up in other things, too opinionated or too hung up on preconceived ideas. My folks, back in Australia, had gone to a Billy Graham Crusade once. As they walked towards the huge arena something written in bright lights over the entrance caught their attention: *I AM THE WAY, THE TRUTH AND THE LIFE: NO MAN COMETH UNTO THE FATHER, BUT BY ME*, it said. (John 14:6)

"I thought the *'ME'* referred to Billy Graham," Dad said later. "I was convinced he said that about himself."

"After the service," he continued, "we went forward as the invitation was given to accept Christ as our Savior. We were serious, even shed a few tears and were counselled and prayed for by a personal worker. But after the crusade, things just faded out. It was like a seed that was sown but there was no soil to grow in."

About six months prior to my decision to turn my life over to God, I remember reading a book by Catherine Marshall called, "Beyond Ourselves." It had explicit and clear explanations about God's plan of salvation for mankind through His Son, Jesus. I was on another long trip with my folks, a friend, Jan, and myself driving through the Grand Tetons, Yellowstone, Glacier Park and the Rocky Mountains. At night, after feasting my eyes on the most incredible rugged beauty of snowcapped mountains, crystal blue lakes and millions of pointed pine trees covering the majestic Rockies, I enjoyed curling up in a comfortable deck chair and getting caught up in reading about the things of God. But it didn't bring me to the point of making a personal commitment. Somehow the "soil" still wasn't ready. However, seeds were sown and planted. They took root and, unknown to us, one day pushed through the soil and started to grow and bloom.

The parable of the sower makes it so very clear. Jesus Himself explains it in the Gospel of Mark in chapter 4: *A man once went out to sow his seed and as he sowed, some seed fell by the roadside and the birds came and gobbled it up. Some of the seed fell among the rocks where there was not much soil, and sprang up very quickly because there was no depth of earth. But when the sun rose it was scorched, and because it had no root, it withered away. And some of the seed fell among thorn-bushes and the thorns grew up and choked the life out of it, and it bore no crop. And there was some seed which fell on good soil, and when it sprang up and grew, produced a crop which yielded thirty or sixty or even a hundred times as much as the seed.*

Then Jesus goes on to explain: *The man who sows, sows the message.*

- As for those who are by the roadside where the message is sown, as soon as they hear it, Satan comes at once and takes away what has been sown in their minds.

- Similarly, the seed sown among the rocks represents those who hear the message without hesitation and accept it joyfully. But they have no real roots and do not last - when trouble or persecution arises because of the message, they give up their faith at once.

- Then there are the seeds which were sown among thorn-bushes. These are the people who hear the message but the worries of this world and the false glamor of riches and all sorts of other ambitions creep in and choke the life out of what they have heard and it produces no crop in their lives.

- As for the seed sown on good soil, this means the men who hear the message and accept it and do produce a crop - some thirty, sixty, even a hundred times as much as they received. (Mark 4:1-8., 14-20 Phillips)

What got our soil ready? I believe it was a combination of things. One ingredient to fertilize mine was provided by Margaret, my fellow student in Brisbane. She persuaded me to go to church with her. Margaret knew what I needed. I didn't. I wasn't ready for it. When her pastor asked me, "Aubrey, are you born again?" I said YES, just to get him off my back. I wasn't ready to see my need for Him. But a seed was planted. After I finally began reading Margaret's Bible and discovered what Christianity was all about, I wrote her. My letter was forwarded to several addresses. Months later, I got a reply.

"I can't tell you how thrilled we were to get your letter," Margaret wrote, "Handley and I prayed for you for two years after you left Brisbane. We were unable to go to the mission field. There were some physical problems. Two years after our marriage, we had twins. Can you imagine short little me having twins on the mission field? The Lord had other plans for us." Margaret and Handley prayed for me for two years! Now there was a definite ingredient to get my "soil" ready. Undoubtedly, the Lord had directed them to do so and because of these prayers God was able to move in and persuade me, at His perfect time, to turn my life over to Him.

It takes a big chunk off our pride and independence to accept Jesus' mandate: *If anyone wants to follow in My footsteps, he must give up all right to himself, carry his cross every day and keep close behind Me. For the man who wants to save his life will lose it, but the man who loses his life for My sake will save it. For what is the use of a man gaining the whole world if he loses or forfeits his own soul? If anyone is ashamed of Me and My words, the Son of Man will be ashamed of him.* (Luke 9:24 Phillips)

We like to be in control, to understand and explain things. We don't understand God, He's too vague, too distant. That's frustrating. We don't bother to read what He has to say to us in His Word. It's easier to brush Him off with some glib, self-righteous indignation: "How can a God of love allow so much suffering in the world?" or "I don't want to be a hypocrite like some churchgoers I know" or like we said, "Sure, I believe in God," while we gave Him a seat on the very edge of our lives with a sign: "Stay right there! Don't call me, I'll call You."

The Bible says this is the work of Satan. But who is Satan? Is he for real? Where did he come from? What's his purpose? I had a very hard time with these questions. Surely he was a myth, an idea concocted by some religious fanatic. But as I began to study the Bible in more detail, I came to see Satan as a powerful force, a former exalted being, close to the throne of God. He was so powerful it got to his head and he decided he wanted to be higher than God. His problem is called pride. Because of that, God ejected him from heaven. Three-quarters of the angels joined him. So here's this powerful spiritual being, trying to instill in us the same pride and value system that cost him his place in heaven. He's very clever and often disguised as a benevolent force of love and concern for our fellowman. The bottom line of his entire purpose, however, is to keep us in control of our own lives, setting our own standards and doing our own thing.

"You deserve the best," he gloats. "If it feels good, do it. You owe it to yourself. You're all right. Stand up for your rights. You're a self-made man."

It goes on and on. His entire purpose, however, is to keep us from surrendering our lives to God through Jesus. Once we begin to consider the significance of the cross, he gets into action and becomes very persuasive in ridiculing the whole idea. Pride takes over - no, we don't need to go overboard with this religious stuff. We may lose our friends, have to change our lifestyle, become weirdos. That definitely won't do.

But God's ways overrule Satan's devices. He uses people who sow and pray. Margaret, in Brisbane, was one of them; my Sunday School teacher in Holland, another; Barbara, the lady I met at the garage sale, yet another. My difficult personal circumstances plowed up some more soil, getting it ready for the seed to grow and blossom. Someone has said that God's trains always run on time. His timing is always on target. He has a plan for everyone and asks us to trust Him. One thing is clear - God was there all along whether we were aware of it or not. He orchestrated all the events. Nothing happened by chance.

My adventures with God in the driver's seat of my life continued. Now, He was about to teach me some interesting things about prayer. Yes, I believed prayer changes things but there's nothing like putting knowledge into practice. The practice came at work. I was "floating" on several floors, relieving nurses on sick leave or vacation. One day, I took a break with Liz, the head nurse on the medical floor where I worked that week passing medications.

"I wish I could work on just one floor," I said to Liz, "I'm getting tired of floating."

"There's a place in surgery," she said. "The head nurse is leaving."

"Head nurse! I've never been a head nurse. I've only relieved them."

"Oh, come on," she encouraged me, "I know you can do it."

She sounded so convincing that a few days later, I got up enough courage to apply for the position. Two weeks later, I got it. The work wasn't difficult, just a lot of added responsibilities, but working with the same people every day revealed some interesting situations. One was that most of the PM staff on that floor did not get along. There was constant bickering and complaining. As the head nurse, I was caught in the middle of it all. Every day was filled with tension and angry outbursts.

"Lord," I prayed at home, "please do something. I'm a nervous wreck. Change me or change them." An amazing thing began to happen after that prayer. There was a complete changeover in the entire PM staff on that floor. Some people were transferred, some quit. Within three weeks the entire staff, from nurses to aides and ward clerks, was brand new. The new bunch was very congenial. We developed an excellent rapport and my new job became exciting and fulfilling.

During coffee breaks, we often chatted. Once in a while, I shared a little about my newfound life in Christ. One day an aide remarked,

"When you talk about these things your whole face changes. You just seem to glow." I looked at her in amazement.

"Really? I had no idea." How wonderful of the Lord to actually shine through His children, I thought. I wasn't really comfortable sharing in detail, remembering my own days of skepticism and annoyance about "religious" people yet His presence was seen by others.

Once in a while, I got together with Muriel from OR.

"Have you met Maria in Central Supply?" she asked one day.

"No, I haven't."

"She's a Mexican lady and a really neat Christian."

The next day, I went to Central Supply to return some equipment. There I met Maria, a lady in her forties, a classic beauty with sharp features, her long hair piled in a huge bun on top of her head. With a heavy Spanish accent she gave me a broad smile and said,

"Praise the Lord. I am so happy to meet you!"

"Want to take a break?" I asked her.

"Sure, let's go downstairs to the cafeteria."

I got to know Maria quite well. She had a fiery burden to lead people to the Lord. I envied her boldness. The problem was Maria did not meet too many people in Central Supply.

"I asked the Lord to open a way to see patients," she said earnestly one day, "and guess what He did?" Her eyes had a twinkle as she held me in suspense.

"What happened, Maria?" I knew I was in for a surprise.

"There was an accident on the Coast Highway the other day," Maria began, "five people were injured and brought to the Emergency Room. They were Mexican people from Arizona and didn't speak any English. Four of them were discharged but one had a head injury. They called in Dr. Williams."

I knew Dr. Williams, a neurosurgeon from Newport Beach. He was a committed Christian.

"Dr. Williams called for me to interpret," Maria continued. "He said, 'Maria, please ask this man if his head hurts.'"

"I was about to do that," Maria continued, "but suddenly I felt a tremendous urge to ask him if he was right with God. So I bent over his face and said, 'Sir, if you die today do you know where you will go?'"

"You didn't!" I gasped. "What did he say?"

Maria chuckled and continued, "He opened his eyes and looked at me, very surprised. Then he said, '...Uh, yo no se.' (I don't know.) So then I said: 'Would you like to know?' and he nods his head." The twinkle in her eye intensified.

"So I pulled out my little red Bible and said: 'OK, repeat after me,' then I read him these verses." She opened a small booklet with Scriptures and began quoting them. "He repeated everything and turned his life over to the Lord." She beamed.

"What did Dr. Williams say?"

"Oh, him?" Maria laughed, "I think he knew what was going on. He just stood there. When I was done, I looked up at him and said, 'Dr. Williams, this man just accepted the Lord,' and he says, 'Maria, that is wonderful, now will you please ask him how his head feels?'"

Incredible. Such boldness. But there was more.

"That night at home," Maria continued, "I thanked the Lord for preparing this man's heart. 'But Lord,' I said, 'there were five people in that car. Surely you want the others to know about You also. If they don't, could You please give me a chance to talk to them as well?'"

"Well," Maria sighed, "that didn't seem possible. You see, they were discharged. I didn't know their names or address and besides, I am not supposed to go to patients' rooms."

"So wait till I tell you what happened the next day," her white teeth flashed in a broad smile. "I was pushing my supply cart to the elevator to restock the supplies on the third floor. Suddenly, I saw these four men coming down the hall. They were going to visit their buddy. He was on the third floor so they had to take the elevator. 'Lord,' I prayed, 'if this is my opportunity, please help me.' There was nobody else waiting for the elevator so when the door opened, we all walked in. And guess what? By the time we got to the third floor they all had accepted the Lord!"

I sat back in amazement. This woman was dynamite.

"As they walked to their buddy's room, Dr. Williams was making rounds and saw me. He asked me to come into the room and interpret again. I said, 'Dr. Williams, these four just gave their hearts to the Lord!' He was so happy. When we got into the room, he wanted the others to come in, too . Then he closed the door and said, 'Let's thank the Lord,' so we held hands and prayed and praised the Lord. Isn't He wonderful?"

Maria's face was aglow by now. I sat back in amazement, speechless with excitement. Maria's faith and boldness were infectious. How I loved listening to this simple yet intense woman. Her laugh was so contagious, her face so full of joy and her simple trust in God a great example and inspiration.

One day I returned some instruments to her.

"We need to pray," she whispered, "right now. Do you have a minute?"

"Sure."

She pulled me inside her domain at Central Supply, ushered me into a tiny supply closet and closed the door.

"It's this woman I work with," she said, "she oppresses me. I don't know what it is but I feel a blackness and a darkness around her."

We held hands and prayed the Lord would lift that oppression. It only took a few minutes and I returned to my floor. That evening, I met Maria again at the time clock.

"Aubrey," she laughed her merry laugh, "let me tell you what happened after we prayed this afternoon." I had almost forgotten about that short prayer. As we walked to the car Maria clued me in.

"When that woman came back from her dinner break, she said the most amazing thing. She said, 'Maria, just now when I came up the elevator, something happened to me. It was almost as though something left me.' She looked so puzzled. 'I don't know what it was but I feel different.'"

"You know," Maria finished as we reached our cars, "she WAS different, I could feel it. We had a wonderful afternoon together. Whatever it was that oppressed her was gone. Praise the Lord."

What awesome power there was in prayer, even a quick prayer in a stuffy supply closet. How personal and always available is our God! *Abide in Me and I in you,* Jesus says. *You must go on growing in me and I will grow in you. For just as the branch cannot bear any fruit unless it shares the life of the vine so can you produce nothing unless you go on growing in Me. I am the vine itself, you are the branches. It is the man who shares my life and whose life I share who proves fruitful. For apart from Me you can do nothing at all.* (John 15:3-5 Phillips)

There were other Christians at South Coast Hospital. One day, I met Linda Francis, a young nurses' aide from Surgical West. Linda still betrayed her former hippie lifestyle with her typical granny glasses and long hair which was wrapped in a tight bun for work.

"Aubrey, could you come over to my floor sometime today?" she asked. "I want us to pray for this patient of mine, Carol Spitz. She's a diabetic and had part of her lung removed."

"Sure," I said. Shortly after lunch, I went over to Surgical West. Linda took me to Carol's room. I saw a petite, blond young woman with a sweet expression on her pretty face. She was sitting up in bed supported by several pillows. A Bible was on her bedside. We prayed for Carol, her husband, Paul, and their two children. It was a sweet moment, one of the first times I participated in personal ministry myself.

Carol made an uneventful recovery and was discharged the following week. Little did I know that Paul and Carol would become very close friends in the future.

"I've applied for a summer job in Africa with YWAM," Linda announced one day. I knew that YWAM, or Youth With A Mission, was an international organization for young people.

"What are you going to do there?" I wanted to know.

"They have a group of us travel and go to different meetings in churches and other places to share and help out," she said. "It's all arranged. We have to pay our own way and I need a passport and visa." She sounded excited and I was happy for her. A few weeks later, I passed Linda again in a hospital corridor.

"Aubrey!" her voice was tense, "we've got to pray."

"What's the matter?"

"I'm leaving in two days and my visa has not arrived. It should have been in the mail two weeks ago." Boldly, I said, "Let's go in here." I opened the door of the sitzbath and turned the VACANT sign around to OCCUPIED. There was not much room in there but we didn't need much. I grabbed her hand, closed my eyes and we bowed our heads,

"Lord, please take care of Linda's visa," I prayed. "Let it come in the mail today. Amen."

We opened the door and stepped out. Nobody saw us. Just as well. When Linda came home that night, her visa was in the mailbox. She left for Kenya the next day.

"Aubrey, is that you?!"

I turned around in the parking lot of our local shopping center facing a tall, blond, smiling man. He looked familiar but who was he? He stuck out his hand. Suddenly, I remembered.

"Steve! What in the world are you doing here?" It was a former classmate from LACC. I had not seen him since graduation eight years ago.

"I just joined a practice here." he said. "What are you doing? How's Bill?"

I brought him up to date.

"So you're still nursing?" he said surprised. "Why don't you get into chiropractic practice? You're a doctor, you know."

"I like nursing. Besides, it takes a lot of money to open an office what with X-ray equipment, adjustment tables, insurance..."

We chattered on about family and other former classmates and promised to keep in touch. At home, I dismissed his suggestion of working as a chiropractor but then I thought, Hey, I'm not in the driver's seat any more. What if the Lord wants me in an office? At least I should pray about it. I can't afford to open my own office so I would need to work alongside someone who is already established. It has to be a Christian and an older, married man so there won't be any potential problems. I smiled. If these were the conditions for a practice for me, then I was safe. I knew all the local Chiropractors and none fit these requirements. Relieved, I forgot about the matter.

But a few weeks later, Joey called. We had worked together at Lambda Sigma Chi, our Christian sorority, and we discussed some details about an upcoming meeting. Then Joey mentioned an old back injury that was bothering her again.

"I just came back from my chiropractor," she said, "and feel much better."

"Who did you see?" I asked.

"Dr. Luschen," she said.

"Oh? Who's he? I've never heard of him."

"You haven't?" Joey was surprised. "He's been here for years. In fact, he is so busy he is looking for a partner. He and his wife want to go on vacation but he can't close the office." I felt a sinking feeling in my chest.

"Is he a Christian?" I asked, holding my breath.

"Oh yes," Joey confirmed. I hung up the phone.

"Is that Your answer, Lord?" I prayed.

I knew I had to follow through on that. This was no coincidence. Besides, there was another matter to consider. After Sandy started kindergarten, he was gone during the morning while I left for work in the afternoon. We hardly ever saw each other anymore. To get off the PM shift, I reluctantly accepted a day job in the Recovery Room which also offered weekends off. However, the Recovery Room was over-staffed and I often had to float again. Lately, I had been stuck on the medical floor where there were many stroke patients and without help from an orderly, it was taxing my strength. I came home exhausted and needed the weekends to recoup my energies.

So I went to see Don Luschen. He was kind and friendly and definitely interested in sharing his office with me. He was also eager to leave on an extended vacation with his wife who was just recovering from surgery. I prayed about it again and two weeks later resigned from my job at South Coast Hospital. The office was small but comfortable. It brought back memories from my days at Moonan Flat - you never knew what kind of people with what kind of problems would show up. Don had built a busy practice. He often saw forty or more patients a day. No wonder he needed a vacation, I thought. I was exhausted after my first week but determined to stick with it.

The next week during lunch break, I saw a car pull up in the parking lot. A man stepped out, then turned to get his wife out. It took ten minutes to get her on her feet. Her back never straightened out, she shuffled ever so slowly at a forty-five degree angle towards the office door.

"Oh Lord," I panicked, "what can I do for this woman?"

They entered the office, I took a history, did a physical and tried to put her on the adjustment table. There was no way she could lay down. I gave her some heat and massage and was able to relax her tight lower back muscles a little. An hour later, she shuffled out of the office more or less the same way she had entered.

"I want to see you again tomorrow," I instructed her.

The scene repeated itself the next day and the next. But every day, she walked a little straighter. Finally after two weeks, she was pain-free and walking normally again. It was a tremendous boost to my sagging morale, working alone in a busy office with no one to confide in or consult. When Don returned four weeks later, I had gained much confidence but was glad he could take the helm again.

We each worked three days a week now. I had more time between patients and was busy writing a publicity booklet for church. One day, a new patient came in. Her name was Donna, a pretty brunette in her forties. She complained about a variety of vague symptoms such as fatigue, backache, headaches, etc. As we talked, she mentioned she wanted to be a writer someday. I said I had written some short articles and the conversation continued along this line.

"Anything you can tell me about writing," she said, "I would really appreciate."

"Why don't you come over to my home next Saturday afternoon?" I suggested.. She was delighted and showed up at the appointed time.

"Sit down," I invited her in. "Tell me about yourself."

A long and sad story followed. With mixed emotions, I listened as she unraveled her story of two failed marriages, children with problems, no job and health troubles. It went on and on.

She doesn't need instructions in writing, I thought, she needs to turn her life over to the Lord and get straightened out.

"Do you go to church?" I gently probed, "do you pray, do you believe in God?"

We got into a deep, serious conversation. Finally, she saw her need for Christ and I led her through a simple prayer. She left with a smile and a Bible tucked under her arm. Delighted, I thanked the Lord for giving me this opportunity to share His love with Donna. Just about two years ago, I would not have dreamed I would do something like this. God was good. He was watering my soil so that the sprouted seeds could grow and bring forth fruit.

I often thought of my friends in Glendale from the Dutch social club, especially my friends, Eric and Ans Hof. I wondered how they were. Oh, how I would love to share my new life with them. Would they be interested? Would they laugh or perhaps yawn? Determined to find out, I wrote them a short note one day, bringing them up to date on my whereabouts and work. Several weeks went by, then I got a note from Eric. They were separated, he wrote, the kids grown and gone. Yes, Eric wrote, it would be nice to see me again. Surprised and saddened, I prayed about this turn of events and suggested we meet after church in Anaheim some Sunday. After all, that was about halfway between Capistrano and Los Angeles where he still lived. But he never replied. Ans wrote also. She was still at the old house in Eagle Rock. Mom had invited me to a special service at the Shrine Auditorium in Los Angeles and I suggested Ans and I meet there. To my delight, I found her waiting for me at the appointed place by a side entrance. She looked well and seemed her old perky self.

"What have you been doing lately?" I asked her, as we found a seat in the huge auditorium.

"Oh, I work at a mortuary," she said, "it's a real good job. I'm also involved in some relief work through a Dutch agency and belong to a debate club."

"What do you debate?"

"Current issues," she said, "philosophies. All kinds of things."

The service started and our conversation ended. She continued telling me about her debate club afterwards but promised to see me again. I drove back to Capistrano and prayed the Lord would reveal Himself to her.

She kept in touch with my folks in Glendale and returned to some of the services at the Shrine. Eventually, she sold her home and moved to Anaheim. There I met her again and took her to my church. Within a year, her debating club was forgotten and replaced by Bible studies and prayer meetings. Ans became a dedicated and energetic Christian who eventually led many others to the Lord. Many years later, we even travelled together through Europe and stayed at Francis Schaeffer's l'-Abri in Switzerland. The following year, it was discovered she had cancer of the liver and she died soon afterwards. Just before her death, she wrote her Christian testimony to be read at her own funeral which she knew would be attended by many of her former Dutch Social Club friends. It was a holy occasion, a homegoing celebration with a clear message from Ans, even across the grave, about God's faithfulness and love for all of mankind. The theme of the message was, *For the man who wants to save his life will lose it, but the man who loses his life for My sake will save it.* (Luke 9:24 Phillips)

Linda Francis returned from Kenya in the Spring of 1971. Excited and full of stories about her travels, we got together for lunch one day. I had stayed in touch with Linda while she was gone and even offered her a place to live at my home if she ever needed one. Now she disclosed the happy news that she was engaged to a wonderful young man, a pastor's son. They would be married in two months. She was staying with her sister and her husband, Joanne and Ben, till that time.

"I'm so happy for you, Linda." I hugged her, "everything seems to be working out so well for you."

But I was wrong. Three weeks before the wedding, the groom got cold feet and backed out. Devastated, Linda cried for days hardly able to pull herself together.

Slowly, however, the shattered pieces were buried and replaced by glimmers of hope. She also got her job back at the hospital. One evening, just after dinner, the front door bell rang. I opened the door. It was Linda.

"Come in," I welcomed her, "sit down. How are things?"

She hesitated, then sat down.

"You know," she began, "when I was in Kenya, you wrote me once and said if I ever needed a place, I could move in with you."

I remembered.

"Well, now that I am not getting married, I can't stay with Joanne and Ben. They're newlyweds themselves and need their privacy. Besides, their apartment is too small."

She paused and looked at me.

"Of course, you can move in here, Linda," I said. "There's plenty of room here. I'd love to have you." I stood up and hugged her and she had another cry. Relieved, she smiled at me through her tears.

"Thank you Beau," she cried, using my old hospital name, "I'll try and be a good roommate."

"I'm sure you will, Linda." I smiled.

Thank you, Lord, I thought, for giving me a roommate after all. Now I have both a piano and a roommate. "*All these things*" have been added but how much more than that have You given me! Living in the Kingdom of God is so much more than "*all these earthly things*" which are merely side benefits. Surely, as Christ said, "*he who will lose his life for My sake shall find it.*"

My cozy house was still a prized possession to me. However, it was not the same as four years ago when I first moved in. Then, it was a therapeutic necessity, a stabilizer in my shaken world. Now it was merely an added blessing, an appreciated comfort. If the Lord would call me elsewhere, even to Africa from where Linda had just returned, I would be eager to go and forsake "*all these things.*" Walking with Jesus was the most exciting walk there was and the only thing that really gave meaning to life. Little did I know that the best was yet to come.

Chapter 11

A FELLOWSHIP IS BORN

"The new San Clemente hospital is almost ready to open," Linda announced one sunny spring day in 1972. We were stretched out on the back patio, cooling off under the shady canopy of the backyard trees, sipping a tall glass of cold lemonade.

"So I hear," I said, "I read in the paper they're taking applications next week. Are you interested?"

"Well, I'm thinking about it," Linda said. "It's a lot closer than South Coast Hospital, I could almost walk from here. It would save a lot of gas and travel time, too."

"Why don't you go and fill out an application and see what they have to offer?" I suggested.

"Yes, I think I'll do that." Linda took a sip of her lemonade. "I've never worked in a brand new hospital. Could be interesting." Then she looked at me and asked, "How about you, Beau? What are your plans?"

"I don't know, Linda," I said pensively, "I don't know."

I had been feeling restless lately at the office. Somehow, working alone in a small area wasn't the same as being in a hospital. I guess I was missing the hospital atmosphere, the contact with different departments, chats in the cafeteria, meeting a lot of people such as staff members, patients, relatives and doctors instead of just seeing one patient at a time. My income was more than adequate but I felt claustrophobic and out of touch with the world.

"Perhaps I'll go with you just to take a look," I promised.

A few days later, we drove up to a sprawling, one-story building still under construction. It was across the freeway less than one mile from my home. It had emerged, rather forlornly, in the middle of an undeveloped grassy area still surrounded by trucks and bulldozers. An army of construction workers were busy unloading all kinds of equipment, huge rolls of carpets, gallons of paint, crates of equipment. The front door was open and the lobby bustled with activity. To our left was a makeshift Nursing Office.

"Hello, Beauchamp!" The voice came from the office.

Who in the world would know me here? I wondered.

A smiling, blond woman walked towards me. It was Aurilee, a Canadian nurse I had met in Glendale almost ten years earlier when we both had to take a make-up Psychology course for the California Board of Nurses.

"Aurilee! What are you doing here?" I smiled, pleasantly surprised.

"I'm assistant Director of Nursing," she said, "what are you doing here? Looking for a job?" I introduced Linda and said, "Well, we both have jobs but we're interested in this hospital because it's so close to home."

"Well, why don't you look around?" she suggested, "it's not finished but you can get an idea what it'll be like. Oh, by the way," she turned to a young man with a friendly smile who had just entered the little office, "this is Harvey, he's our Supervisor."

"Nice meeting you," Harvey said, betraying a charming, British accent. "Are you interested in some applications? I happen to have some right here."

Linda and I walked through the dusty halls, dodging ladders, carpenters and painters.

"This must be the Operating Room, right next to the Recovery Room," I said. The rooms were full of sawdust, a large operating table stood in the corner covered with a dropsheet. We walked on.

"And this must be Central Supply," Linda guessed, "see these autoclaves?"

"Yes, I think you're right and this must be the lab." We turned several corners and continued our guessing game.

"Isn't it neat to see such a new place?" Linda said philosophically, "nothing has touched it yet. It's so fresh and new, just waiting to be used. It's like a beginning, an empty place prepared for action. Like a baby, ready to be born."

"Yes," I laughed at her prose, "you're right. I feel the same way."

"Why don't we pray for this hospital?" she suggested, "let's ask the Lord to bless it."

"Yes, let's!" I agreed. Excited, we retraced our steps through the various departments we had just identified. We stopped in Central Supply again and putting a hand on the large counters, we asked the Lord to bless the people who would be working here. Back in the Operating Room, we touched that heavy, metal operating table.

"Bless the doctors who will operate here, Lord," Linda prayed earnestly, "protect the patients, give them peace and a speedy recovery."

"Father, let Your presence be in this Intensive Care," I prayed as we stood in the empty room with IV poles and nightstands piled in a corner. "Let your peace reign as frightened and hurting patients will be admitted here. Give the staff wisdom and compassion as they take care of these patients. Help the doctors make the right decisions and prescribe the right treatments and medications. Above all Lord, let your love and peace be felt by everyone. Amen."

The medical and surgical floors followed, then OB, the Admitting office, Medical records, the Pharmacy, Emergency Room, Cafeteria, Purchasing, X-ray and Business offices. None of the workmen seemed to realize what we were doing. They were too busy with their saws and hammers and paintbrushes to notice.

Finally, we returned to the Nursing office, sat down and filled out application forms. It won't hurt, I thought, I'm not making any commitments. Excited, we drove home. This had been a special day. A few days later Aurilee called me.

"Are you interested in taking charge of the Recovery Room?" she wanted to know. "We'll only have one nurse there for the time being and she needs to set up the department. You've worked in the Recovery Room at South Coast so you have an idea of what is needed." I promised I'd let her know and hung up. OK, it's decision time again, I thought. What a temptation to be back at a hospital and to have the opportunity to set up a whole department. I earnestly prayed about it and finally shared my thoughts with Don at the office.

"You mean you'd rather work as a nurse in a hospital than be your own boss as a doctor in an office?" he asked, amazed at such a thought.

"Yes, I believe I would," I said. "This has been an excellent experience for me, Don," I added, "you've been very kind to let me work with you here. I've learned a lot. I think the Lord wanted me to get this out of my system so that in the future I would never have any doubts as to what I am supposed to be doing. If I had not worked for you, I would always have wondered if I was doing the right thing. This is a perfect place for anyone to work but I'm just not happy in an office."

He accepted my explanation and we parted as friends. A month later, on August 17, 1972, I began my new job at San Clemente General Hospital. Linda was hired as a nurse's aide on the medical floor.

Being involved in the birth of a new hospital was a new experience for both of us. Each night, we would compare notes at home about our new departments and fellow staff workers. There were not too many patients those first weeks and little orientation. Procedure books were not completed, equipment was unsorted and scattered, crash carts, cardexes, medication routines, everything had to be worked out and routines established. Everyone worked hard, at the same time getting used to one another and finding the location of the different departments. After a few weeks, much had been accomplished. However, at times, personalities clashed and tempers flared as misunderstandings surfaced or communication lines clogged.

"It's like a machine that needs to be oiled," Linda observed one day. "My charge nurse seems very frustrated," she continued, "I don't know if she is capable of running a whole floor. I think she has a lot of personal problems, too. Anyway, it's difficult to work with her. She changes her mind several times a day about assignments and things like that."

"What we need is a support group, perhaps a prayer group," I thought out loud. "You know, I still feel very inadequate dealing with my patients' spiritual needs. We just never had any training in that area. I wish I had some guidelines on how to minister, how to pray with patients and how to comfort relatives."

"You know," Linda said, "when I was in Africa, we attended a meeting of a group called Hospital Christian Fellowship."

"Really?" I was interested. "What kind of a group was that?"

"Well, I'm not sure," she said, "but there were health care workers from all different hospital departments. They sang and had a Bible study, then prayed for each other and their patients."

"Wouldn't it be nice if we could do something like that?" I said wistfully.

"Why not?" Linda asked.

"Yes, why not," I mused, "we could start with a prayer group perhaps right here since we live so close to the hospital."

"Yes," Linda agreed, "maybe once a week. Sounds good."

"Sounds good to me, too. Let's see how many others are interested."

"I already met some Christians at the hospital," Linda was excited. "I can think of several people I want to ask."

Within a week, we had recruited quite a few hospital staff members including Dorothy, a ward clerk on the medical floor; Inez, a secretary from the Nursing Office; Bette, an aide from OB; Lillian, a night nurse on Medical floor; Liz, another nurse's aide; Jean and Sister Regina, both nurses on other floors and Lupe, a little lady from Housekeeping. There was also an orderly, a lab tech, several volunteers and a part-time hospital chaplain. We agreed to meet on Tuesday evening at my home.

About a dozen people showed up for the first meeting. We shared a little about ourselves, read a few Scriptures, sang some choruses and then prayed for each other, our patients, our fellow staff workers, the medical staff and the hospital management. We chatted informally afterwards while Linda served refreshments and we all promised to meet again the following Tuesday.

"We should keep a prayer diary," Jean suggested, "so we can keep track of things we prayed for."

"Good idea," Lil said, "maybe we should also take a small offering to cover expenses." Linda put a small basket on the coffee table. I promised to get a notebook. The following week our living room filled up again. There were some new faces. After introductions I asked:

"Does anyone have a special Scripture to share?"

"I do," said Regina, "Isaiah 50:4. I read it this morning and it really spoke to me." She opened her Bible, found the right page and read: *The Lord God hath given me the tongue of the learned, that I should know how to speak a word in season to him who is weary: he wakeneth [me] morning by morning; he wakes mine ear to hear as the learned.* She looked up. "Isn't this something we all need?" she asked, "to *speak a word in season to him who is weary?*" We all agreed. How practical is God's word and how specific in all its details.

"Let's write down some prayer requests," I suggested, opening our new notebook. We jotted down the names of several gravely ill patients in ICU and a staff problem in the Emergency Room.

"My mother has bladder cancer," Hildegarde from the tissue lab said, "she's in a lot of pain."

"You know," Linda said, "we need to pray again for my head nurse. The tension on the day shift is getting worse. She has such unpredictable outbursts and is easily upset by things."

"So I noticed," I remarked, "I said something in jest to her the other day and she got offended and reported me to the Nursing Office. Well, let's pray for all these requests." We did. When Linda's turn came, I heard her say,

"Lord, please help us on the medical floor. That head nurse is causing so much tension. Please shape her up or ship her out."

"Father," another prayed, "I pray for Doctor McGuire. He doesn't know You even though he uses Your name all day. He has three very ill patients in the Unit. Please give him wisdom about how to treat them. Minister to him, too. Amen."

The following day, I was busy in the Recovery Room when there was a knock on the door. Linda's face peeked in. She looked perplexed.

"What's up?" I asked.

"Beau, you won't believe this," she whispered.

"Try me," I encouraged her.

"My head nurse got fired. She's gone."

"Well, that's what happens when you pray these radical prayers," I laughed.

"Do you really think I'm responsible?" Linda worried.

"No, Linda," I smiled, "I don't think you were responsible. God was responsible. He heard your prayer and chose to answer it this way." Relieved, she left, still shaking her head in astonishment.

Word about our prayer meetings began to spread and new people showed up every week. Others could not come regularly and came just once in a while.

"Did you hear what happened in ICU," someone asked, "after we prayed for Dr. McGuire's patients?"

"No, what happened?"

"One of his patients almost died. He was unconscious but when he woke up, he gave God the glory for sparing his life. He did so well, he walked out of the unit three days later to the surgical floor. You know, patients are usually transferred from ICU on a stretcher. Not him - he walked! The other two patients also recovered and were discharged. McGuire was very surprised. We kept saying, 'Praise the Lord!' He didn't know what to say."

"You know, we need some Bibles in that hospital," Linda said one Tuesday evening.

"Yes," Lillian agreed, "we do. We have some money now. Perhaps that's what we should use it for." She had kept track of our small weekly offerings at the prayer meetings and even opened a bank account.

"We should have something inside the Bibles to say that it is a gift and patients can take them home."

"Well, why don't you look into getting a rubber stamp for that," I suggested, "and I'll contact some Bible Societies and see how much they cost."

A few days later, I had called several publishers and picked up quotes for Bibles in a modern English translation. Then I knocked on the door of the hospital administrator's office.

"Do you mind if we put some Bibles in patients' lockers?" I asked. "We'll pay for them and distribute them." He gave me a surprised look, then shrugged his shoulders.

"Sure," he said, "that's fine with me."

Lillian had a large stamp made which said: "A gift of love from San Clemente Hospital Christian Fellowship. Yours to keep if you wish. God bless you."

"How many Bibles can we order, Lil?" I asked after I gave her my quotes.

"Two hundred," she said.

Three weeks later they arrived, all new and crispy. Excited, we pressed our stamped greetings in each of the fly leaves. That night, after visiting hours, we loaded the boxes on a stretcher and distributed the Bibles to each bedside locker. We also left copies in waiting areas and the Nursing Office. A volunteer, also part of our group, offered some storage space in her office and promised to check the bedside lockers and replace copies taken home. Excited, we met the following Tuesday to give thanks to the Lord for helping us with this accomplishment. Little did we know that within one year over five hundred Bibles would be taken home by grateful patients.

Our Tuesday night meetings continued.

"You know," Bette, a nurse's aide from OB said one night, "there is a small room next to Central Supply which is called the CHAPEL but there is nothing in it. Couldn't we fix it up a little?"

"Yes, why not?" Janet who worked in Central, agreed.

"I have a tract rack," the chaplain suggested, "and some pictures you can have."

"I have some praying hands," Lupe said.

"We have some neat tracts and booklets," Andy, the orderly, added.

"We'd better check with administration first," I cautioned.

The next day, we knocked at the administrator's office again.

"Would you mind if we put a few things in the chapel? There's a couch and a chair in there but nothing else right now."

"Yes, I know," he said. "Sure, if you want to brighten it up a bit, that's fine with me." It seemed that decorating a chapel was not on his priority list but as long as we would furnish the materials, we could do anything we liked. Encouraged, we talked it over during lunch break in the cafeteria one day. A young maintenance man listened in.

"I think a chapel should have a kneeling bench." he said, "lots of people like to kneel when they pray."

"Good idea," I said, "would you like to make one?"

"I'll see what I can do," he promised.

Two weeks later, the chapel was finished complete with kneeling bench, pictures, books, well-stocked tract rack, magazines, a lamp, some Bibles, plants and even a box of tissues. Most items were donated. Soon, visitors from the ER, lab, X-ray, ICU and those waiting for patients in surgery found the room. Even though it was small, it was quiet. Doctors liked to take relatives there to talk after surgery. We used it ourselves at times to say some quick prayers or snatch a quiet moment during breaks.

After several months, our Tuesday night group had settled down to a core group of about twelve people. Six to eight of these showed up each week. "We need some new people," I mentioned one night, "if this is going to be just a bless-me group, we're going to stagnate. It's great that we have Bibles for patients and a functioning chapel but we have to reach out to others. Right now, no new people are getting involved in our prayer group."

"How about a potluck?" someone suggested, "everyone likes to eat."

"Sure," Lupe piped up, "you can have it at my house. I'll cook some Mexican food; you can bring the trimmings." I knew Lupe was an excellent cook. A lively discussion followed and we all agreed on a date and time at Lupe's home.

"What are we going to do for a program?" I asked. Everyone had a suggestion.

"We need some music and a message."

"Any volunteers?"

"I'll bring my guitar."

"What about a speaker?"

"Maybe we need to ask a pastor."

"Let's pray about it."

The next day, I called Jerry, a young, local pastor with a ready smile and a heart for people.

"Jerry," I said, "we're planning a little get-together with some people from the hospital. After dinner, we need someone to present a short, simple Gospel message. Just an outline of what it means to be a Christian - not too long or complicated. Do you think...?" I stopped, wondering what he would say.

"You got it," Jerry smiled, "love to do it. Tell me where and when."

We produced colorful announcements and distributed them all over the hospital. Everyone seemed excited about a Mexican potluck. Many promised to come. The big evening finally arrived. Lupe's modest home filled up with people, seventeen in all. Quite a few had never been to our Tuesday meetings or even showed any interest in our activities. The dinner was delicious, topped off with a rich desert. Animated conversations and bursts of laughter bounced around the room. Time went on.

"It's getting late," I said to Linda, "we have to start." I called for attention. Finally, they all settled down.

"I would like you to know a little more about our Hospital Christian Fellowship group," I began, "I know we've all had a big meal just now so let's sing some songs first." I watched most of the audience, quiet and rather lethargic by now, eye me with blank expressions. Not a very spiritual atmosphere as far as I could tell. Andy strummed his guitar and began leading some choruses. Participation was minimal. Most people didn't know any of the songs.

Everyone seemed full and tired and ready to go home. With a forced smile, I cheerfully introduced Jerry. He unfolded himself from his place on the floor and stepping over several people, he reached my side of the room. He cleared his throat, thanked us all for a delicious meal and then opened a big, black Bible. The room was quiet now and the level of interest seemed to increase. Jerry looked over his audience and began to speak.

It was neat. He got right to the point, quoted some Scriptures, explained what the central message of the Bible was, how much God loves us and how He came to earth and died in our place so we could be forgiven and obtain eternal life. Ten minutes later, he finished. I heaved a sigh of relief. Then something unexpected happened.

"Before we close," Jerry casually suggested, "why don't we take a moment and bow our heads. If there is anyone here tonight who would like to turn his life over to the Lord, why not take care of that right now?"

I froze. He was going too far. This was not a church. What would people think? Well, there's nothing you can do now, my dear, I thought, just pray. Everyone bowed their heads. I peeked at Linda. She looked at me with raised eyebrows. Jerry began to pray. He was very brief. When he finished he said,

"Before you open your eyes, how many of you just now made that decision for the first time? Just raise your hand."

I held my breath, then carefully peeked around the room. Three hands went up...

Jerry concluded his message and I dismissed everyone. They scrambled to their feet, chatted, collected their dishes, said their good-byes and slowly filed out the front door. Back home, I sat Linda down on the couch in the living room.

"Linda," I said perplexed, "what are we going to do with these people?"

"You mean the three who raised their hands?" Linda asked, knowing good and well that's what I meant.

"Right! We're not a church yet we are responsible for them. They made that decision because of a meeting we planned."

"Well," practical Linda smiled, "perhaps the Lord will take care of that, too. I'm going to bed. Good night."

The following Tuesday evening, our entire HCF core group as-
sembled. Excited, we discussed every detail of the potluck, including
the question of how to follow up on the three *new creatures in Christ.*"

"We have to keep in touch with them, get them a Bible and take
them to church," Linda suggested.

"Which church?" Sandy, a nurse and newcomer to our group, asked.
"Our group represents several churches."

"Well, perhaps we could suggest three or four churches and have
them go to each one. Then, they could pick one where they feel comfortable and welcome."

"Yea, sounds good to me," Inez agreed, "then we are not pushing
them to any particular church."

"Right," I agreed, "I know the pastors of quite a few churches in the
area and can alert them when we send them new people."

"Well, I go to church in El Toro," Lillian said, "it's fifteen miles
from here. We have lots of patients from that area so perhaps we can
type a list of area churches we can all recommend."

"What do you say if we try for monthly outreach meetings?" I suggested. "This one was such a success. Perhaps not all of them potlucks,
that's a lot of work, but there are lots of people with large homes. Perhaps we could use some of them and invite special speakers or
musicians to share."

The idea was accepted with enthusiasm and we discussed details.
We needed a literature, refreshments and a publicity chairman, also an
MC and hostess. My past experience with Lambda Theta Chi sorority
came in handy. Excited, we planned ahead for our future outreaches.

We discovered Christian physicians, dentists and other professionals
in the medical field who were willing and pleased to share their faith in
Christ with our group. Several large homes were also made available.

I read a book called "Surgeon of Hope" by Dr. Ralph Byron from
City of Hope in Duarte. Marianne Cook, a fellow nurse in the OR had
worked there for years. She took me to City of Hope one day and introduced me to Dr. Byron. He accepted my invitation to come and drove
sixty miles from his home to Mission Viejo where the meeting was held
that night, to share a dynamic message about his personal daily quiet
times with the Lord and Scripture memorization which included entire
chapters of the Bible.

Dr. Francis Williams, a neurosurgeon from Newport Beach who had
asked Maria to interpret, also came and shared.

Soon, we began to put up posters on our notice boards near the time
clock. Newspapers carried announcements in the entire county and
employees from other hospitals began to attend.

"Please keep us informed of your meetings," they asked, "we like to pass the word and invite other people."

Many lives were touched. A private duty nurse from a local Registry came one night.

"Please tell my boss, Alice, about your meetings," she begged, "there are many Christians with the Registry who would love to get involved with your group."

I did and I had a very interesting conversation with Alice.

"My husband passed away a few weeks ago in your Intensive Care," she told me, "he was not a Christian but someone shared the Gospel with him and he accepted the Lord before he died." She was delighted and promised to tell her nurses about our meetings.

"Why don't you write a little newsletter?" Linda asked. "There are so many people from outside our hospital getting involved now."

"Yes, I have been thinking about it," I said, "we are building up quite a mailing list."

"You know," Linda continued, "I found an address of the International HCF headquarters. Did you say you wanted to write them?"

"Oh, thanks. Yes, I sure do. Here we are calling ourselves Hospital Christian Fellowship but we don't have much information about them. They don't even know we exist."

I wrote a long letter to International HCF headquarters and promptly received a warm, encouraging letter back. Also enclosed was literature and outlines of HCF goals and objectives, together with a Statement of Faith. "We are interdenominational," they wrote, "as well as international and we try not to get involved in denominational issues. Our aim is to bring patients to the Lord, to bring them the Good News of salvation and eternal life through Jesus."

I learned a lot about HCF. It began in 1937 when Francis Grim and his brother, Carl, visited their elderly father in a local hospital. The father was failing in health but as a Christian he was not afraid of death - he even looked forward to it. During their daily hospital visits, Francis and Carl noticed that the nurses were very kind and efficient but not too concerned about their patient's spiritual welfare. Francis spoke to some and discovered they were Christians but never thought about sharing their faith with their patients.

"We really don't know how to," they admitted.

"Would you mind if I teach you?" Francis offered.

They didn't and set aside a time and place to meet. On Christmas Day, Francis' father passed away. This also became the birth of a fellowship that would eventually spread around the world.

Several nurses and students showed up for that first meeting. Francis taught them what the Christian life was all about and the mandate we have to "*go into all the world and preach the Gospel.* That includes the hospitals as well," he stressed. "Patients who never go to church or even think about God, will do so when they are in a hospital, sick and frightened, not sure whether they will live or die or who will carry on their business or take care of their family or pay the bills. They are flat on their back, looking upwards, straight to heaven. A timely word from you may be all they need to turn their lives around for all eternity."

After a while, Francis received several calls from the parents of these student nurses he was teaching. They all said more or less the same thing: "Whatever it is you are teaching our girls, please continue. We see a lot of changes in them - good changes. They're more responsible and concerned about others."

Some even sent a small donation to help with his expenses. Encouraged, Francis continued and started additional groups in neighboring hospitals. Soon, he travelled out of town to teach new core groups. Eventually, he became exhausted with all this extra work and realized he needed to make a choice between his secular job and these newfound fellowships. After much struggle and seeking the Lord, he resigned his job and by faith, continued nurturing his emerging ministry. His brother promised to support him as much as possible.

Francis eventually travelled throughout the continents of Africa, Europe, the Far East, the Middle East, Latin America and the islands of the Caribbean sharing his vision of spiritual care to the sick and dying. Active fellowships among health care workers resulted from these pioneer visits. Scores of patients were brought to the Lord while many others were strengthened, encouraged and nurtured. Francis' first secretary was a pretty, dedicated young girl named Erasmia. Her name and looks betrayed her Greek origin. Many years later "before anyone else snatched her up," to use his own words, Francis married her. She became Mrs. Erasmia Grim and the instant mother of a large HCF family around the world.

Delighted with this pioneer work and it's far-flung results, I stayed in touch with the International HQ, asking questions about outreaches, the need for literature, training materials, etc.

"If you ever come to the U.S.," I wrote Mr. and Mrs. Grim, "please let me know and include California on your agenda." They promised they would.

In the meantime, exciting things continued to happen at the hospital. The three ladies who raised their hands at Lupe's potluck dinner all found a church, followed through on their commitment and eventually had an effect on the lives of their families as well. Joan, a heavy-set middle-aged widow who worked in Central Supply, was one of them.

One day, I went to her department to pick up my weekly order for the Recovery Room.

"Aubrey!" she beamed, "I've got to tell you something. Do you have five minutes?"

"Yes, I suppose," I said, "what happened?"

"You know I am going to get married soon," she began.

"Yes, you shared that last week. I'm so glad for you." I smiled.

"Well, I praise the Lord for bringing Bruce into my life. But wait till you hear this. Last night my heart suddenly started to beat very fast. This had happened before and I had been under treatment by a cardiologist for some time. I called him, took some medication and he met me in the Emergency Room this morning. They hooked me up to the monitor and I could see that little dot of light just racing across the screen. It was much too fast. The doctor said he would have to cardiovert me, you know, shock my heart with those paddles to get it to slow down."

"Yes," I said, "that's quite a drastic procedure."

"Well," Joan continued, "that wasn't the worst of it. What bothered me more was that Bruce was going to marry a sick wife. When the nurse left me alone in the ER, I started to pray. 'Lord,' I said, 'I want to be a good wife to Bruce. A healthy wife. Bruce took care of his first wife for years until she died. I don't want him to go through this again. Please, Lord, let me be a healthy helpmate to him.'"

"You know what happened?" Joan's eyes sparkled, "I felt a hand on my heart. I know that sounds crazy but I did. It was very gentle, just a touch, and when I opened my eyes, my heartbeat had gone down to a regular seventy-four. I saw it on the monitor." Still amazed, Joan shook her head as she recounted the events.

"The nurse came in and noticed it. She called the doctor who examined me, took some tests and discharged me. Not only that, he said I could come to work so here I am."

"Joan," I beamed, "isn't that marvelous? I am so happy for you. Surely, the Lord is good, isn't He?" I related the story to Linda during dinner at home that night. She rejoiced with me.

"I have something to share also," she announced, putting the empty dishes together and taking them to the kitchen.

"What?" I prompted, marveling that we had had so many stories to tell and so many things to share lately.

"Do you remember BB, the lady from Sweden?"

"Yes, I do. Isn't she in the hospital?"

"Yes, she is. She was on my floor with a bowel obstruction. Her roommate, Lucille, had the same thing. They were both in a lot of pain but BB was so peaceful and serene that Lucille got curious and wanted to know why. Well, BB is a neat Christian and she told Lucille she could have that peace. It was a personal relationship with Jesus she needed.

Lucille listened and, the next day, she prayed to receive the Lord. Isn't that neat?" Linda chuckled.

"It sure is," I smiled, "how are they now? Didn't BB have surgery?"

"Yes, she did, last Saturday. In fact, Lucille did, too. They're on the surgical floor now and are doing fine."

"I should see them tomorrow. I wasn't on call last week otherwise I would have recovered them."

"Well, eventually you will see Lucille," Linda said, putting some water for coffee on the stove. "They left a temporary colostomy. It'll be reversed soon."

Indeed, it was. I had almost forgotten about Lucille when one day, her name was on the operating schedule again. I saw her the night before her surgery and found a radiant redhead with curly hair reading her Bible.

"I'm so glad you came to see me," she grabbed my hand, "BB told me all about you."

"How do you feel about your surgery?" I asked.

"Oh, I'll be so glad to get rid of this thing," Lucille sighed, "I'm looking forward to tomorrow."

"Do you want some prayer?" I suggested.

"Please," Lucile responded. We held hands and I asked the Lord to guide the hands of the surgeons and the other OR team members.

The next day, her surgery went well. After the Recovery Room, I transferred her to ICU for observation. Two days later, I hopped over for a quick visit.

"How are you, Lucille?" I asked.

She managed a weak smile and pointed a "One Way" sign with her forefinger. She looked pale, leaning listlessly into a pile of pillows, a nasogastric tube in her nose, IV drip in one arm, a Foley catheter in her bladder. I could tell she was uncomfortable and in pain.

"What's the problem?" I probed.

"Oh, it's the gas," she whispered, rather embarrassed. "The doctor says if I pass gas, he'll take this tube out of my nose and I can drink something. My mouth is so dry, I can hardly talk."

"Why don't we pray about it?" I suggested, taking her hand.

"About that?" she said incredulously. "You want to pray about gas?"

"Why not," I countered, "it's important to you, isn't it?"

"Yes, it sure is," she had to admit.

"Lord, please take care of Lucille," I prayed softly, "do whatever it takes to get her bowel to function properly. In Jesus Name, Amen. Sorry, Lucille. I've got to go. I'll see you when I go home tonight."

I returned to the Recovery Room where all the stretchers were filled with patients. Lab and X-ray techs were milling around. The phone was ringing. Two surgeons sat at the desk, one dictating a surgery report, the other writing post-operative orders on his patient's chart. Dorcas, an experienced nurse who had recently joined the Recovery Room staff, was busy with monitors, tubes and vital signs. I slung my stethoscope around my neck and joined the action.

Around 4 o'clock we were done. Tired, I changed into my street clothes and clocked out. I was almost in the parking lot when I remembered Lucille. Oh yeah, I reminded myself, I promised to go by and see her. As I walked into ICU, my heart suddenly stopped. Lucille's bed was empty. There was no sign of her anywhere. She was gone... Oh my goodness, she died, I panicked. I saw a nurse at the station.

"What happened to Lucille?" I asked, dreading the answer.

"I don't know," she looked up. "I just got here. The bed was empty when I arrived. Let me look at the census sheet. Oh, here she is. She was transferred to Room 312."

"Transferred to the surgical floor? She must be all right then. But so soon?"

"Well, why don't you go and look?" she suggested.

I rushed down the hall to the surgical floor. The door to Room 312 was open. I walked in. There in front of me was a most incredible scene. Lucille was sitting up in bed, no tube in her nose, no IV in her arm, no Foley catheter in her bladder. In front of her was a tray with soup and jello and a pot of tea. She didn't see me because she was reading a newspaper.

"Hello?" I ventured, still hardly able to believe my eyes.

"Aubrey!" she beamed, "guess what? It worked! The prayer worked. He did it." She lowered her voice, "You know... I passed gas."

I hugged her and drove home. Thank you Lord, for what You did for Lucille. My heart was singing. What a beautiful day it was. Look at that sparkling ocean, that clear blue sky. Sheepishly, I remembered the time, not too long ago, when I dreaded praying out loud in front of others. That most embarrassing night in Brisbane when Margaret bailed me out when my turn had come to pray. What happened? When did these changes take place? I didn't even remember. Isn't that amazing? I thought. Last year, we even prayed over the Operating Room table and the equipment here in the hospital. I remembered another occasion, just a few months before.

I had visited Mom and Dad in Glendale over the weekend. Dad mentioned there would be a special performance of Handel's "Messiah" in a local church. Delighted, we went. It was an excellent production with a well-trained choir, a disciplined orchestra, an experienced conductor. But even though I knew that brilliant masterpiece so well, somehow it seemed I heard it for the first time that night. It wasn't the music or the instruments: it was the words that were new. I had sung them before but never realized the significance, the message of the King of kings and Lord of lords, who is the Messiah. Something had changed in me, come alive; something that wasn't there before. Totally absorbed in the message, I marvelled that I had missed the most exciting aspects of Handel's inspired oratorio for all these years. Yes, things had changed. Actually, Someone had changed me. *Therefore, if any man be in Christ, he is a new creation, old things are passed away, behold, all things become new.* (II Cor. 5:17)

Shortly after the incident with Lucille, I was called in on a Saturday afternoon to recover a patient after an emergency appendectomy. The young man was wheeled into the Recovery Room after surgery by the anesthesiologist.

"He's doing well," Dr. Wright said, "when he is stable you can take his IV out."

"OK doctor," I said, making some admission notes on the chart. The OR crew cleaned up and went home.

"I've called housekeeping," the nurse said, as she walked out the door.

Dr. Gordon, the patient's surgeon, stuck his head around the door.

"Everything OK, Beau?" he asked.

"Yes, sir, he's fine."

"Thank you." He was gone. A young man from Housekeeping, dressed in greens, entered the Operating Room. He put a surgery cap on and found a mop and bucket.

"Excuse me," his cheerful face peeked around the corner of the Recovery Room, "which room did they use for this surgery?"

"Room 2," I told him. He went to work and I checked my patient's vital signs again. Then I heard someone singing in the Operating Room. Surprised, I listened. He was singing songs I knew, Scripture songs we sang in church and at fellowship meetings. My patient woke up and I transferred him back to his room. When I came back to Recovery to change, the young man was still at it, singing his heart out as he mopped the floor. Then he emptied the hampers and relined the trash cans.

"I like your songs," I remarked. He looked up and laughed.

"You do?" I saw a tall, tanned young man whose long, sun-bleached hair, tied in a pony tail, peeked from under his cap.

"Are you a Christian?" I asked.

"Sure am. Are you?" He flashed me a big smile. We chatted for a while, then he said, "Can I share something with you?"

"Of course, do you have time for a break? I need to clock out."

We met at the time clock and sat down on the patio surrounding the cafeteria overlooking the bright Pacific ocean in the distance.

"My name is Bill," he started.

"Hi, are you a surfer?"

"Sure am! How can you tell?" he laughed, "I used to be a beach bum. Surfing was my life. Now that I'm a Christian I still love to surf but just in my spare time."

"How much spare time do you have?" I asked, stirring my coffee.

"Not much," he laughed. "I have a wife and two kids, work full-time here and go to Bible School at night."

"Well, that'll keep you out of trouble. What did you want to share?"

"Oh yes," his eyes lit up again, "I usually take my dinner break in the chapel. I like to read my Bible and it's usually quiet there."

"Yes, it is," I agreed.

"Well, last week there were these two ladies there, a mother and a daughter. The lady's husband was in Intensive Care. He was very sick and they were both crying. We started to talk and I asked if they believed in prayer. They said they did. We got to talking about God and the Bible and I found out they really didn't know anything about it. They kept asking questions and we talked for half an hour. Finally, I prayed with them and they accepted the Lord. You should have seen their faces. It was as though a burden had lifted."

"After that," Bill continued, "I have been taking all my dinner breaks in the chapel and I find there are many people there who are so scared and lonely. You know, that chapel is such a needy place. I wish someone could be there all the time."

"Bill, I think that's a great idea," I said. "So often people want to visit the sick but it's just as important to visit the relatives of the sick, especially those in Intensive Care."

I was slowly beginning to discover all kinds of open doors for ministry right there in the hospital. There were so many needs and we were all so busy with our various jobs. But did we really look around us? I remembered a busy Christian doctor walking briskly through the hall one day. A woman was leaning against the wall just outside Intensive Care, crying. The doctor stopped, put his hand on her shoulder and gave her a few words of encouragement.

"Lord, help this lady," he prayed, "give her strength and hope. In Jesus' Name, Amen."

It didn't take two minutes and he was gone. No, she wasn't his patient, he didn't ask her name or what her problem was. He just showed he cared, touched her and prayed for her. Compassion in action.

Soon it was August again. The San Clemente Hospital had been open one year and our monthly HCF meetings were gaining momentum. We often had crowds of forty to sixty people. Linda, however, was getting thin and tired. The heavy work on the medical floor was getting to her. One night after dinner I said,

"Linda, what would you like to do with your life?"

Without a moment's hesitation she said, "Go to Bible School."

"Really?" I was surprised, "I didn't know that. Why don't you apply somewhere?"

"Are you kidding?" she said, "I don't have any money."

"Well, there are scholarships or you can work your way through. Why don't you ask? Which school would you like to go to?'

"Well, I don't know. I like Elim in New York."

We chatted on and I finally convinced her to write several schools, explain her position and wait for a reply.

"The Lord will guide," I said, "but you have to take the first step."

Linda agreed and wrote five schools, three in the US, one in England and one in Canada. They all answered. The only one who offered her a job and a way to work her way through was Elim.

"See? That place was waiting for you all along."

Excited, Linda perked up and began to pack and prepare to leave California. She quit her job, said her goodbyes to the many friends she had made in church, at the hospital and through our HCF group. I would miss her. She had been such a help to me and had actually been the one to get me in touch with HCF. On the other hand, I had been a help to her when she needed a home after her wedding plans fell through. We had needed each other. Now these needs were fulfilled and it was time for her to move on. Another era had ended. Another piece of God's fabric was complete.

Chapter 12

AND HAVING DONE ALL...,STAND!

"There's someone for you on the phone," Dorcas said a few days later. We had only one patient in the Recovery Room with two to come from surgery.

"Hello, may I help you?" I said as I picked up the phone at the desk.

"My name is Richard Dalrymple," a pleasant male voice said, "I'm with the Los Angeles Herald Examiner. Someone told me about your organization. I would like to write a story about it. Do you have time for some questions?"

"I don't know, just a minute." I relayed his request to Dorcas.

"Go ahead," she said, "I'm all right."

There followed an intense twenty-minute session of questions and answers. He was thorough and tough but fair and promised it would be a positive article. It would be in the weekend edition. He'd mail me a copy. Delighted, I hung up. How wonderful to get this free publicity, I thought. Who but the Lord could arrange this?

That Friday, a full page article graced the LA Herald Examiner. A large drawing of a patient with several health care workers around her bed highlighted the write-up. It immediately resulted in a flood of mail. How can we get involved? people asked. Where do you meet? Can you come to Los Angeles? Do you have a mailing list? How can we get on it? Do you have a handbook or some instructions on how to start an HCF group?

I answered each letter as best I could but realized we needed an outline and some specific instructions to mail out. I remembered the voluminous handbook my old sorority had produced with minute details even on how to serve refreshments. No, that wouldn't do. Perhaps a few pages outlining the things we had done in San Clemente like the prayer meetings, chapel supplies, monthly meetings, Bibles for patients and a statement of faith.

One day, I sat down and typed it all up on several sheets of paper. It would make a nice, small booklet. Now, it had to get printed but we had run out of cash. I prayed about it, filed it and waited.

"Would you like to go back to Holland for a visit?" Mom asked a few weeks later.

"I don't know. Why?"

"There's a group of people going to Spain for a convention. They have chartered a plane, will fly to Amsterdam and then take a train to Barcelona. There are some seats available and they need to sell them. It's a two-week trip."

"Sounds good. Let's see, I haven't been back there since we left in 1952; that's over twenty years. I'll let you know." Back home I prayed about it.

"Lord," I said, "if You want me to go, I'll need the time off from work, a baby-sitter for two weeks and the money for the ticket."

That was a tough order but within ten days the hospital had approved my requests for time off and had come across with an unexpected bonus. A good friend offered to take care of Sandy. Excited, I called Mom. We were going. Then another thought struck me. What are we going to do there? It'll be nice to visit friends and relatives but it would also be nice to visit some Christian groups or churches. How could we find out about that? A few days later, I attended a Christian Businessmen's banquet. The man sitting next to me was a world traveller and also happened to be the speaker.

"Do you ever go to Holland?" I asked him.

"Yes," was the answer, "I've been there many times." I told him about our pending visit.

"I would like to meet Corrie ten Boom and Brother Andrew and go to some good churches. Where should I go?"

"Go to Capitol Christian Center in The Hague," was his immediate reply, "they can tell you everything. It's the biggest thing going in Holland right now." Delighted, I called Mom in Glendale.

"Sounds good," she agreed, "by the way, you need a passport."

"Yes, I know. I'll take care of it on my next day off."

The year before I had become a U.S. citizen. Now, I needed an American passport. With warm memories, I recalled the special day at the Music Center in Los Angeles where hundreds of people had proudly accepted American citizenship. I felt so at home here, it was easy to relinquish my Dutch and Australian nationalities. My memories of these countries would always be fond ones and my roots would always be international but now the country of Uncle Sam was my home. The day of my naturalization was special for another reason too. Before the ceremony began, I had some hours to spare in Los Angeles and decided to visit Teen Challenge. I had just read David Wilkerson's book, "The Cross and The Switchblade," and was excited about the things that happened to Dave when he stepped out and trusted God for almost impossible things. The Teen Challenge Center was unique - a large, rambling brick house where men, all ex-addicts from all kinds of backgrounds, were housed and taught from the Word.

I was invited to attend a chapel service where I watched in amazement as a young man by the name of André Crouch was able to teach this motley crew of ex-junkies to actually sing together in unison as a choir. André, I was told, was a gifted young man who had just formed a group called The Disciples. Little did I realize he would one day be one of the world's most acclaimed Gospel singers. Even though the men from Teen Challenge and I were from vastly different backgrounds, somehow there was an instant bond between us, a feeling of belonging to the same family. Indeed, through Christ, we WERE related. It wasn't our nationality, social background, education or geographical location, it was the uniqueness of belonging to the same family, of belonging to the same Father and His Son Jesus that made us one.

Now as a U.S. citizen, I needed a new passport, my third one. The Immigration Department quickly processed my application. The days flew by and before we knew it our charter group filed into the jumbo jet which would take us to Holland.

"Wait till you see Holland," I bragged to my fellow Americans. "It's so clean, you can eat from the streets."

Twelve long hours later, we landed in Schiphol, Holland's international airport in Amsterdam. A bus took us to an old but comfortable hotel with extremely small stairways on the Damrak, a stone's throw from the Central Railroad Station. Before we arrived, someone leaned forward in the bus and said,

"Did you say Holland was clean?"

To my horror, I saw this once-clean city now littered with longhaired, unkempt, dirty people in sleeping bags and ragged blankets. They lined the streets and squares, staring with unseeing, vacant eyes into space. What had happened to my sparkling clean country now littered with drug addicts? At the hotel, a desk man said this had been going on for some time.

"Most of these people are not from Holland," he added, "sometimes the firetruck comes and hoses them all off the streets but it's just a matter of time and they are back."

The next day, we parted company with our group who boarded a train for Spain. Mom and I rented a VW bug and took off for Weesp to see Mom's sister, Frans. To our great relief, it became clear after we left Amsterdam that the rest of Holland had not changed as much as the big city had. The wide, flat pasturelands were still sparkling green with lush grass for thousands of healthy black and white cows. Windmills and church steeples still dotted the horizon. Huge, white billowing clouds moved overhead. A familiar, strong breeze rustled through the willow trees which lined the many waterways. Most villages had kept their picturesque uniqueness. Bright potted flowers flourished in every window sill, accented against immaculate, white lace curtains.

Our visit to Weesp was pleasant and we had a chance to get over our jetlag. Then we headed for The Hague. It was Sunday morning and we were looking forward to church and worship and Christian fellowship in our own home country. We found Capitol and walked into a rapidly filling, converted movie theater. Several people welcomed us warmly in the spacious lobby. There was a well-filled book table, coffee and cookies and a lot of happy, smiling people. Inside, a young man played the piano. The service began with some rousing songs. Even though they were sung in Dutch, we knew most of them. They were Scripture choruses, neatly translated into Dutch. We felt right at home and during the service and even had a chance to be introduced to the congregation to bring greetings from the U.S. The service lasted two hours and was followed by a hot meal, served in the adjacent cafeteria.

"All restaurants are closed on Sunday," someone explained, "and some people come from long distances."

"Are you going to stay for the baptism service this afternoon?" someone else asked.

"Sure, why not. Love to see it," we both said.

We felt an immediate kinship with these people, especially those from Indonesia who had come to live in Holland after 1952. The baptism service was an elaborate, inspiring and joyful affair which lasted three hours. Afterwards, the pastor and his secretary, Gerie, took us across the street to a five-story building where the offices, a print shop and a large Christian bookstore were housed.

"Where can I find Corrie ten Boom?" was one of my first questions.

"She's overseas," Gerie said.

"How about Brother Andrew?"

"Don't know about him, he comes and goes so often, but I'll give you his address."

"Is his book, "God's Smuggler," popular here, too?" Mom asked.

"Oh yes, it's translated into Dutch."

"Tell me about your work?" the pastor asked me.

"Well, I'm a nurse but I got involved in an organization called Hospital Christian Fellowship," I began. "It started out as a local support group for the staff in our hospital but now it's spreading and we're getting more and more involved in a regional outreach. In fact, I just wrote our first handbook. It's rather small. We don't have the funds to get it printed yet."

"Do you have it with you?" he asked. "Is it camera-ready?"

"What's that? Camera-ready?" I gave him a blank look.

"Is it ready to be printed?" he explained.

"It's typed on my typewriter."

"Then it needs to be typeset and laid out," he said knowingly. "No, it's not camera-ready. Why don't you mail it to me? How many copies do you need?"

Surprised, I stammered, "...I don't know. Haven't thought about it really."

"How about five hundred?"

"Sounds great."

"What about the cover? What color paper do you want?" He went on and we discussed further details.

"I'd like to print this first issue for you," he finally concluded with a smile. "There's no charge. The Lord has been good to me, I like to help others especially those who are just starting."

Delighted, we thanked him, praising the Lord for His unexpected provision. My prayer in California was answered in Holland. How remarkable. I didn't know at the time that our friendship with this pastor and his family would deepen over the years, that I would eventually welcome this special couple and several of their children and co-workers to the States, set up speaking engagements for them and their remarkable Indonesian Bamboo orchestra and even translate a book into English relating the pastor's life story. The latter was done in the Recovery Room in between patients.

Our next stop was Harderwÿk, a small village on the former Zuider-zee. We found Brother Andrew's address, a typical Dutch home in a quiet residential street, and rang the bell. A friendly, blue eyed girl showed us to a large office in the back where a blue eyed, smiling man, much younger than I had anticipated, warmly shook our hands. It was Brother Andrew, himself. After some general chitchat I asked him,

"Would you mind if I asked you a few questions? I have a tape recorder with me. Everyone in California has heard about you. They'd love to hear from you personally." He smiled.

"Of course. What do you want to know?"

"What has happened since God's Smuggler was written?"

He launched into a detailed response. The words, highlighted by his characteristic Dutch accent, just flowed from him. We listened, fascinated, as the tape rolled on.

After our interview, we continued our trip through Holland, visited our home in Blaricum, knocked on doors of old friends and relatives. Nothing much had changed, everyone had aged, of course, there were more cars on the road, TV sets in homes, modern appliances.

Otherwise, Holland was still Holland - small, crowded, flat, windy but cozy, a good place to visit and reminisce. Soon, our two weeks were over and we met our party from Spain again. As we winged back across the Atlantic, I was amazed and grateful to the Lord for the way this whole trip had been arranged by Him from finances to a baby-sitter and time off from work and I rejoiced that He had included a printer for our booklet and an interview with Brother Andrew.

True to his word, a large box with neatly printed HCF booklets arrived from Holland a few months later. Delighted, I began mailing them out to the various nurses and other hospital workers who had requested information.

Around that time, I received a letter from Francis Grim, the founder of Hospital Christian Fellowship, announcing a planned visit to the States. "I will be able to spend some time in California," he wrote, "and will be looking forward to meeting you."

What an honor, I thought, to meet this man who over forty years ago began more or less just as we had and was now heading a worldwide fellowship. I wasted no time with my answer and welcomed him to California. What shall we do when he gets here? I pondered. A retreat? Yes, that sounds like a good idea. Where is a suitable place? Someone told me about a Retreat Center in Desert Hot Springs three hours from San Clemente. I contacted the Center and was able to make arrangements for a weekend retreat for about fifty people. Encouraged, I moved to the next step, publicity, and designed a flier, had it printed at a local print shop and mailed out about one hundred fifty to various hospitals and addresses in Southern California. Responses began to arrive - ten, twenty, forty and finally fifty people registered. Encouraged, I called Donna, a local friend who sang and played the guitar.

"Can you come and do some song leading?" I asked. She agreed.

How about a second speaker? I thought. Can't have Mr. Grim do all the talking for the whole weekend. I remembered meeting a young man, a former roller skating champion who had a terrific testimony and was a good Bible teacher. He said he'd be delighted to come. So far, so good. Excited, I continued to plan for this, our first HCF retreat.

Then suddenly, the bottom fell out. The gasoline shortage hit and with it came long lines at the pumps and the fear of driving out too far and being unable to get back. Desert Hot Springs? Too risky. No gas available there to get back to LA. Cancellations began to arrive, first a trickle, then a flood. Mom and Dad had promised to drive from Glendale and help with registrations. However, Dad became ill and they had to stay home. Two days before the event, we had twelve people left including myself, Mr. Grim, Donna, the roller skater and my old friend, Ans Hof, who was going to pick Francis Grim up from LA Airport and drive him to the desert.

"Lord," I prayed, "what do You want me to do? We may as well cancel the whole thing." A Scripture came to mind: "and having done all, to stand." Paul said that in Ephesians 6:16. Well, I certainly had done all so all I could do was to stand. Stand on the promise of God that He was in charge and would work this thing out. I packed my little car, picked up some local people and drove to the desert. As we emerged from the car, I noticed Donna.

"Am I glad to see you," I hugged her. Donna gave me a strange look, then whispered,

"I don't feel too good. I think I have a strep throat."

She looked flushed and feverish.

"Oh no, Donna! Are you taking anything?"

"Yes, I got some medication but it hasn't helped yet." Our accommodations were in a motel six miles from the Retreat Center where we would eat and meet. I drove down there, got Donna settled in her room and returned to the Center where a few people had arrived. Where was Francis Grim? What had happened to Ans? Finally, Ans' compact pulled up on the gravel in front of the Center. Delighted, I dashed outside to welcome our special visitor. Ans bounced out and opened the passenger door. A tall, imposing figure slowly unfolded from the little car. Was he OK? I wondered as I welcomed him, my hand locked in his firm grasp. I didn't have to wait long.

"Aubrey, I don't feel well," were his first words. "I got a cold in Dallas, I believe the air conditioning was too cold. Anyway, I wonder if I can go to my room and rest."

He was definitely feverish. I quickly drove him the six miles down the road to the motel and settled him in his room just a few doors from Donna.

"Is there anything I can get you?"

"Perhaps some soda pop. I'm very thirsty. Or how about some ice water?"

In a daze, I drove back to the Center. Now what? Both Donna and Grim sick. No music, no speaker. The roller skater had arrived at the Center.

"How would you like to be our main speaker?" I asked, explaining my plight.

"No problem," he smiled.

The rest of the weekend, I only remember as a blur driving back and forth from the Center to the motel with ice water, aspirin, penicillin and lots of prayer. Donna recovered but was unable to sing, the roller skater did fine, and our audience of ten was blessed. Francis regained some of his strength and was able to address us once during the Sunday morning service. This was held in combination with a local church which also met at the Center. When it was all over, we packed our bags and I drove Francis back with me to Capistrano Beach. His fever was still high, his throat very red and swollen. A local doctor prescribed Ampicillin shots which I gave him for three days.

A hectic week followed. After sending Sandy off to school, I'd go to work and return on my lunch break to take care of my patient at home. Francis slowly recovered. His huge round-the-world airline ticket had to be rewritten which took two days and was very expensive. Slowly, the fever left and his strength returned. One evening, I invited everyone I knew at the hospital to my home. Over twenty-five people crowded the living room. Francis Grim, seated in my rocking chair, graciously greeted everyone. He was not able to talk too much yet so I asked everyone present to take three minutes to share their testimony. They did and unashamedly poured out their praises to God for coming into their lives. No two stories were alike yet everyone had to go through the same gate - Jesus - to be forgiven, set free and join the family of God.

"I am very impressed with your frankness," Francis Grim finally concluded, "you Americans have a special boldness I really appreciate. I'm sorry, I have not been able to spend more time with you but I'm glad to have met you tonight." His deep voice was both solemn and gentle, his blue eyes clear and penetrating under their bushy eyebrows.

"I would like to invite all of you to come to our World Conference next year in Austria," he announced. "A friend of yours," he smiled at me, "Brother Andrew, will be there as well." We concluded with prayer.

Two days later, I took my special guest to the LA Airport. His visit had been special, I mused as I drove back home, although not at all what I expected. The retreat was blessed in spite of the small turnout, gas crisis and sick people. I had a fresh understanding of Pauls' words "and having done all ... stand." It had been hard for a while, just stand and do nothing but the Lord came through and stood behind His word.

I felt I had passed a test especially designed by God just for me. Encouraged, I pulled up in my driveway, opened the front door and fixed hamburgers for supper for Sandy and me.

"Wouldn't you like to go to Austria?" I asked our group at the next meeting.

"Boy, would I! I've never been outside California." Lupe said.

"Neither have I." Pattie, a young ward clerk from ICU piped in.

"Well, why don't you go?" I asked.

"How much does it cost?" "How long will we be gone?" "What papers do we need?" Everyone talked at once.

"I'll call a travel agent and find out about the plane fare," I promised. "Let's pray about it."

The following week, I gave them some figures. It wasn't cheap.

"How in the world are we going to get that much money together?" they wondered.

"Perhaps we could have a white elephant sale or a dinner or something."

A lively discussion followed. Finally, it was decided our group would sponsor Lupe and Pattie to go to Austria to represent HCF in the U.S. We would ask Jerry, the local pastor who spoke at our first potluck, if we could use his meeting hall. We would sell donated items and offer a Mexican dinner which Lupe would cook. Several people had items to contribute. One of our biggest contributors was Dorothy, a retired nurse raised in China, who had recently joined our fellowship. We all got busy and started spreading the word. Excitement ran high. The Saturday of the great event finally arrived. Dorothy lugged in carloads of plants, vases and an assortment of trinkets. Lupe arrived with her huge pans and bowls with rice and beans and enchiladas. People arrived in droves and quickly filled up the festively decorated hall. Long wooden tables with bright red and white cloths were soon buzzing with chatter and laughter. Some items were raffled, others sold and food disappeared quickly as a busy kitchen crew kept filling empty plates. Finally everyone left, the leftovers were gathered, the hall cleaned up and the intake counted. Sixty percent of the needed funds were there. Not bad. Praise the Lord. Now it was up to the travelers to make up the difference. Family members and neighbors who heard about the planned trip began to get involved, some gave sacrificially, others helped with passports and visa costs. When the day of departure arrived, all the funds were in, all papers in order. Several cars took the excited travelers to LA International Airport where they began one of the greatest events of their lives.

We had done it! We sponsored the first two delegates to an International HCF Conference.

Three weeks later, they returned utterly blessed and inspired by both the beautiful country of Austria and the warm and deep fellowship of Christian hospital workers from around the world. Every continent was represented, they said. I set up a special evening in a local restaurant where Lupe and Pattie gave an official report of their unforgettable experience, describing colorful dresses, strange languages, quaint homes, the huge snowcapped Alps and above all the glowing love of God which drew everyone together into a close and special fellowship.

My mailbox, in the meantime, was filling up. I was spending more and more time answering letters and printing and mailing newsletters. The Recovery Room was busy. Our staff of two had to cover each night and weekend for emergencies. I began to get tired and feel rushed all the time. Perhaps I can slow down or cut back somewhere, I thought. After some discussion with the Supervisor, an extra part-time nurse was hired. I cut back to four days a week.

For a while, this helped. But then another problem appeared. As more and more health care workers wanted information about hospital ministries, I felt more and more inadequate to answer their questions. I was in need of training myself. When Francis Grim was visiting, he had mentioned that a nurse from Africa, Leonora, had felt a call from God to go to Europe and develop HCF there. She travelled to Rotterdam where a doctor offered her a small flat. I got in touch with her and learned that a special Leadership Week was to be given in Holland for Dutch hospital personnel.

"Can I come?" I asked. She answered by return mail.

"Of course, we'd be more than happy to have you."

Go back to Holland again? I had just been there two years ago. Mom didn't want to go again but Ans Hof was interested.

"Let's go to l'Abri in Switzerland as well." she suggested.

I liked the idea. Well, here we go again, Lord. Time off, baby-sitter, money... should I go? Mom and Dad would take care of Sandy this time, the hospital let me off for two weeks and Ans and I soon flew across the Atlantic.

In Holland, she left to visit relatives and I caught a train to a small village in the east of Holland where the HCF group met at a converted farm. After a long and tiring train ride, I arrived and was welcomed by about thirty-five people, mostly nurses. The long summer days didn't darken till about eleven o'clock and roosters crowed around three to welcome the new day. In spite of these changes, I enjoyed the meetings, the rich teachings and the fellowship among health care workers. I met Leonora, who was in charge and a pretty young nurse, Ingrid, who said she wanted to come to the States. There was a fellow named Leo, a male nurse, full of dry, Dutch humor and Ria who coordinated the HCF work in that area. For the final evening, I got a small choir together and taught them some of our California songs, "Father I adore Thee" and "Seek Ye First the Kingdom of God." Afterwards, I drove with Leonora to Rotterdam where I questioned her at length about her work in Europe. She was open and gracious and I learned a lot about administration including filing, record keeping and a host of other details.

I also called my pastor friend in The Hague. He sent a car to get me and take me back to Capitol. This was to be my rendevouz place with Ans. Sure enough, she was there. We enjoyed another excellent service and the next day, we took off for Switzerland. l'Abri was crowded but we found a bed and breakfast chalet nearby and sat in on some excellent teaching sessions by the great, late Francis Scheaffer. How blessed we were, I thought, and what a large family we belong to. We met a pastor from India and one day the three of us climbed an Alpine mountain, passing sturdy wooden chalets, fat cows with chiming bells and a multitude of wild flowers. What a difference to leave Holland where everything is flat and go to Switzerland where nothing is flat. Rested and refreshed, we returned to California. As always, it was good to be home.

The volume of mail had increased. It took me days to wade through it. I accepted a few invitations to speak for groups near the LA area. Work at the hospital continued to be busy. Should I cut back on work again? I thought. After prayer, I dropped another day in the Recovery Room. Three work days a week plus "on call time" offered little income but I managed. What should I do about this growing ministry? I kept thinking.

Our monthly outreach meetings continued. They went well, a steady stream of hospital staff came through these home meetings. Speakers were always available and willing to share. However, setting up these meetings was time- consuming and many of our original core group had moved out of the area. I found myself doing more and more of the tasks that used to be done by others. On one busy, crowded night at the home of a doctor in San Clemente, I found myself leading the singing, manning the literature table, emceeing the program and helping with the refreshments. I also took care of the offering and announced future events. The nurse in charge of refreshments, I learned later, had lost her way and returned home. Other helpers had moved away and had not been replaced.

"Something has to give, Lord," I prayed. "This is not the right way to run an organization. Are You trying to tell me something? Am I supposed to do something different?"

The answer came in a few days, again as a slow but growing, strong conviction. I wasn't ready for it.

"I want you to spread this work across the USA."

"The whole country? No way! That's too big." I balked.

But the thought persisted. I began to bargain.

"What about Southern California? That's about twenty million people."

The answer was silence.

"Well, Lord," I got ready for another approach, "if You want me to give up this local ministry, I want to put out a fleece. If the next two monthly meetings are poorly attended, I will take it as a sign from You to branch out into a larger area."

I had lined up two well-known speakers for the next two months and had even asked for Jerry's hall again. A home would be too small, I figured. A special friend of Brother Andrew, a Bible teacher from Belgium, was to be the first special guest. He had been here before several years earlier and we had had a packed house. Ever since that time, people had been asking me when he would be back. Surely, I thought, a full house was almost guaranteed. But when the big night arrived, instead of the expected two hundred people, only twenty-five showed up, straggling in one by one, barely filling the first two rows of empty chairs. I was crushed. However, the meeting was greatly blessed. One girl brought her husband, who went forward towards the end of the meeting to give his heart to the Lord. It turned out he was a drug addict. The Lord delivered him. My elderly neighbor lady attended also and went forward for prayer. God blessed, yet answered my fleece at the same time.

We had formed a new board to replace those who had moved. A month later, I asked the speaker, a well-known pastor, to dedicate this board. Newspapers had widely announced this meeting. Calls poured in, responses were overwhelming. Encouraged, and secretly optimistic about my fleece, I awaited the big night. When it came, our board of five was there early, full of anticipation. But only a few people appeared at the door. When the speaker arrived with two of his co-pastors, he wondered if he was at the right place. Where was everybody? We waited a little longer and sang some choruses. No one else arrived. There were about twenty-five people again. The speaker delivered an excellent message followed by a special prayer for our new board. It was a holy moment and again I realized the Lord had managed to both bless me and answer my fleece. I had not shared it with anyone but after this meeting, I was convinced I had received my answer. To test it further, I stopped our monthly outreach meetings. Six months went by and no one asked what happened. Ouch! That hurt.

"OK Lord," I relented, "I believe You are folding this phase of our local outreach. Now what about Orange County, right here? That's over ten million people. Perhaps I can handle that." We got together with our new officers and decided on an Orange County Banquet. Energetically, I drove to Santa Ana, made arrangements at the Saddleback Inn for a banquet, then printed invitations. Several people would share during the program - Linda, a nurse friend from Seal Beach, would bring her guitar and sing.

Ticket sales went well. On the night of the banquet, I drove to Anaheim. About a mile from the freeway exit there was an accident. Traffic was backed up for miles. There was also an accident on the lanes going the other direction. I remembered my promise to the maitre d' to be on time. People began to arrive a half hour late. An hour after the appointed time, only half the room was filled.

"We have to serve now, the kitchen people are going home and the food is getting cold." the chief hostess said firmly.

We started to eat. A few more people straggled in. After dessert, about seventy percent had shown up. We got stuck with a huge bill. But the program went well. A pastor from India, a former hospital orderly, shared and challenged us all to be aware of patients' spiritual needs.

"You never know by people's faces or attitudes what they feel like inside," he stressed, "they put on masks. Inside they are scared and lonely and waiting to hear about the love of God."

After the meeting, Merle, a lab tech, came to me.

"Aubrey," he said, "I know you are disappointed that more people didn't come tonight. But I have a great conviction that this ministry will spread and eventually reach the whole country."

Dumbfounded, I looked at him. I had met him at South Coast Hospital quite a few years ago and not seen him since. He didn't know about my fleece or argument with the Lord.

"Thanks, Merle," I said softly, "thanks a lot. I appreciate that."

I knew the Lord had spoken.

Chapter 13

BUCKLE UP!

The USA! How in the world do you cover the whole USA? How many hospitals are there? How much personnel involved in health care? How do you reach them? Confused and overwhelmed, I bombarded the Lord with questions. After a while, I quieted down enough to be able to hear that still, small voice again. When it came it was unmistakable.

"I want you to write a national magazine."

A national magazine? How do you put a magazine together? Where do you get a mailing list? Who's going to pay for it? More questions with no answers. Finally I said, "OK Lord, if You want me to put a national magazine together, You have to show me how to do it."

I remembered my Famous Writer School correspondence course when I first moved into my new home. I also recalled my times with the sorority and later HCF writing press releases and putting newsletters together. Then there was the little handbook. Had all those projects been designed in preparation for this? What articles should be in this magazine? What would the name be?

The HCF headquarters published an excellent periodical called, "Heartbeat." Perhaps I could take some articles from there. Of course, I could write up some of the things that had happened to us in the San Clemente Hospital with our patients and during our outreaches.

I began to jot down incidents and stories. One day, I heard about a Christian surgeon, a friend of Linda's former patient, BB.

"Could we have a fellowship meeting at her home?" I asked BB.

"Please do!" BB was excited.

Over twenty people came. The doctor passed around a tract relating his testimony and recovery from an acute heart attack. It was called, "A New Heart" from a scripture in Ezekiel 18:31. Something clicked inside me as I read that passage at home a few days later: "... *make yourselves a new heart and a new spirit*!" (NASB) That's it! A name for the magazine - "A NEW HEART."

In our church bulletin, I read an announcement about a newspaper some people wanted to start. Volunteers were needed. I attended this meeting and met David, the leader, an expert in writing and publishing. Although in the end, I did not get involved in the church paper, I did get some invaluable information from David about publishing a magazine.

"You need to get some ads," he said, "to offset your cost."

"How do you do that?" I asked.

"Call some Christian TV stations," he suggested, "or health care organizations or book publishers. You also need a rate chart."

"What do you think are reasonable rates?" I wanted to know.

We discussed this and things like a mailing list and bulk permits.

"Are you a non-profit organization?"

"Yes, we did that last year so people could deduct their gifts from their income tax."

"Great! Then you need to apply for a non-profit bulk permit at your post office. How about your mailing list?"

"Well, we have about two thousand names right now."

"Why don't you add a list of hospitals?"

"How do you get that?"

"I don't know. Isn't there a Hospital Association?"

There was, and eventually I got a complete Directory of Hospitals in the U.S. I also drafted and printed an advertising rate chart and contacted two Christian TV stations. They both responded and took almost two pages of ads.

"Make sure their copy is camera-ready," David cautioned.

I smiled and remembered the same question the pastor in The Hague asked me some years before. I'd had no idea then what he meant.

"How often do you want to publish this magazine? How many copies do you want to print each time?"

David continued to ask difficult questions.

"What about quarterly," I suggested, "and perhaps start with about five thousand?"

"Yes," he agreed, "that sounds like a good idea."

I called several printers for quotes for five thousand copies of a twenty-page magazine and realized that these two ads from the Christian TV stations would cover most of our printing costs.

"Now, let me tell you, step by step, what it takes to produce a magazine," David told me as we met in his office a few weeks later.

What followed was a discourse on typesetting, proofreaders, layout, graphics, blue lines, screens, half-tones and a host of other terms all quite foreign to me.

"I just called a lady who advertised in our local paper," he said. "She's not too far from you and said she'd do the typesetting and layout for you. Her name is Barbara. Here is her number."

I called Barbara. She was a pleasant lady behind a huge typesetting contraption. We discussed fees. Hers seemed reasonable and I left her my typed notes for the first issue. A few days later, I returned to proofread her copy then watched her in fascination as she deftly cut up self-adhesive copy, added pictures, lines and screens to produce one very attractive page after another. Next time I can do this myself, I thought. Our non-profit mailing permit came through at the post office. Proudly, I finally took the finished galleys from Barbara to the printer who went to work after discussing paper quality and weight, color of ink and details for screens. Soon, heavy boxes of the first issue of "A New Heart" were lugged into the garage. It was the spring of 1977.

In the meantime, I had acquired another helping hand at home. Since Linda left for Bible school, all HCF correspondence had fallen on my shoulders. Then I received a letter from Ingrid, the Dutch nurse I had met in Holland at the HCF Leadership week. She still wanted to come to the States and had, in fact, arrived in Minneapolis where she was involved in a campus ministry.

"When can you come to California?" I wrote her, "I need some help here."

She arrived just before my sessions with David about "A New Heart" started and helped with typing up mailing labels. I had discovered label sheets we could type names and addresses on, then copy them for future use before peeling them off and attaching them to the magazine. I also discovered that bulk permits require a complicated set of rules. When copies of "A New Heart" were printed, we set up a large ping-pong table in the backyard and began sorting labeled magazines into zip code order. The glossy paper was prone to slip and slide, the legs of the ping-pong table were not too steady resulting in moments of great frustration as magazines kept sliding off the table and onto the ground.

Ingrid had written an article for this issue, called "The Apple Tree." I contributed with "Would You Like To Share Your Faith More Effectively?" and some true stories and testimonies. We even had a directory, mostly of people from California. An excellent article from Francis Grim was used from "Heartbeat." In the back was a subscription and membership application. Exactly nine months had passed between that first directive: "I want you to publish a national magazine" and the actual production of it - the same time it took to carry a baby. In a sense, "A New Heart" was a baby, a newborn, a little clumsy and rather expensive but born nevertheless.

Three months later, getting ready for the next issue, I had a sudden problem. One TV station who had promised a full-page ad in four issues backed out due to financial stress. Undaunted, I figured out a way to type copy on my IBM typewriter and justify both edges. It was time-consuming but saved the cost of the typesetter. Then I cut it to size and pasted it on cardboard pages myself saving further cost for lay-out. Now only the cost of printing and mailing was left. To offset this, I announced subscription rates in the next issue.

Our little handbooks were almost gone and something more sophisticated and detailed was needed. Again, I settled behind my typewriter and slowly began working on an "U.S. HCF Handbook" detailing goals and objectives and the various ways to implement them. Suggestions and pointers from Leonora in Holland helped as did information from International Headquarters.

One day when I was recovering a craniotomy patient in the Recovery Room, there was a soft knock on the door. It opened slightly and the curly head of a smiling, bespectacled woman peeked through. I thought she was a relative of the patient.

"Are you Aubrey?" she smiled.

"Yes, I am. Can I help you?"

"Can we see you when you are finished here? We're from San Jose and want to talk to you about your hospital ministry."

Surprised, I told them to wait in the lobby. Half an hour later, I had returned my patient to Intensive Care and met a pleasant middle aged couple in the lobby. Their names were Charles and Naomi McDonald.

"How did you find me here?" I wanted to know.

"I saw a copy of your magazine," Naomi began, "I called information for your phone number and also got your home address. Then we found your home but you weren't there. So we drove over to your neighbor who said you worked here. The lady at the switchboard said you were in the Recovery Room."

Amazed, I congratulated them on their detective work.

"What can I do for you?"

"I was hospitalized a couple of months ago," Naomi said, "and while I was in the hospital I realized what a spiritually empty place it was. I felt the Lord wanted me to do something about that. Now that I am well, I want to start a hospital ministry but I need your help. I've talked to several people at a hospital near us and many are interested. But we need some more information. Can you come for a weekend in the San Jose area?"

"I don't know," I said thoughtfully, "I'd need to get time off and get a baby-sitter."

"We'll take care of your expenses," Charles announced, "you can fly and we'll pick you up. Of course, you can stay at our home."

I promised to think about it. The next day in church, I spoke with a friend, Charlene.

"Do you want to go to San Jose with me?" I asked her, "I may need some moral support with a seminar they want me to do there."

"I'll be honored. When are you going?" she smiled.

We worked out the details and a six weeks later we flew to San Jose. Naomi, it turned out, was a very energetic woman. She had arranged for a conference room at a local hospital and managed to fill it with about fifty people, most of them health care workers. There was someone to lead the music, a buffet luncheon and even a reporter from a local newspaper. I was glad to have some new handbooks on hand as well as some "Heartbeats." Still feeling rather unprepared in my role as teacher, I earnestly prayed for guidance about what to say. Finally, I decided to give my testimony first then relate how we got started in San Clemente and for the third session, give a Bible study on the various abilities God gives us. I still felt very inadequate and awkward and kept wondering what I was doing here in front of all these people. The reporter got hold of me during a coffee break and asked lots of questions, some rather blunt. His write-up was kind, though. Naomi beamed as she handed me the paper the next day, "Recovery Must Include More Than Medicine," the headline ran. "The business of healing," the article continued, "should involve more than scalpels, antibiotics and stethoscopes - it should include diligent nurturing of the patient's spiritual needs as well according to Aubrey Beauchamp, founder of the U.S. branch of the International Hospital Christian Fellowship."

Encouraged, Charlene, who had been a tremendous support and great company during this weekend, and I returned to San Clemente. The Lord was certainly opening doors. Where would it all lead?

From the Grims, I heard about another international conference that was planned in Wales. After the glowing reports from Lupe and Pattie about their time in Austria, I was anxious to attend this event myself and eager to learn more about the business of ministering to patients' spiritual needs. At church one day I met Flo, a fellow nurse from Westminster, who had started a small support group for nurses. I attended one of her meetings and shared about HCF and the upcoming Conference in Wales. An assistant pastor from a large church approached Flo and me afterwards. "I want you to have this," he handed Flo a small piece of paper, "so you can go with Aubrey to Wales." It was a check, large enough for her round trip plane ticket between Los Angeles and London. Amazed, Flo thanked him. I was elated.

"Now I don't have to travel alone!" I laughed. "Are you coming?"

"I have to discuss it with my husband," she said, rather bewildered.

Things worked out for me. The baby-sitter, the time off and the funds all came together. The months flew by and soon we boarded another jumbo jet, this time for London.

I had never been to London or to Great Britain for that matter. The first surprise came when we landed at Gatwick, an hour by train from London.

"You mean, we aren't in London yet?" I asked a customs officer.

"Train leaves from that platform over there, Ma'am." He pointed. We retrieved our luggage and boarded the train. I hadn't been on one for years. At Euston station in London, we got out. Now we had to find Victoria station for our connecting train. Flushed and slightly out of breath, we pushed our heavy suitcases through the jostling crowd. They were strapped to two delicate little wheels and topped by a bulging bag and an overflowing purse. I desperately tried to keep this contraption together in the heavy, almost stampeding crowd. We learned we could either take the underground or a taxi to Victoria station. We opted for a taxi and patiently waited in a long line for a stately, old black taxicab. The ride through London was almost more than we bargained for. Separated from the driver by a thick divider we soon sat frozen to our seats as the cab careened around corners, narrowly missing pedestrians and constantly tailgating other vehicles.

"Now you know what it feels like to be a criminal and taken to the nearest Police Station," I shouted to Flo as we screeched around another corner.

"Yes," she yelled back, hanging on for dear life, "or an accident victim in an Ambulance taken to the nearest hospital." The cabbie was undisturbed as he pulled up at Victoria Station and hauled our luggage from our little prison in the back.

An hour later, our train left for Wolverhampton where we were to change trains again for Shrewsbury. As the beautiful hilly English scenery sped by, I watched our fellow passengers. Most were in earnest conversation, their speech betraying their English origin. Many others, however, did not look or sound British at all. Some were reading, others napping. How many, I wondered, were going to the Wales Conference?

At Shrewsbury, we boarded a smaller train with only two cars. It seemed that nearly all of the passengers were now foreigners. When the little train finally pulled up in Aberystwyth, our final destination, we were in animated conversation with several of them. Yes, they were all going to the HCF Conference and they were all travel-weary. It was dark and raining when we arrived. A bus was waiting for us and we wearily climbed in. A cheerful young woman welcomed us. She was Julie, one of the Conference hostesses. She promised us a meal, a room and a rest. The University of Wales where the international gathering was to be held, turned out to be a huge complex of enormous buildings sprawled over a vast terrain of hilly and beautifully-kept grounds. Together with about two hundred others, we were dropped in front of our dorm, Pantycelyn (quickly dubbed penicillin). Its interior reminded me of a huge anthill with a maze of intricate tunnels and passageways. However, most of the rooms, after they were located, were single and comfortable.

After a good night's sleep, we met for breakfast. It took a while to locate the dining room at "Penicillin" but when we did, we were greeted by the happy din of hundreds of eating, chatting delegates. After we joined them, my ears tried to categorize the various languages that floated around the table. Here we are, I thought, all of us munching away at the same cereal and scrambled eggs, eating the same food and breathing the same air, yet our languages did not change, we all remained different and unique. As Christians we all take in the Word of God - it's the same Bible around the world - yet we maintain our own identity and specific personality. We are one in the Lord yet uniquely different in expression and form.

After breakfast, we made our way to the Great Hall looming majestically above us on a large hill, overlooking the entire city of Aberystwyth and Cardigan Bay. Here we met hundreds of other delegates who had gathered for the official opening ceremonies led by the Mayor, a lady dressed in an impressive, colorful Welch costume. The mayor expressed her delight in the theme of the Conference, "In His Steps," and stressed the fact that Jesus Christ is not just an example to follow but indeed, He IS *the Way, the Truth and the Life* and our only access to the Father.

An impressive flag ceremony followed as delegates from around the world, one by one, placed a small national flag on the table. When every representative had filed by, a total of eighty-nine flags graced the table from Greenland to the Fiji islands and Australia, from the United States to Korea, Europe, Africa and the Middle East. Some countries, I had to locate on a large map of the world which was displayed on the stage. Colorful costumes lit up the audience. Blacks and whites and orientals all sang together in praise to the Lord. In awe, I realized that there before me was a miniature gathering of the United Nations truly united by the love of Christ, the only bond and hope for lasting peace and unity on earth.

Francis Grim, now in excellent health and full of strength and energy opened the Conference with a stirring challenge.

"God," he said, "is looking for individuals. Individuals who will rule with Him. The Bible states that we shall rule with Christ. But," he cautioned, "are we rulers over our own lives? Do we rule our tongue, our thoughts, our appetite? We cannot rule in any area of our lives but by the power of Christ within us. Let us always endeavor to follow in His steps so we can be rulers indeed in this dark and perverse generation."

I shared a coffee break with a bearded man from the Faroe Islands located one hundred miles north of the Norwegian coast. He was a nurse and had met Francis Grim the year before when he visited his country. He had wanted to come to the conference but finances and time off from his job made it appear impossible.

"But God delights in impossibilities," he smiled, "a sick patient needed to be transported to Denmark. An escort was required and I was chosen to take him, at government expense. From there, it was easy to go to Wales. I worked extra time and accumulated enough days off to come to the Conference."

On Sunday morning, Ian Muir, a Scotchman, spoke on the many avenues of worship.

"This is missing," he said, "among most evangelicals."

"God demands our worship," he stressed, "because of Who and What He is. In Revelations 5:9, we read that He has redeemed and purchased us. Our worship to Him should be part of every aspect of our lives and not be limited to pleasant and joyful occasions only. Worship during difficult times is of utmost importance. Only then can God's grace and power be fully realized in our lives."

The evenings were set aside for Continental Focus programs. There was Africa, the Middle East, Europe, Latin America, North America and Australasia. Each Focus evening was preceeded by a morning session of prayer specifically directed to the continent to be featured. Leaders included pastors from the Philippines, Africa, a businessman from the Middle East, a pathologist from Ireland, a doctor from Venezuela, a layman from India and a surgeon from the U.S. This made us aware of the needs and conditions in other parts of the world.

Many delegates spoke no English so nine interpreters, hidden in little booths at the back of the auditorium, translated all sessions. We learned how to pray Korean style. Korean Christians are known to be prayer warriors. Their style is unique and effective for larger groups. After the morning message, we all formed small groups of three or four and prayed out loud for the specific requests and needs mentioned. Personal requests, praise and worship were also included.

"Twenty minutes of such intercessions by nine hundred believers," Francis Grim said, "equals three hundred hours of prayer."

A chaplain spoke on "Total Patient Care" and quoted Isaiah 6:8-10:

Whom shall I send, and who will go for us? Then said I, Here am I; send me. And He said, Go, and tell this people, Hear ye indeed, but understand not; and see ye indeed, but perceive not. Make the heart of this people fat, and make their ears heavy, and shut their eyes; lest they see with their eyes, and hear with their ears, and understand with their heart, and convert, and be healed"

"Only Christians can truly give total patient care," she said, "they have that added spiritual dimension and sensitivity only Jesus can give."

This was elaborated on in another message by Francis Grim when he spoke on counseling:

"Unless we are filled and guided by God's Spirit," he stressed, "counseling will be of little effect to anyone. Jesus said: 'Without Me ye can do nothing.' We need both God's love and guidance to effectively help and counsel others." (John 15:5)

I was struck by the excellent and detailed preparations made by the staff. Everything was saturated by prayer. Small matters were never neglected, all things handled with a personal touch and done with loving care. At one meeting a medical doctor from Tanzania made a thought-provoking statement:

"Not only do more people pass through the hospitals of the world than through its churches, the hospitals of today may well become the church of tomorrow. In some countries where churches have been forcefully closed, this is already the case. Let us never take our hospital mission field lightly."

Many golden nuggets were presented by another pastor, this one from England as he expounded his message, "The Approach to the Patient":

"We must always stay aware of the following facts:" he stated, "One, God is actively in control of every detail of our life; Two, unredeemed man is separated from God and Three, when speaking to your patients say to them what God says in His word. In other words, know who God is, what man is and what to say."

On a practical level, he challenged what we must be. "God is more concerned with what you ARE than what you DO," he said, "In addition to knowing God's salvation in our lives, we must be clean, confident and honest. Be yourself. Don't copy others. Do your job well and set an example. Go the extra mile. Let the Holy Spirit guide you in all matters and above all be a good listener."

In order for the delegates to digest their spiritual food, several bus trips were arranged during a free day. To my delight, I came to sit next to a sweet young girl from Holland. She was from Laren, right next to my birthplace of Blaricum. In our minds, we visited familiar streets, buildings and schools. She shared that she had lost her job because she had prayed with a dying patient and his young wife. The wife had been most grateful and comforted but the prayer had cost her job and training.

"However, God is good," she stated, "He gave me a better job in a Christian doctor's office."

One afternoon, I was privileged to speak on "Problems and Successes in HCF Outreaches." I used our first retreat at Desert Hot Springs as a great example of unforeseen problems.

"Our biggest challenge is to get along and respect each other," I said, "and to know how to handle disappointments and discouragement. Once when things locally were going downhill, the husband of a close friend of mine said, 'Aubrey is just beating a dead horse.' But the Lord was trying to get my attention away from local outreaches so He could prepare me for a national one something I would never have considered if it had not been for that 'dead horse.'

"Reaching hospital staff with the Gospel takes dedication, perseverance and patience," I concluded, "if we do our best and leave the results up to the Lord, we will never be disappointed."

A highlight for most was a powerful message by Loren Cunningham, the founder of Youth With A Mission ministries. With a smile, I remembered meeting Loren in California the year before. We found him after an almost impossible search through Los Angeles during Francis Grim's second visit. Francis was determined to find him but it was like locating a needle in a haystack. After what seemed a senseless, wild goose chase, we literally bumped into Loren and even had lunch with him. At that time, he accepted Francis' invitation to the Wales Conference. His topic was: "Humility, both Christ's and Ours."

"We have to be willing to be known for who we really are," he declared, "willing to admit when we are wrong, willing to expose our real self and admit our mistakes."

"Pride," he continued, "is an effort to be known for what we are not. In His humility, Jesus chose to become a servant. He also chose to give up His rights and His reputation. In Philippians 2:5 the apostle Paul says, 'Let this mind be in you which was also in Christ.' This clearly means we have to be willing to give up our human rights, our freedom, our privacy, our family, food, friends, fashion, home, nationality, reputation and finances. God wants us to be free yet the only way to have His freedom is to lose ours. We cannot have God's reputation until we lose our own."

In another session, Loren spoke on Mark 5:1-17, the story of Jesus releasing the demon-possessed man. The demons entered a herd of swine who then drowned in the sea. As a result, the local population begged Him to leave the area. The swine were their livelihood, their source of income. The loss of their job was more important to them than the fact their possessed brother had been set free and had been restored to his right mind. They never considered that Jesus could re-direct their lives. They wanted their pigs back!

"Let's take a look at the pigs in our own lives," he challenged. "Are we willing to give up everything and follow Christ?"

At the last session the often baffling question of "Why Do The Innocent Suffer" was discussed.

"Jesus," Loren stated, "was the most innocent Man who ever lived yet He suffered more, physically, mentally and spiritually than anyone else. Jesus, the most innocent, died so that the most guilty may become innocent! Jesus has limited our suffering and promises us that He will not ever permit us to suffer beyond our endurance. Yet spiritual suffering, the suffering of loneliness and guilt, is far more intense than physical suffering. Jesus was more concerned with spiritual suffering than with physical pain.

"Yet the Bible states that Jesus, though innocent, learned obedience through suffering so it is clear that we can learn through suffering as well. Jesus' suffering gave credibility to His message and helped to spread God's Word throughout the world. For example, the strong, suffering church behind the Iron Curtain today is challenging all Christians in the free world. Paul, in Colossians 1:24 sums it all up when he says, *[I] now rejoice in my sufferings for you, and fill up that which is behind of the afflictions of Christ in my flesh for His body's sake, which is the church.*"

Dr. William Reed, a surgeon from Florida, spoke on "The Care of the Dying." The question of euthanasia came up. When is a condition terminal or hopeless?

"Although the medical profession is commissioned to reverence and maintain life," Dr. Reed said, "let us keep in mind that the word euthanasia means 'natural death'. There comes a time when we doctors, after earnest prayer, have to decide when to allow natural death to take place."

As to the definition of "terminal" he stated, "In a sense, we are all terminal but as Christians, we will never die. The subject of death and dying is very popular in America today," he continued, "a focus on this was long overdue and on the whole I agree with their approach. However, I feel that one important thing is missing: Jesus and the hope of eternal life! Only Christians have this hope but it was given for the whole world. It is our duty to stress and proclaim this hope to all who will hear us."

Among the many new people I met were Ken and Faith Ragoonath from Trinidad in the West Indies. It was the beginning of a strong friendship followed by many visits to the States in the years to come. Ken had been instrumental in the growth of a strong fellowship in the Pittsburgh area started by a nurse, Margaret Malcomson. Margaret and her husband, Bill, were also at the Conference. Ken, himself, headed the Caribbean HCF. He was a pastor and former hospital worker. One morning he spoke on fear.

"King David said:" he quoted, reading from II Samuel 9:1-8, "*Is there yet any that is left of the house of Saul, that I may show him kindness for Jonathan's sake?*"

"He found out," Ken continued, "that one of Jonathan's sons was still alive but lame and hiding in a cave at Lodebar. The young man was very much afraid to appear before the king who only wanted to put him in a place of honor at his own palace.

"How often are we afraid to come out of our hiding places?" Ken looked around the quiet auditorium, "afraid that we will find an angry King? But our King is waiting for us and anxious to give us a seat of honor at His table. Let us come out of hiding and come to where He is."

One evening, Margareta, an occupational therapist from Sweden, and I took a walk along one of Wales' narrow, winding, hedged-in roads. An old car stopped. The driver was a Welchman and he offered us a ride.

"I just live in the next valley," he explained, "and the wife and I would just love to have you over for a cup of tea."

Why not? we thought and hopped in enjoying the beauty of the passing hills. It turned out the man and his wife had attended some of the Focus Evenings which were open to the public. They were Christians. He was a printer. Their modest but cozy home was warm and clean and we were treated like royalty. Before leaving, we prayed for this precious couple and thanked them for their hospitality. I thanked God for the unexpected visit in the home of this Welch couple.

Songs and faces of this Conference linger on. I will always remember the smiling, upturned face of Godfrey from the island of Barbados, singing that beautiful Caribbean melody "I was Born to Serve the Lord," playing the piano not only with his hands but his whole body, expressing the soft, swaying rhythm of the moving lyrics. I still see the earnest face of an Egyptian doctor urging all fellowships to care for and comfort other groups, uplifting them when they are discouraged and keeping in close touch. Neither will I forget the sweet face of a Latin American girl, one of the Spanish translators, and her pleas to come and help in Latin America.

"You can come by plane, by boat or by car," she pointed out, "but please come!"

For the U.S.A. focus night, we had concocted a mime surgery taking place in an American hospital. Dr. Reed first read a paraphrase of the Good Samaritan. Then the play began. I was the patient admitted to the hospital for surgery. We had few props but conveyed the usual signing of papers and consents, an explanation by the nurse of all the gadgets; TV, intercom, bed controls, etc. The bedside phone kept ringing as the patient was asked to get into a hospital gown. Then she was given some shots and asked to give up her dentures. People were going in and out constantly, the surgeon, the anesthesiologist, the dietitian, the EKG, X-ray and lab technicians. Finally, an orderly took her on a cart to the Operating Room where she was put to sleep, prepped, draped and operated on. Dr. Reed did get one prop. It was a huge, colored mop he had put on his head for a wig. The audience roared.

In the middle of surgery, it became apparent the patient was in serious trouble. The surgeon took a break with his assistant (a hospital administrator from Canada) and discussed the hopelessness of the situation. (Margaret, at the head of the table and the anesthesiologist, kept her hands over my face in lieu of a mask. She tickled my nose.) The surgeons returned and Flo, the circulating nurse, helped them sew me up, bandaged my abdomen and returned me to my room. They all left.

I woke up and hurt. Nobody was there to help me. Finally, a cleaning man came in with his broom. This was Bill, Margaret's husband, who earnestly began to sweep the floor. I begged him to help me. He shook his head, "Sorry, I can't." Then a thought hit him, he peeked around his shoulder, produced a little Bible from his pocket and began to explain the Gospel to me. Can he pray for me? Yes, I nod. He did and I relaxed, calmed down. A background choir sang, "Amazing Grace." A modern, humble Good Samaritan ministered peace when medicine could do no more.

The Conference ended with a sweet communion service, an appropriate closing for this momentous occasion. Now, years later, I still see the colorful costumes, the display tables; I hear the sounds of strange instruments from faraway shores and see the joyful faces of the delegates. Some thoughts expressed by some of the conferees said it all:

FROM TRINIDAD: "The truth brought out from the Word of God by the various speakers really blessed my heart very much. I have a great burden to pray for the world of which I am now a part."

FROM SWASILAND (Africa): "We praise Him for the simplicity of His Word which unloosed all doubts, fears, discouragement and weakness of faith."

FROM A FORMER HOSPITAL PATIENT: "I was in that position of being on my back, looking up to God. What a comfort it was to know that He was with me. I would like to say thank you to all doctors, nurses and others who have dealings with the sick. You have all brought great joy to my heart."

FROM A YOUNG DUTCH NURSE: "Refilled with the Holy Spirit and God's love, I am going back to my own country and hospital. The Lord has filled me with a great desire to do His will and I pray that the same compassion Jesus had for the lost, He will give in my heart for the lost in my hospital. I also pray the Holy Spirit will move mightily in our HCF group as only He can."

FROM NORTHERN IRELAND: "This has certainly been a most unique conference. Here we are, people from many nations, tongues and color, all one in Christ. (Both Northern and Southern Ireland were represented.) The prayer of our Lord Jesus has been answered in a small measure at least, when He prayed *that they may be one* (John 17:11)."

After the ten-day conference, most people left including Flo, my travel companion. I was invited to stay for another week of Staff meetings. This provided a great opportunity to meet with other staff members and get to know them on a more personal level. At the beginning of the Conference, I had also met Mrs. Erasmia Grim, Francis' wife, a gracious and lovely lady. After many years of correspondence, it was good to finally talk to her face to face.

"If you ever come to the States again," I urged the Grims, "please let me know. We'd love to have you." They promised they would.

Tired and travel weary but greatly encouraged and uplifted, I finally returned to California. My vision had been deepened, my burden for the lost had become more urgent. And with it came a renewed determination to follow the Lord in whatever future paths He had for me.

Chapter 14
MIRACLES CONTINUE

By now I had accumulated a typewriter, several file cabinets and many boxes of office paraphernalia. It was all crammed under and on top of a large, rather unstable kitchen table in a corner of my bedroom. The production of The New Heart was done on a wobbly card table and my lap. It was obvious, I needed more space - a real office. But how and where? Renting space was expensive and besides I would be away from home and Sandy. Using my only guest bedroom upstairs would not be very practical. What other possibilities were there?

I asked the Lord but He seemed silent until one day when suddenly, He provided a very clear answer. It was Sunday morning and Sandy, now ten and an early riser, had crawled in bed with me. We chatted about this and that. Suddenly, he said:

"Mom, why don't we build another room on this house for a den?"

"That's it!" the Lord seemed to say, "build an office on your house."

"Sounds like a good idea, Sandy," I responded, not revealing that I agreed with the room idea but not with its use. Sandy had plenty of space to play in. The Lord merely used his suggestion to provide an answer to my office dilemma.

I found the Lord often works this way. We have a problem and ask His guidance. Nothing happens until something apparently quite unrelated comes up and suddenly the answer is there. The directive of the Lord regarding extra office space was unmistakable: build an addition onto your home. It certainly would be a marvelous solution, I thought. The backyard was large enough. The room would have to be attached to my bedroom; its windows would become the door into the office. But how do you go about building a room? I discussed it with Beverly, a nurse in the Operating Room. Her husband was a builder.

"I'll ask him to come over and take a look," she promised.

Konnie, a bearded, heavyset German, came over. Yes, there was plenty of room for an addition, he agreed. No, he wasn't able to do it - too busy.

"First thing you need is a blueprint," he explained, "and have it approved by the Building Commission. I can do the blueprint for you," he promised.

We discussed details, dimensions, windows, closets, utilities, etc. The following week, true to his word, he brought a blueprint over. No charge. The Building people approved it and gave me a permit. Now what?

"You need to get some quotes," Konnie advised.

I called several people. They came, looked around, scribbled on scraps of paper, frowned and scratched their heads.

"We need to remove that acacia tree," they said, "and part of the pine, just a branch but it's a big branch. It'll be difficult to dig trenches for the foundations because of all these roots."

Finally, I began to see a financial picture emerging. To build the office, including wiring, windows, roofing, painting, carpeting, shelves and desks would cost about $10,000. I told two builders they could have the job but I had no money yet.

"Call us when you do," they said and left.

"OK, Lord," I said, "I've done all I can do. I have the blueprint, the permit, the quote and the builders. Now I need the money."

Nothing happened but somehow I wasn't worried. I was beginning to learn to trust the Lord for seemingly impossible things. He had given me a clear order. I had done all I could. Now it was His turn. I wonder how He is going to do this, I thought. I didn't have to wait long. Just a few weeks later, the Lord gave me the surprise of my life.

It was almost 8:00 AM, time to start my day in the Recovery Room. Walking through the halls, I decided to check the prayer request box in the chapel. We had no set schedule for this, whoever passed by and had a minute to spare would check it. The chaplain came in most often. The little chapel was empty when I entered. The tiny black, wooden box in the shape of a treasure chest, stood on the kneeling bench. It had a small slit in the lid and "PRAYER REQUESTS" written on top. The lid was not locked. I opened it and found three prayer requests, small folded pieces of paper. The first one was written by a visitor, a woman requesting prayer for her husband in Intensive Care. The second one was from a patient who wanted someone to visit her. When I opened the third piece of paper I saw, to my surprise, that it was not a prayer request but a check. How strange, I thought, for someone to leave a check in the prayer request box. It was made out to Hospital Christian Fellowship for $25.00 and signed by one of the hospital staff doctors. I didn't know him very well. The date, I noticed with even greater surprise, was eight days ago. Nobody had checked that box for eight days? Very unusual. I glanced at the check again and read the scribbled second line, repeating the amount. Suddenly, I froze.

Oh no! It can't be!

I held my breath, my hand turned cold. I stared at the amount again.

It couldn't be! But it was!

There was no dot between the 25 and the two zeroes that followed. The check was not for $25.00 but for $2,500.00! How could this possibly be? Nobody had ever given that much. Nobody knew about the office plans. How could that check have been there for eight days? Why would this doctor give us that much and why would he leave it in a prayer request box?

Perhaps it was a joke?

Lord, I breathed, I have to go to work. If this is for real and not a joke, please, somehow confirm it right now. In a daze, I stuck the check in my pocket, left the chapel and headed for the Recovery Room just down the hall. At that precise moment, a doctor came around the corner and headed in my direction. It was the one who had written the check!

"Hi..." I stammered, "uh.., I just found your check."

He slowed down, gave me a quick glance and said, "Oh, that's fine."

"Excuse me," I persisted. I had to know. " Why did you do that?"

A quick smile crossed his face. He continued to walk.

"Oh," he said vaguely, "the Lord has been good to me." He rounded another corner and was gone.

I had my answer. It was not a joke. Thank You, Lord, I breathed. In a state of shock, I floated into the Recovery Room and called Mom and Dad in Glendale. They were stunned. All they could say was "Praise the Lord!"

I wasted no time calling the builders.

"You can start," I announced on the phone, "I don't have it all but there is enough for the foundation and the frame."

They went to work and began removing trees and limbs and digging trenches for the foundation. It was hard work but progress was made.

Lord, I thought, this is wonderful. What's next? I prayed expectantly. The answer was already on its way. A letter arrived in the mail the next day. It was from Dr. Robert Orr, a retired medical missionary in Dallas. He had met Francis Grim on one of his trips and was on our mailing list.

"I'm about to receive an inheritance," he wrote, "and rather than share it with Uncle Sam, I want your organization to have it. I will be mailing you a check before the end of the year." It was late November. How much would he send? I wondered. Nothing to do but wait.

In the backyard, the foundation was poured, the frame almost up. A building inspector came and approved the effort. Just before Christmas, the check arrived from Dallas. With trembling fingers, I opened the envelope. I closed my eyes. Take a guess, I thought. No, I couldn't. Come on, take a look, I chided myself. You can't stand here forever. Slowly, I opened my eyes and looked at the unfolded piece of paper. The check was made out for $3,600.00! I screamed and jumped for joy.

"Thank you, Lord!" I shouted. "Thank You! You're amazing!"

The work continued uninterrupted. I wrote Dr. Orr, thanked him and explained why his gift had come in so very handy at this time. He wasted no time and wrote: *I'm so glad I could help. Seems to me you need some more though, to finish your office. I will talk to a doctor friend of mine and see if he can help also.* A week later another check arrived in the mail from Dallas, this one for $1,250.00!

Delighted and greatly excited, I watched my builders complete the roof, put in windows, electricity, doors, shelves and sliding doors. The painter would be followed by the carpet installer and then the furniture. I was still about $2,600.00 short but had no worries that it would be supplied. However, as the weeks went by, no more donations came in. Nothing.

Now what, Lord? I wondered. We're so close. Is there something I should do?

There was.

The Lord gently reminded me that I had a small savings account. Sandy had also received a small inheritance from his grandmother, specifically designated for college, which was also kept in a savings account. Together, this amounted to $2,600.00. Should I really use this? I wondered. I'll have nothing left at all. If I use Sandy's money, I said to the Lord, You will have to help me replace it before he needs it.

Finally, I felt an inner peace about this and emptied both savings accounts. Somehow, I knew the Lord was pleased but in spite of that, I also felt as though I was walking on water. Each step could be my last. Look to the Lord, not to your circumstances, I kept reminding myself.

The office was completed. We had an official dedication ceremony led by our hospital Chaplain, Dan Plies. What a luxury to have all this space. I began spending more and more time in my new domain. The amount of mail increased, "The New Heart" had to get out, orders for "Handbooks" and newly produced introductory brochures needed to be filled. Small donations came in now and then and I began adding some to Sandy's savings account. In less than two years, every penny had been replaced. I also began tithing to International HQ.

As my time in the office increased, my days in Recovery decreased. From three days of work a week, I cut down to two, then one. Finally, I only took weekend calls. My paychecks were greatly reduced yet somehow, it stretched to pay the monthly bills. There were always emergency surgeries over the weekends so there was always plenty of work. However, I needed the weekends to rest from what was now my five-day workweek in the office.

One Saturday, I sat in the Recovery Room next to a sleeping patient who had just parted with his appendix. I was tired. What am I doing here? I wondered grumpily. I can't talk to my patients. When they wake up, I take them back to their room and go home. Before, when I still worked full time, I made rounds and often chatted and prayed with patients before and after surgery. On weekend call, I couldn't do that. Besides not being able to interact with patients, I was also tired, bone weary, ready for a day at the beach. I need some time off, Lord, I complained. Perched on a stool next to my patient, I flipped open my Bible.

Ho, everyone that thirsteth, I read in Isaiah 55, *come ye to the waters, and he that hath no money; come ye, buy and eat: yea, come buy wine and milk without money and without price.* Sounds good, Lord. Is that for me? Then I was in for a surprise.

Wherefore do ye spend money for that which is not bread? Isaiah continued. *AND YOUR LABOR FOR THAT WHICH SATISFIETH NOT?* (Is. 55: 1,2) The words leaped off the page. I stopped short. Why DO I spent my labor on that which satisfies not? To pay my bills, of course. Shouldn't I be a responsible parent? A responsible citizen? Confused, or perhaps reluctant to consider this suggestion, I flipped back a few pages and stopped at chapter 44. *For I will pour water upon him that is thirsty, and floods upon the dry ground: I will pour my spirit upon thy seed, and my blessing upon thine offspring* (Is. 44:3).

Relieved yet scared, I realized the Lord wanted me to quit my job altogether. And live on what? HCF expenses were barely being covered. Francis Grim and all other staff workers, I knew, lived entirely by faith, trusting the Lord for all their needs. But can we do that here in America?

Gently, the Lord reminded me of His financial provision for the office. Yes, that had been miraculous, I had to admit. But nothing much was coming in right now. Could I trust Him for daily, weekly and monthly bills all the time? How about insurance? Would quitting my job be faith or presumption?

But the Lord asked in His Word: *Why spend your labor on things that satisfy not?* O Lord, give me some time, I finally begged, I hear You but it's too big a jump right now.

Sandy was fourteen now, a tall, energetic young man. Since third grade, I had been able to put him in private Christian schools. He was an average student, lively, not able to sit still for long with a short concentration span. He seemed to be an emerging leader but needed more supervision and guidance than either his schoolteachers or I could give him. There were spells of rebellion and disobedience at home with an occasional tantrum. I felt the acute vacuum of a father figure in his life. How can I handle this, Lord? I prayed, I can't be a father to him. Again, unknown to me, the answer was already on its way.

The next day at work, Hildegarde, the gal from the Tissue Lab across the hallway, rushed into the Recovery Room. She was a Bolivian and had joined us for several HCF meetings. We prayed for her when she was hospitalized with a mysterious kidney infection, and she made a rapid recovery.

"Here," she thrust a slip of paper in my hand, "find out for me before tomorrow night what kind of school this is. It's very important."

She was gone. I read the name of a Boy's Ranch in the panhandle of Texas. I'd never heard of it and didn't know anyone in that area. Why did she ask me? What was the rush? During a coffee break, I looked her up in the lab. I knew she was a single parent raising two boys.

"I heard about this place," Hildegarde explained, "and need to find out if it has a good reputation. My boys are getting out of hand. They need more discipline than I can give them. The Ranch said they could come but I don't know anything about this place. This may be their only chance. Please see what you can find out!"

I remembered a local pastor who had mentioned once that he had graduated from a Bible school in Texas. I called him. He wasn't home but his wife said he really didn't know anyone there. "However," she added, "I know a lady who is very influential. She knows a lot of people and has many contacts."

"Could you please call her," I begged her, "ask her to call Hildegarde, not me, if she finds out anything."

The following evening, I heard from a delighted Hildegarde on the phone.

"This lady from Texas called me," she began, "she had never heard of the school but contacted lots of top-notch people including several officials in Washington DC. She said she found out that this school is the second best in the nation!"

"Wow!" I agreed, "that's marvelous, Hildegarde."

"I've called them already. Someone will be out here soon to talk things over."

A few weeks later, a friendly Texan spent a whole afternoon with Hildegarde and her boys, explaining Ranch life in all its details.

"The boys are housed in dorms," he said, "each dorm has about twenty-four boys. They're all different ages. Each dorm has two dorm parents who live there also. There are about five hundred boys at the Ranch altogether. We take them at any age but not older than fifteen. After they graduate from High School, they have to leave."

He showed pictures of rodeos, a dairy farm, herds of cattle, agriculture, construction shops, a small zoo, a theater, sports fields and comfortable dorms, all built around a large steepled church.

"We have a strong discipline program also," he warned, "but it's fair. Nobody ever gets punished for doing something they didn't know they shouldn't do. They also get plenty of warnings. Most kids adjust quickly. There's so much to do and see, we keep them too busy to get into much trouble," he chuckled.

The best part was the cost. There was none. The entire ranch was supported by private donations. Delighted, Hildegarde got her boys off to Texas. She travelled with them and returned a few days later with glowing reports of the Ranch. Her boys had a rough time for a while accepting their loss of freedom, she said, and adjusting to the increased discipline, but pretty soon they shaped up and were doing well.

"Why don't you send Sandy there," Hildegarde asked.

Send my son away? That's kind of drastic, I thought. All the way to Texas? Was that really necessary? I kept a close watch on Sandy at home and spoke with his teachers at school. They all seemed to think this Ranch would be good for him. Reluctantly, I began considering this option. Sandy was strongly opposed to the idea. Nevertheless, I finally wrote for application forms. There was lots of red tape. Transcripts were needed, health certificates and references. As I took care of all these details, the conviction that this indeed was the right thing to do began to take firm shape.

The Texan came out again, this time to talk to Sandy and me. We talked, asked questions, looked at pictures. Sandy was unconvinced. I knew it would be a tremendous change for this water-loving, carefree, beach boy.

"Let's try it anyway," I decided.

Three months later, he left. His first letter was brief and to the point: *"This is definitely not the place for me, Mom,"* it read, *I miss you, my friends and the beach. Please let me come home!*

Determined, I wrote back that he was going to stay. I would visit him during Christmas recess. *It's up to you whether you are going to be miserable or happy*, I wrote.

It worked. Three months later, I began getting optimistic reports from his counselors and dorm parents. "He is doing well," they wrote. "Once you got through to him that he was going to stay, he shaped up. He gets along with the other kids, signed up for a building program after school hours and is making good grades in school." Relieved, I thanked the Lord for this Ranch. Yes, I missed Sandy very much but knew he was in good hands and in a better environment than I could provide.

At the office, things were moving along. I had received invitations from other states to come and speak for health care groups. I still could not go very often because of my hospital job. Was this the time to quit? I wondered. Was I supposed to travel? In the past, I had limited travel to be home with Sandy. Now I was alone.

Then there was Ingrid, the nurse I met in Holland. She had lived with me for about a year and not only helped with chores and office work but taught me how to play the guitar.

However, Ingrid had left again after she enrolled at a local Bible school and met her Prince Charming in the form of Marlon, a tall, blond, handsome student from the Midwest. They were married in 1975. So here I was by myself again, at home and in the office. Was this the time to cut the umbilical cord of my dwindling paycheck?

Finally, I made the decision and quit my weekend call time at the hospital. Then I accepted an invitation to go to Tulsa where an HCF group was forming under the direction of Helen, a Nursing Supervisor. I flew to Dallas first to meet our great benefactor, Dr. Orr. He introduced me to some other physicians. One of them arranged for me to speak at a medical school. Dr. Orr then put me on a bus to Tyler, where Dr. George Hurst, the medical director of a large hospital, was waiting for me. He had also met Francis Grim on a previous visit and had arranged a meeting for me at his hospital. In Tyler, I stayed at the home of the hospital chaplain, Elwood, and also met a very special couple, Dr. Gerry and Denise Landry. Little did I know then that the Landrys would eventually join the full time HCF staff, run a French HCF training center in Switzerland for a couple of years and that Gerry eventually would travel around the world as an HCF promoter.

In Tulsa, I received a wonderful and warm welcome from Helen. She had invited a large number of Christian health care workers to her home. They covered her entire living room, including the couch, chairs and floor. I shared about the HCF vision, our aims and objectives and some details about the tremendous Conference I had attended in Wales. I felt right at home in Oklahoma and afterwards kept in touch with Helen who proved to be an excellent leader and communicator.

In the meantime, I had heard from the Grims that they were planning to visit the U.S. again. This time they were traveling together.

Wait till you see this new office, I wrote. Instead of going to the desert, I decided to try a retreat in the mountains for them. Mom and Dad had discovered a place called Forest Home that seemed just perfect. I contacted the Registrar who sent me details. Finally, I signed a contract for a minimum of forty and a maximum of eighty people. Excited, I drafted a flier, got it printed and mailed them out to everyone on our mailing list in the west coast. The results were overwhelming. Registrations poured in. Our maximum of eighty was reached. More registrations came in. The Registrar made additional space available.

The Grims arrived by plane from Hawaii, their last stop on a world tour. What a pleasure to welcome them both in my home. The upstairs guest room had become a "prophet's chamber," a place for visitors and guests working in the Lord's service. With Ingrid gone, they moved in and had a perfect, private little world up there.

When we finally made our way to the majestic San Bernardino mountains and Forest Home, we had one hundred twenty people signed up. What a difference from the first Retreat at the desert just four years earlier with the gasoline crisis and the illness of Francis Grim! This was a great celebration. Everyone loved Forest Home, the meetings were blessed and inspired, meals and accommodations just perfect. We really met the Lord in the mountains, made many new friends and returned to the beach totally refreshed and inspired to press on in the service of the Lord.

I had a precious time of fellowship with the Grims at home and realized again how God was using this special couple to bring His message of life to hospitals around the world.

"Tell me about the new Training Center," I asked them one night as we sat on the back porch after dinner.

"Well," Francis began, "Leonora needed some extra space for her office in Holland. She was still living in that tiny flat in Rotterdam and her travels across Europe were taking a lot of time. The need for a training center and additional office room became acute. She began looking around and came across an empty hospital that was for sale in a small village in the center of Holland. It was fairly large, big enough for a training center, but expensive. It also needed a lot of work and renovation. She got together an ad hoc committee which included Brother Andrew. They all thought it was a great idea but the final decision and responsibility was on her shoulders. We advised her to seek the Lord's leading and that we would stand behind her decision.

"So she signed the contract and began cleaning the place, room by room. A friend came to visit and help and decided to stay. Her name is Bertie. Then a Dutch girl, Magda, came to help them out for a year. She decided to stay, also. The Lord moved on several people to help with the financing. Eventually, they got the place ready for training. A small class of students from various parts of the world signed up for the first nine-month course."

"It's a lovely place," Erasmia added, "very pretty and comfortable. The village is pretty too. You must come and take a look sometime, Aubrey. I just love Holland, it's so clean and pretty."

"I'd like to," I responded, "I also hope we can persuade some Americans to take this training. I'll mention it in 'The New Heart'."

The Grims left and made stops in Dallas, Tulsa and Philadelphia. In Dallas, they met Drs. Orr and Hurst again. In Tulsa, they stayed with Helen and her HCF group. While in Philadelphia, they enjoyed the company of Rita, an emerging HCF leader and Joe, a local hospital employee who had joined the group recently. The Grims stayed at Joe's home and were able to lead his mother to the Lord - a special blessing.

A few months later, I received a note from a nurse in North Dakota. Her name was Wanda. She was interested in going to Holland to take the training course, she wrote. Delighted, I encouraged her to go and sent her details. She was accepted and left for Holland just a few months later. Then one day, I received a call from a nurse near Kansas City. Her name was Pat and she was interested in starting a fellowship.

"Can I come to California and see what you're doing?" she asked. I smiled. A kind of internship? Interesting idea.

"Let me think about it and let you know," I said and hung up the phone.

What do you want me to do about that, Lord? I prayed. The idea of seminars came to mind. I had attended several in the past on a variety of subjects. I liked the idea of having an audience for a whole day. What sort of a program could we present? Where would we hold a seminar? Why not several seminars? Perhaps travel from one location to another? Preparing for one seminar would take a lot of time so I might as well repeat it at other locations.

Slowly, a schedule began to emerge: a trip through southern California with stops at places where we had contacts. I began to call and write people and soon had classrooms in hospitals and churches lined up in the cities of Lake Isabella, Palmdale, Bakersfield, Fresno, Lodi, Monterey and San Jose. Then I wrote Wanda in Holland. *Would you like to come to California after you graduate?* I asked her. *I'm planning to take a three-week trip through California and do some seminars with a nurse from the Midwest. I need your help.* Wanda wrote back that she was willing to come. Pat agreed also, so we firmed up our dates. I printed and mailed fliers which soon resulted in a brisk flow of registrations.

The same day Wanda arrived in Los Angeles from Holland, Pat flew in from Kansas City. As I drove to the airport, I wondered how I would find two people I had never met before at two different air terminals in the huge LA airport. Wanda's plane was late and arrived at a different gate than scheduled. Well, I'll get Pat first, I decided. I'll just walk to the gate when the plane arrives and look for her. But when I arrived at the check-in counters, all tunnels to the gates were closed to visitors. All I could do was to stand at the end of one of these huge tunnels and watch arriving passengers from dozens of flights flowing towards me. I stopped a few of them, asking where they had flown in from... Hawaii, New York, Miami. Nobody from the Midwest. Finally, when there was a lull in the stream of arrivals, I noticed a pretty, petite, short girl coming through the tunnel. She looked at me.

"Are you Pat?" I ventured. She was. I welcomed her to California.

"We need to go to another terminal to find Wanda." I said, picking up one of her bags. Her plane had finally arrived but there was a glut at the customs. Thirty minutes later, I met Wanda, also short but a brunette with large, expressive eyes and a slow, sweet smile. Neither she nor Pat had ever been in California.

"You're in for a treat," I promised as we drove home. Much needed to be done before our departure. We collated handouts, packed folders, prepared name tags, registration lists, books, magazines, notes and personal belongings. It all came together and a few days later we took off.

The first seminar at a hospital in Palmdale went well. We met in the cafeteria with about thirty-five health care workers from the Antelope Valley. Pat gave her testimony, Wanda shared about her time in Holland and I presented several sessions about our HCF outreach in San Clemente. I also presented a session on leadership and the methodology for starting an HCF group. The responses were good and some seemed pleasantly surprised when we started each session with prayer and singing. Encouraged, we moved to our next location. In the meantime, both Pat and Wanda were enjoying the California scenery.

"Look, are these real orange trees?" Pat squealed in delight, "let me take a picture."

"Wow! what enormous mountains!" Wanda said in awe. We sidetracked to Sequoia National Forest, still one of my favorite places.

In Lodi, we met in a church building. It was my birthday and I was presented with a huge cake. A bubbly, active nurse named Barbara was in charge of this seminar. We met Charles and Naomi again in San Jose and in Monterey, we spent time with Dr. Kabat whom we had met earlier at our Forest Home retreat. He had set up a seminar room for us at his hospital.

Three weeks later, we returned to the office, tired but happy and excited. It had been a good trip, a sort of experiment, but worth the effort. Both Pat and Wanda had gained a lot of practical experience. Perhaps in the future, after a few more trips, they could go without me. Pat returned to the Midwest while I persuaded Wanda to settle in my home, occupying the "prophet's room." She helped at the office and worked part-time through a local Registry.

I had become used to living without a paycheck by now. HCF began covering travel expenses and utilities. Somehow, the refrigerator was never empty. Clothing and food was often dropped off unexpectedly. Dorothy, a retired nurse found many ways to help. Small gifts for personal use came in once in a while.

Meanwhile, I had received some letters from Helen suggesting we plan a national conference in Tulsa. The idea wasn't new and had been discussed before. In fact, the Grims thought it would be an excellent idea and had looked over a possible facility with Helen when they were there. Now I had to face this challenge. Were we ready for it? A national conference would be a costly affair. Did we have enough people to support such an event?

What about speakers? Helen listed a few. She also called frequently with suggestions. Dr. Ralph Byron, the surgeon from City of Hope in California; Dr. Maurice Rawlings, a cardiologist from Tennessee; Elisabeth Eliot, famous author and missionary; Kay Arthur, a nurse and founder of Reach Out ministries also in Tennessee.

"What about Brother Andrew?" she asked me one day, "didn't you say you met him in Holland?"

"Yes, I did," I began, "but..."

"Isn't he involved with HCF in Holland?"

"Yes, he's on the Board there."

"Well, maybe he will come."

"What about cost? If we pay for all these people's travel, we'll be broke."

I remembered that just recently Brother Andrew had opened an office in California. His ministry was called Open Doors. I had met some people from there. Perhaps I could give them a call. One day, I did and also officially wrote Brother Andrew in Holland.

Almost by return mail, he answered. Yes, he would come to speak and would take care of his own plane fare. Open Doors would also mention it in their US national magazine. Delighted, I relayed this good news to Helen. We printed the fliers on glossy paper with pretty pictures of Tulsa provided by the Chamber of Commerce.

"I would like to go home and see my family," Wanda said one day. "I also need my car which is still at home. Perhaps I could fly home to North Dakota and then drive down to Tulsa and meet you there."

"Sounds like a good idea, Wanda." I agreed.

"How are you going to get to Tulsa?" she asked me.

"Well, I was going to fly but I have a lot of stuff to carry. I was also talking to Linda. Do you remember her?"

"The Jewish nurse who plays the guitar?"

"Yes, she helped me out at that banquet for Orange County. I asked her to do some song leading in Tulsa. We may just take our time and drive, a sort of mini-vacation."

It all worked out. By now, about a hundred and twenty people had registered for Tulsa. Linda and I left California and drove through

Arizona and New Mexico to Oklahoma. Helen had recruited a lot of volunteers who took care of transportation for the speakers, hostesses and those working in registration and literature distribution. Some of the Open Doors staff had come down also. One man, Johnny, offered to help take a special offering so all our expenses could be met. The HCF Caribbean coordinator, Ken Ragoonath from Trinidad, flew in with a planeload of happy, colorful people. Brother Andrew arrived and gave several stirring messages on Jonah, how he ran from God but was later greatly used in a city he despised. The other speakers had challenging messages as well. It was great to meet so many health care workers from all over the country. I met Rita from Philadelphia. Joe was there also; Minnie, a glowing little Philippino nurse from Detroit; Margaret and her husband, Bill, from Pittsburgh; Pat from the Midwest and so many others.

A friend of Linda, a nurse named Bonnie who lived in California, shared our hotel room. At the close of Kay Arthur's message, Bonnie gave her heart to the Lord. Her life was greatly changed.

"I always thought I was a Christian," she said later, "and have been active in my church for years. But only now do I see there was no personal commitment to the Lord, no personal relationship, no new life."

After the conference, we spent some quiet days in Tulsa relaxing and wrapping up some details. A milestone was behind us, our first National Conference. It was the summer of 1980. Linda and I were housed at the home of a pharmacist and his wife. Tulsa was hot and dry. One afternoon, I began to marvel at the incredible things that had happened to me since that first prayer meeting in my home, just eight years ago.

"Just as well I had no idea where it would lead me. I would have crawled in a hole and died," I laughed.

"Yes, you better keep your seatbelt buckled when you give your life to the Lord," Linda agreed. "I may go to Thailand next year!"

"Thailand?!" I said. "That's a long way, Linda."

"Yes," she said. "It's a hot, difficult place for Christians to work."

"You'll have to learn the language, won't you?" I ventured.

"Yes, and the customs, the food, everything. It's scary but I know the Lord is leading me there."

If I could have seen into the future, I would have seen that Linda would go to Thailand. She learned the language and loved the people. Then, because of her health, she returned to California where she headed an Asian outreach at a huge church, a job tailor-made for her.

And where would I be? Much to my surprise, I would be in Thailand also, although only for a month, attending another International Conference. But that would not be for another six years.

Chapter 15

SETTLING IN THE SADDLE

Joe, the young man from Philadelphia, signed up for training in Holland. When he had been there a while I received a letter from Leonora. *We would like for Joe to do his practical training in the U.S.*, she wrote. *Bertie, my co-teacher, will travel with him. Would that be all right with you?* Wanda, who knew Bertie from her time in Holland, was delighted.

"You know, for my practical training, I travelled with Bertie and another student to the Philippines," she remembered, "we had a great time. Bertie is such a delightful person, a good leader, really positive, a good speaker and teacher. She loves the Lord."

"What can we do for her and Joe if they come, Wanda?" I asked her.

"How about more seminars? Bertie could speak at some local churches or Christian groups as well," she suggested.

I wrote Leonora and relayed our decision to her. We would be honored to have Bertie and Joe here, I said. We decided on another California seminar tour, this time to cities we had not been to before. But first Wanda was due for a vacation and went home to her family in North Dakota. A few weeks before the arrival of our overseas guests, Joe's Mom became very sick and he immediately flew from Holland to Philadelphia to be with her. Bertie arrived alone. We hit it off right away. She was a pretty brunette with a quick wit and proved to be a capable leader.

"Good grief!" she said when she saw her schedule, "when do I breathe?"

I laughed. "We're putting you to work, my dear."

Joe called to say his Mom had passed away. It was not a sad occasion, he reported, but rather a glorious homegoing. He arrived in California the following week just before the seminars began. Wanda, in the meantime, had returned from North Dakota. She had brought a friend, Laurel, to help her with the driving. My house was full again.

We found a place for Joe at the home of Dorothy, our retired nurse friend. Laurel and Wanda shared the prophet's room upstairs and Bertie was made comfortable in Sandy's old room. Laurel, a quiet, sweet, pretty girl said she'd be glad to go along on the trip to help at the book display and set up the rooms.

Soon, the five of us, Bertie, Joe, Wanda, Laurel and I, departed in two cars. Our team clicked and we smoothly moved from place to place. Attendance was good, the response warm. People seemed grateful we touched on spiritual matters in health care.

"You know," I said to Bertie one night as we relaxed after dinner, "we recently had a new law passed in California. All nurses here need to renew their license every two years. In the past, it was just a matter of filling out a form and sending it in with a fee. Now, we also need thirty hours of approved continuing education to get our license renewed. I thought these courses would only be given through nursing schools and education departments in hospitals but I have been receiving fliers offering approved courses that are given by organizations."

"Perhaps you can offer them, too," Bertie suggested.

"Yea, I think I'll write for information."

"Aubrey," Bertie said earnestly, "these classes can be vital to hospital staff, especially nurses. They need to know how to recognize and deal with spiritual needs. Nothing like that is taught in nursing schools."

"How well I remember," I said wistfully.

"You can apply spiritual care in so many areas," Wanda, who had been silent so far, added, "like care of the elderly, terminally-ill patients, care of the relatives and what about things like the sanctity of life, euthanasia and abortion?"

"Yes," I agreed, "but you also need qualified instructors."

"True, but I'm sure you can find them."

Encouraged, I wrote the California Board of Nursing after our trip and asked for an application for a provider number. I studied the outlines and realized we could qualify if we had the right faculty. Mentally, I listed several professionals I knew including doctors, psychiatrists, nurses, counselors and some clergy and chaplains who would meet both the Nurses Board and our own HCF standards. It seemed that an open avenue was stretching before us. I determined to pursue it.

The Lord was good to us. Besides obvious blessings like the many health care workers we were reaching with the Gospel, there were also personal blessings, unexpected yet delightful. One of them came a few days before Bertie's departure. At a home meeting where she had spoken, she met Matthew, a scientist and his wife, Ingaborg. They became good friends. When Bertie was about to return to Europe, they called asking if they could come over and say goodbye. One evening, they arrived just after dinner. We all gathered in the living room and chatted.

A little after nine o'clock, Laurel's eyes grew heavy and she excused herself. Wanda, who had spent hours in the kitchen preparing dinner, soon followed. Well, I thought, these people are here to see Bertie so they don't need me. I also said my good nights and left. As I was about to exit the room, Matthew said an odd thing. He looked at my piano and asked,

"Aubrey, does that thing work?"

"Sure," I smiled, "do you play?"

He didn't answer but got up, seated himself at the piano and softly began to play the second movement of Beethoven's Pathetique sonata. I knew it well. It was simple and lovely, one of the few pieces I played fairly well myself. I waited politely for awhile, thanked him and left the room. As I was getting ready for bed, however, I became suddenly aware of a waterfall of flawless music coming from my living room. Surprised, I recognized a very brilliant and difficult composition by Chopin.

Was that Matthew playing?

Was that my piano?

I stood still and listened carefully. The whole keyboard seemed to come alive. Quickly, I slipped into my bathrobe, opened the bedroom door and tippy-toed back into the living room. There was some noise upstairs too, a door opened, sounds from the stairway and soon Wanda and Laurel appeared. Silently, we all sat down, engulfed in a glorious cloud of exquisite music. When he finished, Matthew had a wildly applauding audience of five.

"More! More!" we clamored.

"I thought you were a scientist!" Bertie said, "are you a concert pianist also?"

"Yes, he is," Ingaborg said, "he has played with symphony orchestras and given many recitals. But it's just a hobby." Matthew launched into Debussy, Beethoven, Mozart and many other composers. I grabbed my tape recorder and starting to tape this impromptu concert.

"I didn't know my piano could sound like that." I laughed.

Then Matthew shifted gears and began playing hymns and praise songs. We gathered around him and joined in, singing our hearts out. It all ended at midnight with a prayer meeting. In awe, I remembered how much I had wanted that piano and how the Lord had miraculously provided it many years ago. Now He had supplied a pianist as well. He certainly gives *abundantly above all that we ask or think* (Eph. 3:20).

Bertie's time came to an end. Both she and Joe returned to Holland. Joe graduated and joined the staff at the Training Center. His family roots were in Italy and he felt a deep desire to live and work in his country. However, the time had not yet come. First, the Lord needed to further prepare and shape him. Laurel also left so Wanda and I were alone again.

"I would like to do some seminars in Washington and Oregon," I said to Wanda one day. "I hear it's pretty. We don't know too many people there so it's time we discover who our neighbors are."

The year before, Wanda and I had visited Seattle at the invitation of a Dr. Richard Carlson and his wife Lois. He wanted people to hear about Hospital Christian Fellowship and had rented a small auditorium for an introductory meeting. Through newspaper announcements and phone calls he spread the word about our visit. We had a good meeting with about thirty-five people in attendance and also enjoyed staying at the Carlsons' lovely home. Of course, we climbed Seattle's space needle and saw the salmon struggling upstream in the locks at Puget Sound. I felt it was time to explore the area north of us a little more. Wanda agreed and was able to get time off from the Registry.

I also approached Paul and Carol Spitz. Carol was the patient at South Coast who had lung surgery. Linda and I had prayed for her about seven years earlier. She was also a diabetic and had gone blind during the last several years. That and many other medical problems had kept her in and out of hospitals almost constantly. After she lost her sight and in the midst of other diabetes-related problems, she became pregnant again, something her doctors had felt was impossible. They strongly suggested an abortion.

"You won't survive this pregnancy," they counseled her, "and chances that the baby will be normal are almost nil."

After much prayer and agonizing, they decided against an abortion. A complicated pregnancy followed. However, Carol delivered a normal, chubby baby girl named Jenna Joy without the aid of a Caesarian section as had been planned! Jenna was in perfect health.

Paul and Carol had often shared their story. I asked them if they would like to come along with us to Oregon and Washington. By this time, Paul had spent so many hours in the hospital, he had developed quite a ministry talking and praying with other patients. They both agreed to come, made arrangements at home and soon our two cars were on their way north.

I had also asked another nurse friend, Marie, from Bellingham, Washington, to join us. We had met in Tulsa at our National Conference. She agreed, boarded a bus and met us in Medford, our first stop in Oregon. Wanda and I were bone weary, tired from a weekend retreat we had sandwiched in at Mount Hermon (near San Francisco) before our trek up north. I had rented seminar rooms at Holiday Inns in Medford, Eugene, Bellingham and Richland. The seminar in Medford was attended by about twenty-five people. Response was good. Before the seminar ended, I mentioned that our team would like to go to church the next day. If anyone had any suggestions as to where to go, we'd be open. One nurse approached us afterwards.

"You're welcome to come to my church," she began, "but it's about twelve miles from here in Applegate."

"Give us directions and we'll go," we decided.

"There are two services," she said, "my husband and I teach a class for kids during the first one."

"We'll look for you in the second service," we promised.

The next day was bright and sunny. The beautiful Oregon scenery, green and hilly, flowed by as we made our way to Applegate. Soon, the residential areas of Medford were behind us. Nothing but trees and rolling hills here.

"Can't be a very large church," Marie observed.

I agreed. The road continued. Rounding a curve, we noticed a small shopping area. Just a few buildings with a gas station, some stores and a restaurant. A small sign said: Applegate.

"Well, this must be it," I said and parked the car among perhaps forty others, mostly trucks. We saw a few people entering one of the storefront buildings and followed.

To our surprise there were several hundred people present.

"Where did they all come from?" Wanda asked in surprise.

More were coming in, whole families and large groups piled out of arriving trucks and station wagons. Pretty soon, the hall was full. And this was the second service? Amazing! A bearded young man in jeans strummed a guitar and began to sing. Everyone followed. The songs were familiar, mostly Scripture songs. He led from one into another.

A young preacher, also in jeans, settled on a tall stool, opened his Bible and began to preach. It was a simple but powerful message. Afterwards, when we got up to leave I spotted our nurse from the previous day. We chatted a while and went next door to the coffee shop for lunch. It was then I noticed that Marie had not said much.

"Did you like the service?" I inquired, stirring my coffee.

"Oh," she said, "did I ever! I have never been in a service like this."

"What do you mean?" Wanda asked.

"In my church, everything is different," she said, shaking her head. "Everything is... kind of routine. You know what songs to sing, the exact order of the service. Things are more formal. It's good," she added hastily, "but there are so many young people and they're so totally absorbed in the service. Nobody gets fidgety or sleepy. It's amazing," she marvelled.

We all agreed that it had been a special service. It was so good to know we belonged to such a large and varied family. That afternoon,

Wanda and I drove to Crater Lake, about eighty miles from Medford, while Marie stayed at our motel and rested. It was an unforgettable trip with a most spectacular view: a huge, quiet lake cradled at the top of a snowcapped mountain.

Our next stop was Eugene. We filled the room with over fifty people. Marie got into a discussion with a troubled nurse when the seminar was over. We watched her from a distance. Before long she was able to pray with this nurse and lead her to the Lord.

"If nothing else happens on this trip," she beamed later, "I don't care. This is what it's all about. What a day this has been."

Many years later, I met this nurse again at a retreat in California. Her life, she said, had never been the same since that prayer.

There was more in store for us that day. Paul, after days of driving and standing at seminars, was in need of some exercise. He loved to play volleyball.

"Can you take Carol back to the motel?" he asked after the seminar. "I want to play some volleyball. I'll meet you there later. Don't wait for me for dinner."

When we got back to the motel, there was a message for me from an old friend, Beaver. She and I had sung together in a choir some years earlier but then she had moved to Arizona. Now, she was visiting her daughter in Eugene and somehow had found out where we were staying. She had left a phone number which I immediately called.

"Let me take you all out to dinner," she suggested, "there's a homey restaurant here."

I relayed the invitation to the rest of the team. It resulted in squeals of delight. To conserve our meagre budget, we lived on very simple meals during seminar trips. Crackers and cheese, soup and peanut butter sandwiches were our usual fare. Paul often kidded about his "new job with this severe boss who didn't feed or pay her people." A real dinner sounded divine.

"What about Paul?" Carol asked.

We realized we didn't know where he was. Besides, he had said not to wait for him.

"We can leave a message telling where we are," I finally suggested. Everyone agreed and we took off to find the restaurant.

Eugene is not an easy city to find your way around but eventually, we arrived at the given address. Beaver and her daughter were waiting. We arranged ourselves around one of the comfortable tables and were soon in animated conversation. The meal was served, fresh salad, steamy vegetables, baked potatoes, chicken and beef. The dessert, specialty of the house, came last.

"Peanut butter pie is Paul's favorite," Carol sighed. There was still no sign of him.

"Let's take him a piece," Wanda suggested. Around nine o'clock, we returned to the motel. Paul had just arrived and had found our message.

"I don't believe this!" he fumed as Carol and Marie walked in, "you went without me? After eating cheese and crackers for days, you went without me? Don't you know I like to go out for dinner?" We knew he wasn't serious just putting up a front. I had never seen Paul really angry or offended. He'd gone through too much for that but he was a great kidder.

"The least you could have done is bring me back some peanut butter pie," he yelled in mock anger. Carol said we did.

"Where is it?" he demanded.

"Aubrey has it." she confessed. Paul rushed out of his room and started banging on my door. I knew what was coming.

"Yes?" I said, opening the door for him. He stormed in like a hungry tiger.

"Where is it?" he demanded.

"Where's what?" I said innocently.

"You know what," he grabbed me by the shoulder, "my pie!"

"What pie?" I tried to wiggle loose.

"The pie you brought from the restaurant!"

"Oh, that pie?" I suddenly remembered, "we ate it. After all, you weren't home and..."

"You did what?!" he roared. "I don't believe you! Wanda," he turned to where she sat on the edge of her bed, grinning from ear to ear. "She's lying, isn't she?"

"All right," I finally relented, "here it is. Eat your heart out, brother." Then, seriously, I added, "Sorry you missed dinner, Paul. It was fun."

In Portland, we had a small basement classroom in a hospital. Seventy-five people crowded in. We visited Mt. St. Helen and later picked up dust from that earthshaking eruption as far as Yakima. Another special treat was a drive to the majestic Timberline Lodge on snowcapped Mt. Hood. Two major hospitals in Seattle had opened their doors to us. In spite of the rain, we had a good crowd. We also renewed our friendship with the Carlsons. The Bellingham seminar had to be cancelled. Only a few people had signed up. We took this as from the Lord since we were all in need of some time off. We relaxed in Marie's comfortable home and enjoyed meeting her husband and two children.

The Spitzes visited friends in Seattle where Paul was offered a job as Assistant Pastor. He accepted and they moved from Southern California to rainy Washington. But that's a whole different story, related by Paul himself in his own book.

After a few days' rest at Bellingham, we continued to Spokane where we were royally welcomed by the pastoral care department of the huge Sacred Heart Hospital. One more seminar followed at Richland and our mission was completed. Marie boarded a bus back to Bellingham, Paul and Carol had already left and Wanda and I took our time driving south on I-5 to balmy Southern California. We were weary but excited and thanked the Lord for giving us these opportunities to speak to health care workers and also, as a special bonus, to enjoy tremendous sightseeing spectacles.

"Serving the Lord really pays off," I said to Wanda.

"Yes," she agreed, "there is nothing like it."

When we got home, I received a letter from Ingrid, now happily married to Marlon. They were pastoring a small church in Collinsville, Oklahoma.

"Aubrey," she wrote, "I met this nurse from England. Her name is Judy. She has a tremendous testimony and recently moved to California. She's working with Joni Eareckson now. Maybe you would like to have her speak for you sometime."

I contacted Judy. No, she was not a regular speaker and was really too busy to come.

"How about Joni?" I asked, "would she be willing to speak?"

She said she would. What an opportunity for health care workers to hear Joni, the young girl who broke her neck in a diving accident when she was seventeen. Though paralyzed from the neck down, she had overcome great obstacles and clung to an ever-increasing faith in God to become a well-known speaker, author and singer. Her talents as an artist were also outstanding even more so because she had to hold her pencils and brushes in her mouth.

What about another National Conference? I pondered. San Diego seemed a good place. We travelled to the San Diego State University and met with some people there to look over the facilities. Everything worked out and soon our announcements were printed and mailed with the theme: "Approaches to Healing." People from all over the country responded - three hundred of them. For music, I had contacted a large church and talked to the Music Director, a pleasant, bearded, middle-aged man. He promised to cover all the music periods. What he did was much more than I expected. On opening night, he showed up with a large brass band complete with background singers, all decked out in colorful outfits. They were splendid and immediately set the tone for the entire conference. On other evenings, he provided smaller choirs and some guitarists. Overwhelmed, I tried to thank him.

"Don't mention it," he waved his hand, "it's our privilege to have you in our city."

"Remember the music we had in Tulsa at the first conference?" Wanda reminded me. Yes, I did. The Grace trio, an outstanding combination of voices and instruments, blended their talents into several unforgettable performances. The Lord was certainly good to us inexperienced nurses, and provided liberally to cover all the details so well. The San Diego Conference was a great success. Joni was very special and much appreciated. Several physicians and Paul and Carol Spitz were also on the program and delivered powerful messages as well. As a result, the San Diego Conference became the springboard for annual National Conferences. These conferences resulted in the most amazing tales. One of them was Nancy.

A pretty hospital secretary from Rocky Ford, Colorado, Nancy received a flier in the mail one day announcing our National Conference in San Diego. What caught her eye was Joni Eareckson. She had always wanted to meet her. Together with her friend, Marsha, she signed up for the Conference. Impressed with the HCF goals and vision, she later invited our team to Colorado for a seminar. She also received "A New Heart" and read about the Year Of Life program at our Training Center in Holland. After what she felt was a nudge from the Lord, she applied. Her application was accepted and a few months later just after our team conducted a seminar in Rocky Ford, she was on her way to Holland. In just a few weeks, she was engaged to Peter, also a nurse and a full-time staff worker. Within a year, they were married.

"All I did was go to San Diego to hear Joni," she said, "and look what happened to me. I'm married, live in Holland and I am even learning Dutch."

After San Diego, more surprises were in store. Francis Grim returned for another visit. He mentioned a doctor he wanted to meet who lived in my area. I contacted this physician and suggested he visit us and meet our founder, Francis Grim. He accepted. Francis' schedule was hectic, however, and it was only the day before his departure that we were able to get together at my home. When he and his wife were seated, the conversation turned to Corrie ten Boom.

"How is she?" Francis asked, "I know her well but have not heard from her for a while."

Corrie, a very special lady, had lived in Holland during the war. Her parents hid Jews from their captors. Later they were betrayed and transported to a camp in Germany where Corrie's sister and father died. Corrie was released by mistake, a few months before the war ended and had since travelled the world, speaking to people everywhere, sharing the Gospel. Her book, "The Hiding Place," has been a bestseller for years.

"Corrie's retired," the doctor said, "she lives here in Southern California with her companion, Pam."

"I would love to see her," Francis said wistfully, "but I am leaving tomorrow."

"I could call her," the other doctor suggested.

"Really? Please do," Francis smiled. He walked over to the phone and dialed a number. Soon he was talking to Corrie. He handed Francis the phone.

"Hello, *tante* Corrie," Francis said, "how are you?" (*Tante* means aunt in Dutch and is also a term of endearment used for older people.) Stunned, I sat glued to my seat. Corrie ten Boom was actually talking on my phone? I had missed her in Holland so many years ago and now she was speaking on my phone? I gathered that Francis was going to make his conversation a short one. Quickly, I beckoned him. Do you mind if I listen in on the extension in my bedroom? He shook his head. No, go ahead. I rushed over, quietly lifted the receiver and heard the familiar voice with the strong Dutch accent. She was about to say goodbye. I found my voice and suddenly said, in Dutch:

"Hello, *tante* Corrie. How are you?"

"Who's that?" I heard her surprised voice.

I introduced myself. Francis said goodbye and hung up.

"Do you live here?" Corrie asked. "Why don't you come and visit me sometimes? We've just moved here and don't know many people. Bring some knitting or something along so you have something to do while we chat. Of course, you have to stay for lunch." Honored, yet in a daze, I accepted her invitation.

"I'll call you back," I promised and hung up.

"Does she mean that?" I asked the doctor as I returned to the living room.

"Of course," he smiled, "she loves company. Well, we'd better be going. It was so nice meeting you both." A few days later Francis left.

I thought again about the many wonderful people I had met over the past ten years or so. Godly people who had gone through much, it seemed, to be molded by the Lord. And now I was about to meet Corrie ten Boom. When should I call her? I waited three weeks. Then we set a date. In great anticipation, I drove the thirty miles to her home, named Shalom, and rang the doorbell. She opened the door herself.

"Hello, Aubrey," she said in Dutch, "I'm so happy you could come. Please come in."

Delighted, I looked at the frail yet energetic figure before me. A little stooped, her grey hair tucked in a tight roll around her smiling face, she had the familiar round, metal-rimmed glasses and tiny dimples on her healthy, tanned face.

"You must tell me all about yourself," she beamed, offering me a chair in the cheerful, comfortable living room. "Would you like a cup of tea?"

I nodded, looking at the portraits of Corrie's father and other relatives. They were all so familiar.

"Pam is not here," tante Corrie continued. She shuttled back and forth to the kitchen. Soon we were sipping our tea and enjoying some real Dutch cookies. We chatted on, I shared about myself, our family travels and the Hospital Fellowship. Yes, she knew us well and had also travelled much with Brother Andrew. She showed me her gifts from Indian tribes (people she had worked with) including an elaborate feather headdress. We had lunch and played the little organ.

"I really need to go, tante Corrie," I began several times. I enjoyed her company but felt I was overstaying my welcome.

She objected, "Please stay, there is so much to talk about."

In the late afternoon, Pam came home - a beautiful, gentle girl in her late twenties. She spoke Dutch fluently without a trace of an accent.

"Where did you learn to speak such perfect Dutch?" I asked her in amazement.

"Thank you," she said modestly, "I worked in Holland for Brother Andrew for many years."

We chatted on. Soon, Pam moved to the kitchen where she cooked a very tasty, hot meal. I had to stay for dinner as well. After dark and many hours after dinner, I finally took my leave. What a wonderful day it had been. How inspiring and peaceful to be in the presence of people who walk so close to the Lord.

A few weeks later, I took Mom and Dad over for an afternoon of reminiscing with tante Corrie. It was just a few months before Corrie suffered her first stroke which paralyzed her vocal cords. I saw her again just a few times and for short visits after that. For five years, Pam and a small team of dedicated friends and professionals took care of tante Corrie. "Shalom" remained a house of peace through all those years. Finally, the Lord quietly took her home when her days, numbered from birth, were up. Her task was completed. I kept in touch with Pam who later shared about her "silent years" with Corrie at an HCF retreat. Her favorite verse was, *Our times are in Your hands* (Ps. 31:15 LB).

Shortly after my meeting with tante Corrie, there was another International HCF Conference scheduled in Exeter, England. Afterwards, there would be a four-week refresher course at Rehoboth, the training center in Holland. Bertie wrote and asked if I would take some sessions and share about our outreaches in the USA.

There are some people coming from your country, she wrote, *Lavonia and her sister Nina from Mississippi and Minnie from Detroit.*

Exeter, we found out, was easier to reach than Wales. Over 1,200 people from well over 100 countries arrived. There were forty-five from the States. When the ten-day conference, equally as impressive as the Welch one, concluded, we boarded a night boat to cross the Channel.

Back in flat, windy, green Holland, I had that familiar feeling that I still belonged here. Leonora recovered her car from the hold in the ferry and drove us to Rehoboth in the village of Voorthuizen. It was my first visit to the Training Center. It was all I had imagined it to be - clean and cozy, permeated with prayer and love. About thirty people had gathered for the refresher course at the Center. I shared several times and enjoyed interacting with these people from around the globe. Joe was there, too. He seemed to be everywhere, tending the garden, fixing things around the house and making visitors welcome. He still wanted to go to Italy and was biding his time, waiting on the Lord. Erasmia Grim was there as well.

"I just love your country," she beamed as she took my arm one day.

"Come, let me take you to the duck pond."

Framed between some retirement homes, a small pasture and some willow trees, we found the secluded pond and watched the ducks conducting a noisy mini-convention in the center of the water. Here we are, I thought, two people living across the world from each other, two people who responded to the Shepherd's voice, *Go ye into all the world*, who were called into the same ministry, meeting in Holland. I knew Erasmia had weathered many a storm, as I had, yet she had grown lovelier and wiser as the years passed by.

I thought of the millions of others who had made the same commitment and were led by the same Shepherd Who has a place for everyone - everyone, that is, who chooses to follow Him.

In a sense, I now felt settled in the saddle, my personal saddle prepared for me by the Lord. The many years of preparation for this particular position were over. How long I would be in it or which direction it would take in the future, I didn't know nor did it matter. I wasn't the driver anymore. It meant a lot to share this moment with Erasmia.

We were gravely aware of our responsibility to the millions who yet live in spiritual darkness. Sitting side by side on that soggy bench, we quietly absorbed the scene in front of us, thankful, grateful, aware of the Lord's admonition, *Without Me you can do nothing*, and His wonderful promise, *I will never, ever leave you nor forsake you.*

EPILOGUE

Today, many years later, after attending yet another international staff conference, I find myself at the duck pond again. The willow trees are trimmed, a few well-fed cows graze in the adjacent pasture. The tidy row of homes is sparkling clean, as before. Familiar red geraniums and white lacy curtains are clearly visible through the large windows. The ducks suddenly interrupt their pond meeting to paddle excitedly towards a wobbly, squealing toddler dressed in a little red jacket. With a mixture of fear and excitement, he holds out his carefully saved bread crusts to the quick, loud duck platoon.

Can they be trusted? he seems to think.

Insecure, he looks back at his Mom for reassurance.

She smiles and nods her head. "Go ahead! It's all right. I'll be right here."

It reminds me of us grown ups, reaching out to touch others, the hungry, the lonely, the sick and the discouraged. Sometimes they seem to make fearful noises. Shall we proceed? Will we be rejected? We glance back to our Father and see Him nodding.

"It's OK, go ahead." He smiles. "I'm right here, watching you."

How interesting, I mused, that I would return to Holland so often after all these years and stay in this HCF Center with its international spectrum of staff and students, all of whom are health care workers.

I was a nurse (I had never wanted to be a nurse). I was English-speaking (a language foreign to me and hard to learn). I was a Christian (like those narrow-minded Bible believers I had wrinkled my nose at for so many years).

I marvel as I think about "A New Heart", the magazine now in its thirteenth year. The Lord had to twist my arm to get my attention and cooperation! The circulation has doubled and copies go to people in all fifty states. Every time I finish an issue, I feel completely drained and empty. There's nothing more to say, I think. This is the last issue. Yet three months later, there's always copy and ideas on my desk again. I remember Corrie ten Boom's graphic example of the train ticket.

"When do you get your ticket?" she used to ask, "weeks and months before you go or just before you leave?"

The point was clear: when you need information, inspiration, strength, wisdom or courage you get it. When you don't need it, you don't have it. I smile. It sure keeps our trust and dependence on God fresh and alive.

The ducks waddle back to the pond. A weak, watery sun peeks through the fast-moving clouds. The toddler and his mother are leaving. My mind returns to my happy years in Blaricum and I marvel at the intricate pattern that has been unfolding thread by thread over the years. I am reminded again of that graphic example tante Corrie used so often of an embroidery cloth with many threads crisscrossing all around in every direction, an apparent mess.

"This," she would say, holding up the cloth for all to see, "is how we usually see our lives."

"But this," she turned the cloth around, "is how God sees it."

On the other side, the right side, was a perfectly embroidered crown!

I remember all the "threads" that crossed in our lives, seemingly at random. Take Joe, for instance. He felt the Lord wanted him in Italy. He didn't know anyone there nor did he speak the language but eventually he went and enrolled in language school. He kept corresponding with his U.S. friends. One of them was Wanda. Eventually, his letters conveyed more than friendship. Wanda responded and a year later they were married. Then Wanda had to learn Italian and, eventually, she had to learn how to raise their little bambina, Gloria Joy.

Sandy, my son, graduated from high school in Texas with honors and was given a scholarship. He enrolled at a nearby university but after two years, he quit. He couldn't quite make it and lost his scholarship. Broke and not sure what he wanted to do, he moved back home. For a year, he worked at various odd jobs. He was well versed in all branches of construction and able to convert a little toolshed in our garage into an extra bedroom. He also designed and installed a roof over the back patio, shielding it from the many pine needles that rained down regularly.

Interestingly, it was during that year at home that Sandy began to take the Lord seriously. He started to attend church because he wanted to, not just to meet his friends as he had done before. He studied the Bible, went to Bible studies, had lots of questions and prayed for direction. He was also baptized again.

"When I was six, I was baptized but I wasn't serious," he confessed, "now I want to do it for real." One Sunday he asked, "Why do I always cry during worship, Mom? I'm not ashamed or anything like that; I just wonder why?"

I smiled. "I don't know, love," I said, "guess you're just being blessed."

After a year, he joined the Air Force and began attending evening college. Suddenly, his brain shifted gears and he developed an interest in business, economy and real estate.

"Guess I am a late bloomer," he said. "I love to go to school now. I want to get a degree in business and management."

"Well, you asked the Lord what He wanted you to do and here's your answer."

"Yes, I guess you're right but sometimes I wish I had more detail about the future." he sighed.

"Remember," I reminded him, "the Bible says: *Thy word is a lamp unto my feet* (Ps. 119:105) - not a floodlight. A lamp only gives you enough light for what you need to see right now."

Another interesting thread in the messy side of my tapestry was Bill. After our divorce, we kept in touch from time to time, exchanging brief notes, mostly progress reports on Sandy. One day he called. I sensed God was dealing with him. He talked for two hours, was having problems, didn't think God would accept him. Then suddenly, he prayed the sinner's prayer and accepted Jesus as Lord. Another thread was pulled into place. Another life transformed.

Helen, my sister, moved to San Luis Obispo on the coast of Central California. Eventually, she returned to school and became a certified mental health technician. She often helps with seminars and retreats when we're in the area. The Lord is central in her life, too.

Mom and Dad retired from LACC in Glendale and moved to San Clemente in 1979. Still active and healthy, they offered to help with my mounting administration tasks, volunteering their time from their home at their own pace. They recently turned eighty still full of life and vigor.

Our National Conferences continue. After Tulsa and San Diego, there were others in Missouri, Indiana, Louisiana and Kansas. There are frequent weekend retreats throughout the country. Seminars continue at an increasing pace. Our HCF teams have now crossed the entire continent from coast to coast and border to border several times. We have had radio and TV interviews and newspaper coverage.

After Wanda's departure, new staff workers came and lived in my home. After several years we were so overcrowded, we all needed some breathing space. We prayed, waited, looked for solutions and eventually were led to open a Midwest Base in Springfield, Missouri.

Another buried thread recently reappeared again. After Helen showed the first chapters of my manuscript about my childhood years to some relatives, my Uncle Henk in Holland asked, "What happened to Mickey?" Mickey? My former sandbox playmate? Helen didn't know. Neither did I. They moved to Canada fifty years ago. I believe it was Alberta. That's a long time ago.

But the question lingered in my mind and one day I picked up the phone, dialed Information for Alberta, Canada and asked for his number. Luckily, his last name was rather unusual. The operator only had two numbers. Excited, I dialed the first one. No one answered. Then I tried the second number. A young girl answered, "Hello?"

I swallowed. Now what?

"Did your father live in Holland when he was little?" I asked her, realizing that was a weird question.

"Yes, he did." she said.

It was Mickey's daughter!

Her parents were not home but I got their address and sent Mickey my first chapter about the sandbox incident. Less than two weeks later, there was a long, eight-page letter in the mail from a surprised and delighted Mickey, now Warden Manager of the Pacific Region of National Parks. A long-lost thread had surfaced again.

Remember Donna, the lady I met in the Chiropractor's office? We became friends. A few years later, she went to see her Mom in Liberal, a small farm community in Kansas and her former home town. Her Mom was hospitalized. When she returned to California she said: "That hospital in Liberal does not have a thread of Christian evidence anywhere. No Bibles, no literature, no Christians. Nobody prayed with Mom all the time she was there."

I gave her some HCF literature which she distributed on a subsequent visit. Many years later, several nurses at a National Conference shared their burden with me for a Christian Fellowship at their hospital.

"Where are you from?" I asked.

"Liberal, Kansas. We only have one hospital there," came the answer. It was the one Donna had prayed for while visiting her Mom! Today, Liberal has an active and vital HCF group.

I realize now that our lives are really a string of intricate events, carefully knit together by a loving Father who wants our attention and our trust. We need Him because there are many valleys between the mountaintops of our lives. Disappointments, frustrations, feelings of bewilderment and confusion are baffling realities, throwing us again and again upon the mercies of a faithful Father and a renewed dependence on His guidance.

I clearly see the danger of consistent success in life. It is bound to lead to independence and self-sufficiency, away from our constant need to be close to the Father. That is why my favorite psalm is Psalm 139. It reveals the fact that God knows us and carefully knit us together even while we were in our mothers' womb. He is aware of our sitting down and rising up.

"But God has limited Himself," my pastor said recently, "to leave His message in the hands of people. People like us, imperfect and self-centered. Only by keeping our eyes and mind on Him can we become more like Him and be able to hear His voice, carry out His mission and reach our full potential."

Then he made a startling announcement: "Let us always allow God," he solemnly warned, "to take any measure He deems necessary to keep our full attention focussed on Him."

Search me, O God, and know my heart:

Try me, and know my thoughts:

And see if there be any wicked way in me,

And lead me in Your everlasting way.

(Ps. 139:23-24)

For more information, write to:

Hospital Christian Fellowship

P. O. Box 4004

San Clemente, CA 92672

v